This book starts in autumn
but because of the
cyclical nature of the
seasonal celebrations
you can begin during any
season of the year.
See page 10: *How to begin.*

A Way of the Mountain
book

EARTH FESTIVALS

Seasonal Celebrations for Everyone
Young and Old

Dolores LaChapelle and Janet Bourque

Illustrations by Randy LaChapelle

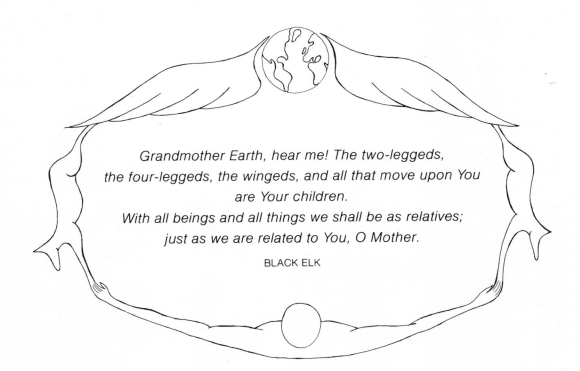

*Grandmother Earth, hear me! The two-leggeds,
the four-leggeds, the wingeds, and all that move upon You
are Your children.
With all beings and all things we shall be as relatives;
just as we are related to You, O Mother.*

BLACK ELK

Finn Hill Arts, Publishers

P.O. Box 542
Silverton, Colorado 81433

P.O. Box 295
Kirkland, Washington 98033

Printed in the United States of America
Library of Congress Catalog Card Number: 76-15321
International Standard Book Number: 0-917270—00-2

Acknowledgments

Permission to quote extensively from the following works is gratefully acknowledged by the authors:

The quotation from Black Elk which appears on the title page is from *The Sacred Pipe: Black Elk's Account of the Seven Rites of the Oglala Sioux*, Edited by Joseph Epes Brown. Copyright 1953 by the University of Oklahoma Press. This quotation is also used on pp. 31, 67, and 122. When it is first introduced in the text on page 31, ellipses indicate the words which have been omitted from the original text. One other excerpt from *The Sacred Pipe* appears on page 22 of this work.

From *Seven Arrows* by Hyemeyohsts Storm. © by Hyemeyohsts Storm. Reprinted by permission of Harper & Row, Publishers, Inc. We want to acknowledge with gratitude the help and encouragement given us in the early stages of our ms. by *Seven Arrows'* editor, Douglas H. Latimer. We also wish to thank Clayton E. Carlson of Harper & Row.

"A Song of Chalco" by Angel Maria Garibay K. Adaptations from POESIA INDIGENA, by Angel Maria Garibay K., published in 1952. Reprinted by permission of the Universidad Nacional Autonoma de Mexico. Published by Doubleday & Co., Inc. in SHAKING THE PUMPKIN, edited by Jerome Rothenberg. Copyright © 1972 by Jerome Rothenberg. Reprinted by permission of Doubleday & Co., Inc.

By permission from YAQUI MYTHS AND LEGENDS by Ruth Warner Giddings, Tucson: University of Arizona Press, copyright 1959.

From *Akwesasne Notes*, Mohawk Nation, via Rooseveltown, N.Y. for excerpts from "The Non-Progressive Great Spirit" by Gayle High Pine. Reprinted by permission.

From *A Sand County Almanac with other essays on conservation from Round River* by Aldo Leopold. Copyright © 1949, 1953, 1966 by Oxford University Press, Inc. Reprinted by permission of the publisher.

From "Attunement" by David Spangler. Reprinted by permission of the Findhorn Foundation, The Park, Findhorn Bay, Forres, Moray, Scotland.

From DOES IT MATTER? by Alan Watts. Copyright © 1968, 1969, 1970 by Alan Watts. From BODY TIME: PHYSIOLOGICAL RHYTHMS AND SOCIAL STRESS, by Gay Gaer Luce. Copyright © 1971 by Gay Gaer Luce. Reprinted by permission of Pantheon Books, a Division of Random House, Inc.

From *Ecology Action Educational Institute*, Box 3895 Modesto, California 95352 for their "Unanimous Declaration of Interdependence." Reprinted by permission.

From *Foundations of Tibetan Mysticism* by Lama Anagarika Govinda. Reprinted by permission of Rider & Co., London. Published in the United States by Samuel Weiser Inc.

From *Hollering Sun* by Nancy Wood. Copyright © 1972 by Nancy Wood. Reprinted by permission of Children's Book Division, Simon and Schuster, Inc.

From *Lord of the Dawn* by Tony Shearer. Copyright © 1971 by Anthony Shearer. Reprinted by permission of Tony Shearer and the publisher, Naturegraph Inc.

From *Man and His Symbols* edited by C. G. Jung. Copyright © 1964 by Aldus Books, London. Published in the United States by Doubleday & Co., Inc. Reprinted by permission.

From THE PSYCHOLOGY OF CONSCIOUSNESS by Robert E. Ornstein. Copyright © 1972. Reprinted by permission of W. H. Freeman and Company, Publishers.

From *Psychology Today*, for "Lessons From An Indian Soul, A Conversation with Frank Waters" by James Petersen. Copyright © 1973 Ziff-Davis Publishing Company. Reprinted by permission of *Psychology Today* Magazine.

From "The Commentary" of C. G. Jung in THE SECRET OF THE GOLDEN FLOWER translated from the Chinese into German and explained by Richard Wilhelm; English translation by Cary F. Baynes. Reprinted by permission of Harcourt Brace Jovanovich, Inc.

Gary Snyder, REGARDING WAVE. Copyright © 1968 by Gary Snyder. "Song of the Taste" was first published in *Poetry*. Reprinted by permission of New Directions Publishing Corporation.

John G. Neihardt, BLAC ELK SPEAKS, copyright John F. Neihardt, 1932, 1959, 1961. Reprinted by permission of The John G. Neihardt Trust, Hilda Neihardt Petri, Trustee.

1. Published by special arrangement with Shambhala Publications Inc., Berkeley, California. By Michael Fagan from MAITREYA I, edited by Samuel Bercholz and Michael Fagan. Copyright 1970 by Shambhala Publications.

2. Published by special arrangement with Shambhala Publications Inc., Berkeley, California. By Lama Anagarika Govinda from MAITREYA II edited by Samuel Bercholz and Michael Fagan. Copyright 1970 by Shambhala Publications.

3. Published by special arrangement with Shambhala Publications Inc., Berkeley, California. From MANDALA by José and Miriam Argüelles. Copyright 1972 by José and Miriam Argüelles.

Taken from THE CRACK IN THE COSMIC EGG by Joseph Chilton Pearce. © 1971 by Joseph Chilton Pearce. Used by permission of Crown Publishers, Inc.

THE COLLECTED WORKS OF C. G. JUNG, ed. by G. Adler, M. Fordham, H. Read, and W. McGuire, trans. by R. F. C. Hull, Bollingen Series XX, vol. 9, *The Archetypes and the Collective Unconscious* (copyright © 1959 by Bollingen Foundation and © 1969 by Bollingen Foundation), reprinted by permission of Princeton University Press: short quotes from pp. 352, 357, 363, 388, 389. Vol. 11, *Psychology and Religion: West and East* © 1958 by Bollingen Foundation, reprinted by permission of Princeton University Press: short quotes from pp. 533 and 535.

We want to thank Betty, Jim, Rees and Eloise, Ed, Marilyn, Brian, Fred, and Amy. Without their help this book could never have been completed or published. We also want to gratefully acknowledge the help of Nurmi Hansen, typographer and Howard Vierling of Craftsman Press, Printers, and the King County Library System.

contents

about the book

What this book is about

Words, whether printed or spoken, do not bring us into a living relationship with the earth, yet only such a relationship can end the desecration of earth.

Only by bringing your whole being, mind and body, into contact with the whole of the earth, represented by all the living beings in your particular "place," can you enter into real relationship with the earth. We, who have few rituals today that celebrate this unity of body, mind and spirit, are trying to find our way back into the earth family without a guide to show the way.

Long ago the Celts called this relationship with the earth "the Ancient Harmonies," the American Indians, "Living in Harmony with the Earth," the Balinese, "when the world was steady." Until very recently in the earth's history, man acknowledged the necessity of moving through the earth's seasons with balance by celebrating festivals, particularly at the equinoxes and solstices. Complex stone structures such as Stonehenge in the British Isles and Chaco Canyon in our own southwest marked the time of these seasonal festivals.

Seasonal celebrations are a unity, a wheel of life. Each moves into the next, developing out of the previous season and flowing into the next. We have no rituals for this harmonious, unfolding whole. You don't just suddenly relate to the earth. You either relate all the time and with your entire being, or it's merely the intellectual assent of an alienated being which can in no way prevent USING the earth for any purpose we may find expedient, completely unmindful that, "the organism which destroys its environment destroys itself," or, as Chief Sealth said to the whites in 1854: "Continue to contaminate your bed and you will one day suffocate in your own waste."

To celebrate a festival means: "to live out, for some special occasion and in an uncommon manner, the universal assent to the world as a whole." You temporarily live complete and whole, in a total relationship with YOUR world. This total relationship allows for the gradual assimilation of inner awareness into daily life, which is more lasting than the sudden mind-exploding flash of unity which comes from the use of consciousness-expanding drugs and brings more lasting power. Because you are not only part of the whole but the whole is part of you, you have access to all "the power" of the whole. True festivals give us the gift of experiencing for a moment this "power" which brings renewal and transformation.

This book *Earth Festivals*, provides detailed instructions for arranging seasonal festivals which help bring about a living relationship with the earth.

Who this book is for

This book is for anyone trying to become whole. This cannot be done alone. It must be done with others. For millennia, it was done with others on a festive occasion. But to have real festivity you must have playfulness and make-believe and this cannot be valid without bringing children into the festival.

From the Pygmies of the Congo with their "molimo," the voice of the forest, to our own southwestern Indians who have "kachinas," spirits visiting them, valid festivals have elements which are ostensibly for "the children." In reality, these elements are just as much for the continuing education of the adults and the reintegration of everyone into the on-going cultural relationship with the earth. Real learning, just as much as real festivity, demands the presence of all ages. These festivals are for adults AND children.

How the book started

My parents grew up on small farms but raised their family in town. Their respect and love for growing things, their feeling of oneness with nature, involved our family in a very special relationship, not only with life, but with each other.

Such a special relationship has been so important in my own life that I have always tried to help others in their search. I have found that many parents today are looking for a way to enrich their family relationship and provide their children with a strong sense of "self." They want very much to be able to provide learning experiences for their children that will give them the tools for living fully in an ever changing society. *Earth Festivals* provides these learning experiences.   *Janet Bourque*

For me, the beginnings of the festivals in this book came from years of isolated living with children of various ages in true wilderness — on a seemingly barren outcrop of rock surrounded by glacier ice. In such a setting I watched children relating to the rock and the water and the few plants in a total manner — the way "natural peoples" have done for thousands of years. I began to relate in the same manner, learning from the earth. Later, I discovered similarities between what we were doing and many of the rituals in American Indian cultures.

Dolores LaChapelle

Later, we developed the rituals, not only in our own families but through working with groups such as nature study camps, communal groups, experimental classes in public schools, church groups, Girl and Boy Scouts, and a group starting a "new town." We amplified some aspects of the rituals and dropped others which we found to be too difficult for temporary groups to handle.

We gratefully acknowledge our debt to the Indians. They kept such practices alive through hundreds of years of persecution, patiently waiting for the dominant white culture to learn, hoping it would learn before it was too late — for them and for the earth. This white culture is beginning to learn, now, so it is actively seeking help from the Indians — learning how to be American. This does not mean we try to become Indians but that we use some of their techniques for achieving wholeness, to BECOME ourselves, so we no longer feel we have to conquer and subdue the land. This means, as Wilfred Pelletier, an Odawa Indian, pointed out "that the stubborn land the pioneers cleared and cursed will be loved, respected, and revered by the great-grandchildren of pioneers. And the native creatures of that land will also be loved and fostered, including the original American human: the Indian."

There is an ancient Indian legend concerning Venus, the Morning Star and the period of nine hells, which began, in the words of Tony Shearer, when "we became more involved with our own creations rather than with our earth mother and her gifts." This beginning of the first hell coincided with the year Cortez landed in Mexico. The last, the ninth, will end in 1987. Toward the end of the ninth hell there will occur a great longing for unity — for wholeness.

The return of the Lord of the Morning Star, Quetzalcoatl, will herald deliverance from the ninth hell.

From South America to the Great Plains in our own country and from the time of the Toltecs down to the present, the Morning Star has continued as a central symbol in Indian thought. This mysterious star, which appears and disappears, brilliantly suspended between night and day, symbolizes the union of opposites — day and night, right and left, conscious and unconscious — holding all in balance.

Venturing out into space, seeking to learn the secrets of the stars, man saw his first earthrise and the uniqueness of life on this blue-green globe rose into his consciousness. Earth is beginning to acquire a sacred dimension. Astrophysicist Carl Sagan reminds us that way out in space, from Mars, EARTH is the Morning Star.

How to use this book

Cycles

The book is arranged in cycles, based on the yearly progression of the seasons. The first two cycles are concerned with relationship: between one human being and another, between the inner and outer realities and between man and the earth. When these relationships are sufficiently clear there comes a flow of energy. The next two cycles are concerned with this energy. From the energy of relationship comes the vision. The last cycle is concerned with vision.

Sessions

The sessions in each cycle present the material needed to celebrate the four great Earth Festivals with "understanding": fall equinox, winter solstice, spring equinox and summer solstice; however, each session in itself provides a small celebration. The sessions are planned for an hour once a week. This material may easily be expanded to fill two hours. As a framework for everyday use, amplify the content of the sessions by referring to the *Useful Books* appendix.

Everything necessary to arrange these celebrations is provided. This partly accounts for the complexity of the layout of this book. The other factor in this complexity is due to the fact that we have no familiar words in English and no symbols at all for giving directions for such

celebrations. Our way out of this difficulty comes from the work of Silas John, an Apache shaman who started a new religion in 1916 by writing down the 62 prayers he received in a vision. His writing encodes information calling for nonverbal behavior as well as for speech: "symbols that tell what to say" and "symbols that tell what to do."

Each session contains material under the categories listed below. Each of these categories has a corresponding symbol so that it can easily be seen during the course of running the session.

 "ceremonial leader"

This symbol is based on the idea that a true leader has traditionally been a kind of guide — one who clarifies an issue by throwing more light on it — so we use a symbol for light.

Whenever this symbol is used it means that the leader is discussing or explaining. Most sessions begin in this manner.

The term "ceremonial leader" means just that — one who leads the ceremony for that particular time. The word, *leader*, should not construe up images of a person who has authoritarian control.

The discussions written alongside this symbol are based on notes taken during actual sessions. The language may seem strange because the discussions originally were brief, random phrases, used to communicate complex ideas in as simple a manner as possible so that the children in the group could understand. These were put together in a continuous whole and cleaned up grammatically for use in the written form. Teachers and leaders of youth groups will be familiar with this type of material as it is included in any printed curriculum as an aid to the adult, who may be familiar with a new and unusual field of learning in his head, but is often unable to discuss this in terms which may reach a child. Traditionally, fables and fairy stories are told in children's language although they are not for children only.

An 8 to 12 year old will have heard most of the words used in these discussions but may not necessarily understand them all. Often, the understanding comes through the later actions in the session.

Do not attempt to memorize these discussions or read them verbatim. They are given only as a guidance to show which points should be covered. Adapt them to your own group and your own part of the country.

During these sessions clearly verbalize for the children present the fact that they are travelling in different states of consciousness — all equally valid, but different. If they have achieved a sense of peace and unity with nature through a meditation or chant, be sure they are brought back into "this reality." When no adults are present children may freely travel in other states but often feel guilty or afraid. The advantage of the relationship achieved in these celebrations is that the adult can facilitate the child's re-entry into "this world." This encourages flexibility and relationships to many levels or states of consciousness with no anxiety.

 directions

Specific directions for art activities, dances, rituals, etc. are always preceded by this symbol.

The two symbols above will be seen throughout the book under every aspect of the sessions. The following symbols indicate specific parts of each session.

 movement in general: dances, chants etc.

 closing

Material used at the end of each session to pull all together into a cohesive conclusion.

 creative art activity

The original meaning of the word, *create* is *to cause to grow.* The art activity provides a way for learning to take place through the interaction of body and mind together.

Concerning specific material in the sessions

Music

Outside of recordings for specific purposes no music is listed in these sessions because pre-teen agers are more deeply involved in the "top 40" current music than any other age group. Each group using this book can only experiment and decide what best suits it. Advice and sources are given in an appendix.

Chants

Extensive use is made of the classical Tibetan chant: OM MANI PADME HUM. This may seem strange as it certainly was not developed in our land, but this chant seems to work better than any other in many different contexts. Baba Ram Dass may be correct when he says, "I've run dozens of Western songs through ... and they've had their moments of delight, but they don't have something, see. They're not OM MANI PADME HUM: maybe ultimately, OM MANI PADME HUM isn't Tibetan but merely the highest vibrational instrument ... a universal symbol."

Quotations

The careful juxtaposition of quotes on the session pages provides the key to greater understanding for the adults. When an idea is first presented in language geared to children, the adults easily see how this can be applied to their own life. By reading the quotes on the page, which are the words of an expert in a particular field, the rational mind grasps the full implications. Then, by using the same idea in a ritual or an art activity, it reaches the whole person not just the rational mind and thus becomes integrated and transforms life itself.

Physical setting

These sessions are specifically designed so that they may be used in cities or suburbs as well as open country. You do not need a large expanse of nature to enter into a real relationship with nature. In Japan, a tiny wall shrine with a single flower epitomizes this relationship. In this country, one man in solitary confinement in prison developed an entire life on a relationship with a bird who flew to the bars of his window.

If you do not have even a vacant lot or secluded corner of a park, create a miniature outdoors in your ceremonial tepee area with discarded material from florists or become friends with gardeners in city parks and use their discarded materials from routine maintenance work.

Each session makes use of two areas

The meeting area — used for discussion and projects.

The ceremonial tepee area — By having an area set apart, the group automatically becomes more collected and enters easily into a quiet, receptive mood with no necessity for words to remind them. Sounding a gong is very useful when first entering the ceremonial tepee area. A three quart stainless steel mixing bowl makes a good substitute. Turn the bowl upside down, balance it on one finger and hit it with any type of wooden implement.

Ideally, the two areas should be in separate rooms; actually, the same room may be used if the ceremonial tepee area is clearly marked off. Use a circular rug or make a circular line of tape on the floor.

Materials needed

At the end of each session a specific list is given of all the materials for the sessions. Full details of where to procure these materials are given either at this time or in the *Supplies* appendix.

Most of the materials listed are inexpensive or free. Because the impact of human population in or near cities is destroying our relatives, the living beings of the earth, it is no longer valid to make use of extensive plant material or animal skins. Full use is made of recycled materials. Use your own imagination in adapting seasonal commercial items. For example, we use Christmas tree icicles for fringes on the winter solstice shields. Although this may bother some white purists, Indians freely make use of such things as plastic juice jugs for water in sacred sweat bath ceremonies and all sorts of adaptations of plastic throw-away junk materials for costumes in Indian dances.

How to begin

Although this book begins in autumn, because of the cyclical nature of the material you can begin during any season of the year. If you are beginning in autumn start at the beginning of the book. If you are beginning in any of the other three seasons of the year follow this procedure:

FIRST   Because the autumn equinox cycle contains all the introductory material necessary to start, begin with the first two sessions of this cycle relating the material to the season you are in.

SECOND   Then, using the calendar, decide how many weeks are left before the next main seasonal festival: winter solstice, spring equinox or summer solstice. Continue with the sessions related to your present season, reserving the last

week before the festival for the preparation for the festival: session 9 of the Relationship cycle for the winter solstice, session 2 of the Vegetation cycle for the spring equinox and session 7 of the Vision cycle for the summer solstice.

THIRD   Celebrate the festival for your season. Then continue with the sessions following that festival in the book.

Earth Festivals may be used over again each year following the seasons and building on the preceding year's learning. This is how seasonal rituals have always been done by mankind. Each year provides greater depth of insight and you will be adding material; however, the sessions are complete in themselves and may be used just once in situations where this is necessary such as schools and nature camps.

About the authors

Janet Bourque holds the degree of Master of Education in Supervision and Curriculum, and teaches at Bellevue Community College in the Home and Community Education Department. She is the Advisor for two cooperative preschools and teaches Parent Education. During the 1975-6 academic year she also instructed on three reservations, helping Indian teachers qualify for their Child Development Associate Certification.

In the field of outdoor education Janet Bourque and her husband, Fred, have been on the staff of the Institute for Survival Education and worked on outdoor education curriculums for the public schools as well as worked extensively with the Boy Scouts.

She is married and has three children: Tom, John and Renée.

Dolores LaChapelle taught in a "community school" in Utah and an experimental high school in Seattle and now teaches Tai Chi at Fort Lewis College in Colorado. She has an extensive background of mountain climbing and skiing. She has been doing free-lance writing for a number of years.

Dolores is married and has one son, Randy. Her husband has done extensive research in ice and snow, providing the family opportunities for mountain and wilderness living.

Dolores and Janet have collaborated on three previous books and produced a children's record.

We began to realize that ecology always has been the basis of Indian life. But there is a great difference. To Indians the earth is not inanimate. It is a living entity, the mother of all life, our Mother Earth. All her children, everything in nature, is alive: the living stone, the great breathing mountains, trees and plants, as well as birds and animals and man. All are united in one harmonious whole. Whatever happens to one affects the others, and subtly changes the interlocked relationships of the parts to the whole. FRANK WATERS

The sign, which we now call the *peace sign,* has its origin in the Indian sign language for the word, *medicine.* The Indians used the idiom, "making good medicine." In making the sign language for this term, the right hand is held level with the heart and then sweeps outward and up to the sign for medicine which is the usual peace sign with palm outward, index and second fingers separated and pointing upward. The origin of the *peace sign* is not ordinarily attributed to the Indian sign language because of our limited definition of peace. We define peace as the absence of war. To the Indian peace has a much broader meaning somewhat similar to the Hebrew word, *shalom.* Man cannot have peace unless he is at peace within and with his natural surroundings. This is what the term, "good medicine" means: that all is harmonious both on earth and with "the Powers." ("Good medicine" can have other meanings.) Making "good medicine" would mean making things harmonious and balanced so that peace can reign.

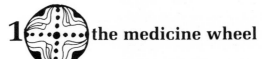

1 the medicine wheel

For this beginning session it is important that a tent or yurt be set up outside for the ceremonial area. This sets the tone for the entire program. An indoor area may be used for the remainder of the weekly sessions. The group gathers in the meeting area first. Strike a gong to get the group together. Ask everyone to sit down in a circle, Indian style. Give the peace sign. Almost everyone will probably spontaneously respond with it.

Did you know that the Indians were the first people to use this sign for peace? We learned it from the Indians.

Each small tribe had its own spoken language which was different from every other tribe. It's just as if everyone who went to one school spoke a different language from those who went to another school. Since Indians very often came into contact with other tribes a universal hand sign language was developed. This peace sign was one of the signs the Indians used. Another sign was used for a greeting. You grasp the other person's right arm at the elbow with your right hand, while at the same time he grasps your arm at the elbow. Try this greeting with someone next to you.

The Indian not only tried to live in peace with his friends in the tribe, he tried to live in peace with all of nature: the land, the plants and animals. He took only what he needed to live without destroying the land or polluting the rivers or fouling the air. Today, we're going to begin a journey into the past to try to learn from the Indians how to live with the land and all its creatures.

◆ The group moves to the ceremonial tepee. Ask everyone to be seated in a circle. The charcoal block is lighted to burn the natural incense. Strike the gong for attention.

♦ One hundred years ago the Cheyenne Indian child grew up with no school buildings. He didn't learn from books. There were none. Instead he learned through stories told and retold. He also learned from what he did each day with other members of his tribe.

Today I'm going to tell you about one of the most powerful teachings of the Cheyennes, the *medicine wheel*. What do you think the word, *medicine*, means?

◆ Discuss, get a few ideas from the group but don't spend much time on this as a fuller understanding of the word, *medicine*, will be developed over the next few weeks.

♦ In the center of this circle is a skull. I want you to lay down and look at it. Now stand up and look carefully. See if you see it any differently. Now let's move around in a circle. Sit down and look carefully again. Do you see it from a different side? There are many ways of seeing one thing — from high and low, close up or from far away. You also have feelings as you look: fear or joy or curiosity. Walk around the circle again. Look carefully again. Close your eyes and see it within your mind. Lay down and look at it again. Has the skull changed? No, but your seeing has changed. As we moved in the circle our way of seeing changed. This seeing of things from all different viewpoints is part of the idea of the *medicine wheel*. Draw a medicine wheel with me.

◆ Distribute paper and pencils. As you explain the wheel, lay it out using small stones. At the same time draw the wheel on the large piece of paper so it will be clear. Begin by placing a small circle made of seven stones in the center. From the top stone put three stones straight up. This is North. To the right put three stones in a line. This is East. To the left put three stones in a line. This is West. Now put three stones in a line toward the bottom. This is South. These are the spokes of the medicine wheel. At the end of each spoke place a larger stone. Complete the outside circle by putting two stones between each large stone. There are now twelve stones around the outside of the wheel. The medicine wheel is now ready to teach us.

♦ Among the Indian the first teachings are of the four great Powers of the medicine wheel. On your diagram above the northern dot write these words: north, white, buffalo, wisdom. Near the dot on the right, write: east, yellow, eagle, understanding, sees far. Near the dot on the left write: west, black, bear, undecided, looks-within-place. Below the bottom dot write: south, green, mouse, innocence, trust, seeing near things.

Look carefully at what you have drawn. Where do you place yourself on the medicine wheel? If you think of yourself as being very smart, your medicine animal is the buffalo and your color is white. Are you shy? Are you not eager to try new things? If so, your medicine animal is the mouse and your color is green. Do you worry about things? Do you worry about what might happen or that you might have said something wrong? Are you undecided? If so, your medicine animal is the bear and your color is black. The eagle of the east sees clearly and makes his plans carefully. His color is gold or yellow.

Each of us has a beginning place on the medicine wheel. This is how we first see things but if you just see things from one direction only, you are not really seeing the whole thing are you? Remember when we walked around the skull. If you had stayed in one place you would never have really seen the whole skull as it really was. If you stay all your life as an eagle, for instance, you never really see all of anything. You are only part of a person. You must learn from the buffalo, the mouse and the bear before you can see from all the directions and then you can become a complete and balanced person. You must turn the wheel to learn the medicine of each direction.

You all know some Indian words. Who can think of any? You notice Indian names are easy to chant as you say them. Whenever Indians came together in a large group they would frequently chant together. Let's try this.

Begin clapping hands in rhythm: 1 - 2 - 3 - 4. The hard beat is on 1. The group will usually join in quickly. Sway with the rhythm of the clapping. When the rhythm is established begin chanting to the beat: STILL - a - gua - mish; YA - ki - ma - a; O - ka - na - gan.

When the group has the chant and the beat, stand up and stomp on the beats with a hard stomp on the first beat. Continue chanting and stomping. Move around in a circle until you have gone around to your original spot. Sit down there. Do not clap or chant. Sit quietly. It may take a few minutes but the group will follow example and sit down quietly.

How many times have we moved in a circle or used the word, *circle* or *round* or *wheel*? (discuss) What is round in nature? (discuss) Everything the Indian did was in a circle because he believed the power of the world always worked in circles. The sky forms an arc above us. The earth is round. The wind moves with its greatest power in a circle. The sun and moon are round and we move in a circle round the sun. The moon moves in a circle round the earth. The seasons of the year form a great circle in their changing: spring, summer, fall, winter and then it's spring again.

In the time to come we will learn more about the circles in nature and in our own lives.

The Indians learned much from stories but also from dreams. Dreams were thought of as messages from "the Powers" and were discussed by the family or with the wise men to understand their meanings. Do you think you can learn something from your dreams? Tonight, listen to your dreams. In the morning think about them and write down whatever you remember. Save this paper and next time we meet we will talk about dreams and how the Indians interpreted them.

(Pick up the round basket of sunflower seeds.) One of the things Indians often shared were sunflower seeds. This is my "give-away" to you today. This is also our "give-away" from the earth today. Pass them around the circle so we can share.

When the basket has completed the circle, exchange the arm grasp with those near you and then go out the door first so you can take the group back to the meeting area.

About the "give-away"

The "give-away" is a Plains Indian term used by such tribes as the Blackfoot and the Cheyenne. Almost every session will further develop the full range of this concept.

About the medicine wheel

The wheel is a common symbol in the collective unconscious. Hyemeyohsts Storm derived his ideas of the medicine wheel from Cheyenne teachings; however in European writings the wheel is a favorite symbol in alchemy for the circulating process leading to the goal represented by the *philosopher's stone* in Jungian terms, the individuation of the "self." In alchemy this wheel must be turned by the four seasons and the four quarters of the universe.

In a footnote in Jung's *Psychology and Alchemy* there is a drawing from an alchemical manuscript dated 1610. This drawing which explains the "squaring of the circle," has the same form as Storm's

You have noticed that everything an Indian does is in a circle, and that is because the Power of the World always works in circles, and everything tries to be round. In the old days when we were a strong and happy people, all our power came to us from the sacred hoop of the nation, and so long as the hoop was unbroken, the people flourished. The flowering tree was the living center of the hoop, and the circle of the four quarters nourished it. . . . Everything the Power of the World does is done in a circle. The sky is round, and I have heard that the earth is round like a ball, and so are all the stars. The wind, in its greatest power, whirls. . . . The sun comes forth and goes down in a circle. The moon does the same, and both are round. Even the seasons form a great circle in their changing, and always come back again to where they were. BLACK ELK

medicine wheel. According to the 1610 manuscript the circle in the center is "the mediator" which makes "peace between enemies ... rather he alone effects the squaring of the circle." Using medicine wheel terminology, this drawing may be explained by saying that the center, the true "self", makes peace between:

outside — represented by the four quarters of the universe: east, west, north and south
inside — the four ways of seeing

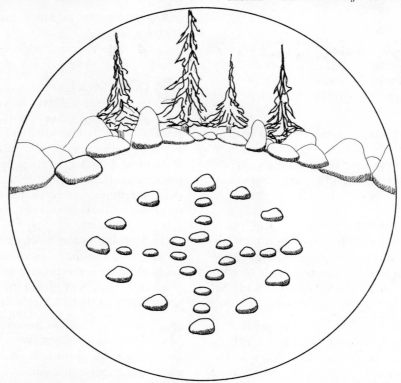

meeting area	
gong or stainless steel mixing bowl as a substitute	wooden implement to hit it
ceremonial tepee area	
gong and wooden implement round bowl or basket containing sunflower seeds containing sunflower seeds 31 small round rocks skull	matches one large cardboard and felt pen natural incense. See appendix stiff paper and pencil for each person *Seven Arrows* by H. Storm

Very little attention is paid to the essence of man, which is his psyche. . . . The really complex and unfamiliar part of the mind, from which symbols are produced, is still virtually unexplored. It seems almost incredible that though we receive signals from it every night, deciphering these communications seems too tedious for any but a very few people to be bothered with it. Man's greatest instrument, his psyche, is little thought of. C. G. JUNG

There exist within us two major modes of consciousness: one analytic, the other holistic; one rational and linear, the other intuitive and nonlinear. One of them — the "dominant," verbal-intellectual, rational one (Ornstein calls it the "day" side of consciousness) has at times been paid great attention by orthodox psychologists. The other — the "night" side of our conscious life, the mode of the dreamer, the artist, the mystic — has been largely ignored except by "esoteric psychologists," that is, persons trained in such systems as yoga, Buddhism, and Sufism. . . . [There must be] a complementary interaction of the two modes of consciousness if man is to realize his highest potential. . . . It is not that intuition is better than intellection or that verbal knowledge is worthless but rather that the two modes of knowing must go together — that the night side of consciousness must be acknowledged as real, experienced, and integrated into the obscuring brilliance of the day. ANDREW WEIL

2  dreams

 Last time we met we talked about the Indian medicine wheel and about the symbolic animals of the four directions. Let's do an Indian chant about these four animals.

✦ Everyone stands in a circle. As the chanting is done move around in a circle. Hands are clapped loudest and feet stomped hardest on alternate words as indicated below.

Chant of the Four Directions
(Repeat each line four times.)

SOUTH is GREEN and MOUSE and IN - no - CENT trust
WEST is BLACK and BEAR — un - DE - cided, LOOKS - with - IN - place
NORTH is WHITE and BUFF - a - LO and WIS - dom
EAST is YEL - low AND ea - GLE, under - STAND - ing, SEES far

 (Everyone is again seated on the floor.) Since last session have you noticed any of the traits of the buffalo of the north in you or the mouse of the south. Maybe you hadn't realized you had these before. (discuss)

Yes, some of you realize that at times you are moving along the medicine wheel. Do you realize that you are a different person at night when you sleep than you are during the daytime when you are

Symbolization . . . is the starting point of all intellection in the human sense, and is more general than thinking, fancying, or taking action. For the brain is not merely a great transmitter, a super-switchboard; it is better likened to a great transformer. The current of experience that passes through it undergoes a change of character, not through the agency of the sense by which the perception entered, but by virtue of a primary use which is made of it immediately; it is sucked into the stream of symbols which constitutes a human mind.
SUSANNE LANGER

awake? Remember I asked you to write down your dreams. Can anyone tell me a dream?

◆ Discuss. If there is any clear symbol in any of the dreams let them discuss what it means to them. Allow the discussion to continue as long as the group is interested but do not analyze the overall meaning of any dreams.

What we have just been doing, talking about our dreams, isn't done very much in our life in this country, but there is a tribe of people called Senoi Indians who live in the high mountain jungles of Malaya, across the Pacific Ocean, who think it is the most important thing that people can do. Every morning the parents and children talk about the dreams they had. Difficult dreams are taken to the tribal expert, called a halak, to figure them out. Dreams are very important to the whole tribe because the Senoi Indian believes that in dreams he can contact the spirit world and learn from it many important things or bring back very beautiful pictures which he has seen in the spirit world to share with others in the tribe.

Many of you have had dreams of falling. How did you feel when that happened? (discuss)

Among the Senoi Indians if a child had been frightened when he dreamed of falling and the fear woke him, the father of that child would say to him, "You should not have tried to wake up because everything in your dream has a good purpose. You should relax when you feel yourself falling. If you are falling in a dream it means that the spirits are calling you to them because they like you and want you to come to their land. When you finally meet them you might be frightened at first because they are so powerful but you don't have to be because they only want to show you something entirely different which you've never seen before so that you can tell others about it."

Another interesting thing is what the Senoi Indians think of dreams about fighting. Let's say a child named Sintu dreams that his friend, Matu, has attacked him in a fight. Sintu tells his father of this dream. His father tells Matu's father about it. Matu's father explains to Matu that he has caused trouble to Sintu without wanting to do it because he has allowed a bad person in Sintu's dream to use his face as a disguise in the dream. So Matu is told that he should give some kind of gift to Sintu and try extra hard to be friendly toward him to prevent this bad person of the dream from ever using Matu's face again. As a result the boys become even better friends than before the dream.

If someone dreams of floating away somewhere he is told that he must float somewhere in his next dream and find something to please his friends —

One state of mind does psychological harm to children: anxiety. Or, more precisely, the defensive excesses of thought, feeling and behavior which we tend to develop against chronic expectations of anxiety. . . . By virtue of being human, we are always imagining, and we are sometimes alone and helpless in the process. When we are all of these simultaneously — imagining and alone and helpless — we are in a state of anxiety. . . . [Some teachers] avoid anxiety by way of helping them to avoid their imaginations. . . . All too often, however, what we find is the teacher falling into such a course by default, for lack of methods and materials which can help the children avoid anxiety by way of being less alone and/or less helpless with their imaginations.
RICHARD M. JONES

Thus the circular movement also has the moral significance of activating all the light and the dark forces of human nature, and with them, all the psychological opposites of whatever kind they may be. It is self-knowledge by means of self-incubation. . . . The conscious will cannot attain such a symbolic unity because the conscious is partisan in this case. Its opponent is the collective unconscious which does not understand the language of the conscious. Therefore it is necessary to have the magic of the symbol which contains those primitive analogies that speak to the unconscious. The unconscious can be reached and expressed only by symbols, which is the reason why the process of individuation can never do without the symbol. The symbol is the primitive expression of the unconscious, but at the same time it is also an idea corresponding to the highest intuition produced by consciousness.

C. G. JUNG

such as a new song or a picture he can make or a dance he can teach the tribe. Because of this way of thinking about dreams there is no violence among the Senoi because all angry or hostile feelings do come out in dreams and then the Senoi deal openly with them by positive ways. The Senoi had not had a violent crime or a war among themselves for 300 years when the first white men visited them. All the other tribes in the lowlands of Malaya were afraid of the Senoi because they thought they were magical because of the amazing things they had learned in their dreams.

The American Indians didn't go into dreams the same way the Senoi Indians did but they did pay a great deal of attention to their dreams. The American Indians made paintings on shields of the dreams or visions they had. We are having a special festival next week. Let's make a shield painting of our dream for that festival. It will be a gift from that spirit world we visited in our dreams.

♦ Pass out a piece of railroad board to the group. Have them share the felt pens or crayons in small groups.

♦ Divide your shield in half with any kind of line you want. On half of it you can put your daytime self. For this use the symbol for the kind of person you are — a buffalo person of the north or a bear person of the west or whatever. Put a sun in this section to show that it's day. In the other section put a moon and show what you learned in your dream while you visited the spirit world.

Make all parts of your drawing big so that it can be seen at a distance. When Indians carried these shields in special ceremonies it was important that everyone could see them well.

♦ Conversation with each person about his dream will help him decide on which symbols to use for his shield drawing.

♦ We will use these gifts from the spirit world to decorate our ceremonial tepee circle when we celebrate the Autumn Equinox Festival next week. (Gather the shield drawings to save.) Let's turn the medicine wheel with the chant we learned today.

♦ Do the chant which they learned earlier today.

Remind everyone to bring something to give-away at next week's Autumn Equinox Festival. They could bring any kind of fruit or vegetable to eat or fall leaves to decorate the ceremonial tepee.

We find a fundamental conformity in mandalas regardless of their origin in time and space.
. . . they are endeavouring to express either the totality of the individual in his inner or
outer experience of the world, or its essential point of reference. Their object is the self in
contra-distinction to the ego, which is only the point of reference for consciousness,
whereas the self comprises the totality of the psyche altogether, i.e., conscious and
unconscious. It is therefore not unusual for individual mandalas to display a division into a
light and dark half, together with their typical symbols.   C. G. JUNG

About ritual preparation

In Indian ceremonies all parts of the ceremony are equally important. The making of an object is just as sacred as the use of the object in the actual ritual. In fact, the Hopi emphasis on preparation for rituals consists of three parts:

announcing the coming ritual

preparation of materials to be used

inner preparation — praying, meditating and putting forth good mental energies for the coming ceremony

Without this concentration on inner preparation by every member of the tribe, the final ritual will not fully succeed.

only the meeting area is used this session	
one piece of 12 x 12 in. railroad board for each person	watercolor felt pens or crayons

A share in the superhuman abundance of life . . . the fruit of the festival, for which alone it is really celebrated, is pure gift; it is the element of festivity that can never be "organized," arranged, and induced. . . . Thus, when a festival does as it should, men receive something that it is not in the human power to give. This is the by now almost forgotten reason for the age-old custom of men wishing one another well on great festival days . . . the real thing we are wishing is the "success" of the festive celebration itself, not just its outer forms and enrichments . . . but the gift that is meant to be the true fruit of the festival: renewal, transformation, rebirth.

JOSEF PIEPER

3 autumn equinox festival

Today is one of the greatest of the earth festival days so the time allotted for the meeting should be open-ended.

For today's special festival day, the ceremonial area should be decorated in greater detail. See directions for this at the end of the session.

Before the session begins you should mix the ingredients for the Indian Bread so it will be ready to cook later.

Let's take a look at your dream shields. What do they show you as you look at them?

Discuss. Be sure to bring out the idea that often a person is on a different place on the medicine wheel at night from where he is in the daytime.

Have you ever thought about the fact that there is a different amount of light and dark each day during the various seasons of the year and that this might have an effect on us too? During the fall months we gradually get a shorter and shorter day and a longer night. Do you think this has any effect on us? How do you feel when the days get shorter and there's more darkness? (discuss) What effect does this growing darkness have on the plants?

Today is the autumn equinox. That means the earth has moved into such a position that the sun gives us just as much darkness as light on this one day. Equinox comes from the word equal — equal darkness and light.

We have six months ahead of us where the nights are longer than the days. That will certainly change us some won't it? What changes will that make in you? (discuss) So it's a good idea to think about these things ahead of time so you'll be ready for it. If our part of the earth changes and gets darker we have to change just a bit, too, to remain balanced. We can't act just exactly the same way we did in the summer and expect to remain in harmony with the earth.

The Indians knew this very well and, since the most important thing to them was to be in harmony

The principle of Indian dancing is stomping . . . the foot is raised flat from the ground, put down again flat, and then, as it were, pushed down into the earth by a bending at the knee. There is thus produced a combination of heaviness and springlike ease.

JAIME DE ANGULO

with the earth, they celebrated the autumn equinox as a very important festival day so they could get themselves back in balance with the changing earth.

If you're going to have less light in the next six months what things do you have to do to balance that out — to make up for it? (discuss)

Gloomy, dark days make some people cross or sad so we should be aware of that and balance things out. The Indians managed to do this during the fall and winter months by having more get-togethers such as parties, by telling funny stories and by more dancing and singing and chanting. That's what the Autumn Equinox Festival does for us.

Each of you has brought something for the feast so now we can all together make the festival. Indians celebrate by eating and drinking something the earth gives-away to humans and by dancing and chanting as a give-away back to the earth.

Let's begin by dancing. Indians dance with their feet solidly on the ground so they really feel part of the earth and so they can get strength from the earth. We will learn the step first and then do it to the Indian music.

The step: Begin with both feet flat in full touch with the ground and with your weight on your left foot. While slightly bending the knee slide the right foot over to meet the left foot. The left foot then takes a step sideways to the left, slightly bending the knee and shifting the weight of the body to the left foot, so that the foot hits the ground on the drum beat. Repeat the slide-step continuously. This dance is very easy to learn.

The dance: The group stands in a circle. Each person stands with arms down. As the drum beat begins, slowly raise the hands, palms up until the arms are straight up. As the drum beat increases, the arms are brought down and put on the shoulders of the persons to either side. The whole circle moves to the left, each person using the slide-step described above.

Dance to the music of band 4 of side 1 of *American Indian Dances.*

Then everyone goes into the ceremonial area. Each person carries the item he has brought for the give-away. The fruit is put in the bowl; the leaves and flowers into the jars.

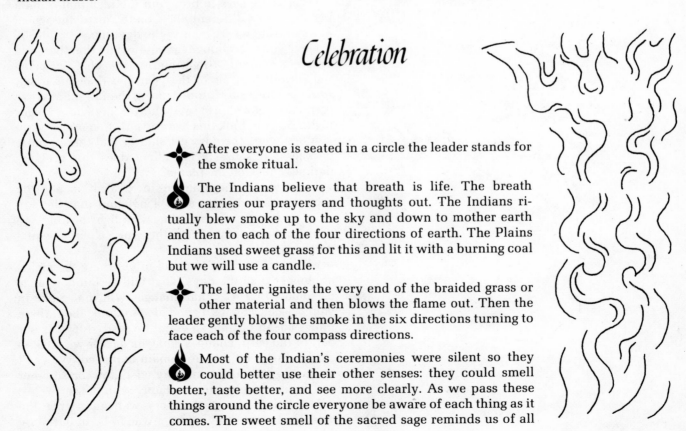

Celebration

After everyone is seated in a circle the leader stands for the smoke ritual.

The Indians believe that breath is life. The breath carries our prayers and thoughts out. The Indians ritually blew smoke up to the sky and down to mother earth and then to each of the four directions of earth. The Plains Indians used sweet grass for this and lit it with a burning coal but we will use a candle.

The leader ignites the very end of the braided grass or other material and then blows the flame out. Then the leader gently blows the smoke in the six directions turning to face each of the four compass directions.

Most of the Indian's ceremonies were silent so they could better use their other senses: they could smell better, taste better, and see more clearly. As we pass these things around the circle everyone be aware of each thing as it comes. The sweet smell of the sacred sage reminds us of all

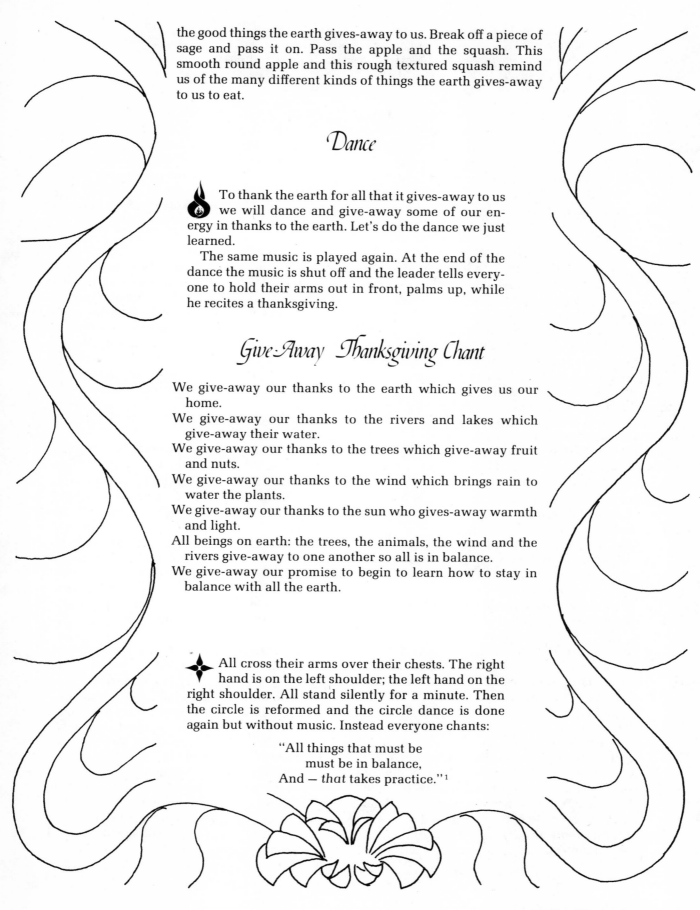

the good things the earth gives-away to us. Break off a piece of sage and pass it on. Pass the apple and the squash. This smooth round apple and this rough textured squash remind us of the many different kinds of things the earth gives-away to us to eat.

Dance

To thank the earth for all that it gives-away to us we will dance and give-away some of our energy in thanks to the earth. Let's do the dance we just learned.

The same music is played again. At the end of the dance the music is shut off and the leader tells everyone to hold their arms out in front, palms up, while he recites a thanksgiving.

Give-Away Thanksgiving Chant

We give-away our thanks to the earth which gives us our home.

We give-away our thanks to the rivers and lakes which give-away their water.

We give-away our thanks to the trees which give-away fruit and nuts.

We give-away our thanks to the wind which brings rain to water the plants.

We give-away our thanks to the sun who gives-away warmth and light.

All beings on earth: the trees, the animals, the wind and the rivers give-away to one another so all is in balance.

We give-away our promise to begin to learn how to stay in balance with all the earth.

All cross their arms over their chests. The right hand is on the left shoulder; the left hand on the right shoulder. All stand silently for a minute. Then the circle is reformed and the circle dance is done again but without music. Instead everyone chants:

"All things that must be
must be in balance,
And — *that* takes practice."[1]

Teach us to know and to see all the powers of the universe, and give to us the knowledge to understand that they are really one Power . . . The first peace, which is the most important, is that which comes within the souls of men when they realize their relationship, their oneness, with the universe and all its Powers, and when they realize that at the center of the universe dwells Wakan-Tanka, and that this center is really everywhere, it is within each of us.

BLACK ELK

Festival Shields

During some festivals Indians painted festival shields so that they could ask "the Powers" to help them be in harmony with the earth as it changed and to thank "the Powers" for all that was given to them. These festive shields were their give-away to "the Powers."

You have to pay close attention to the earth to be in harmony with it. You have to listen to the earth too. You can't just go your own way and still be in harmony. The earth and everything on it speaks to you if you'll just listen. The Indians knew how to listen. They knew when to be silent and listen to the earth speak to them. When you paint a festival shield you must do it in perfect silence and if you do that the earth can speak to you through your design. A Navajo Indian medicine man said, "The painting is a visual prayer and one should not interrupt a prayer with words." First, I will give you directions and then you will work in silence so you can hear the words of the earth.

The shield painting we are making today is to help us balance ourselves as the earth's season changes.

- Take your cardboard and draw a very light pencil circle about 2 inches inside the rim. It doesn't have to be perfect. This is just so you will keep that space free to put the border around later.
- What is most important to you, now, in the autumn? Is it playing in leaves or playing football. Draw a tree or a football or whatever is important to you now on the left side of your shield. (Hold up the circle sketch and show them.) Remember our medicine wheel has the four colors of the four directions. Each of these colors also stands for a season of the year. (Point out on your sketch where each

direction lies.) This is the Autumn Equinox Festival so we want to draw a picture of what is most important to us this fall, right now.

- What was most important to you last summer? This is your personal symbol for summer — maybe swimming was most important so you'd show wavy water or maybe tree climbing was most important so you'd draw a tree. Or maybe a dog was most important. Put the drawing of whatever was most important to you on the bottom of the shield because that's summer's place.
- Now look forward to the winter. What is most exciting for you as you think of winter. Maybe it's skiing. If so, draw a skier or snowy mountains. Or maybe it's sledding. Draw a sled. Put this at the top of the shield because that's winter's place.
- We won't draw spring because that's too far off. But we will put a sun there in that space.
- Now each of us has the things we are most interested in on our autumn shield but we haven't shown how we really feel yet inside. Indians always drew symbols of their inside feelings too. Let's do that now.
- Supposing you are a bear person of the west. Your color is black. But if you are feeling particularly wise lately you are beginning to move on the medicine wheel and so your color would be white right now. You would be a white bear because you are not only looking-within as the bear does but you are becoming wise which is the color of the buffalo of the north — wisdom.
- If you are green mouse of the south but lately you've begun to see farther than you used to you would be a yellow mouse because you have moved along the medicine wheel and can see far like an eagle.

continued

continued

- So, think of yourself as you are now in the fall of the year. Draw the symbol of yourself: bear, buffalo, eagle, or mouse. If you are changing be sure to put the color of the direction you are moving in. This is an autumn equinox shield so put the symbol of yourself in the autumn part of the circle. (Point to the circle sketch.)

- Now, think back to last summer. What were you like then. Were you just as you are now or were you different. What way were you different? Decide which of the four colors fits your difference and then draw your animal symbol in that color at the bottom of the shield — the direction of summer.

- Now, think of yourself in the coming winter. What do you think you will be like? Draw your animal symbol in that color at the top of the shield.

- Those of you who have finished can now put a special design around the outside of the entire shield to show that it's a continuous movement around the circle of the year through the seasons. I have some Indian designs in these books. You can copy any design that appeals to you or make your own design.

- The last step is to separate off the four seasons by doing a design between each of the four sections. It can be the same design or a different one. It could be a design which means fall to you.

(When the drawing is finished) I have here dried corn husks and dried leaves. You can string these together with needle and thread and tie them onto the bottom of your autumn shield. Put four of these strings of leaves on your shield. They stand for each of the four directions. Use the paper punch to make the holes for the strings.

When all have finished their shields, leave them in the ceremonial area and move to the meeting area to bake bread.

Bread Baking

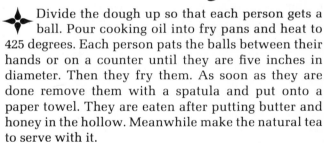

Divide the dough up so that each person gets a ball. Pour cooking oil into fry pans and heat to 425 degrees. Each person pats the balls between their hands or on a counter until they are five inches in diameter. Then they fry them. As soon as they are done remove them with a spatula and put onto a paper towel. They are eaten after putting butter and honey in the hollow. Meanwhile make the natural tea to serve with it.

Closing Ritual

(When everyone is finished) Look at your shields. See how the earth changes each season. We, too, change just as the earth does. The earth is like a gigantic medicine wheel turning through the seasons. We can dance with our shields.

Turn the record player on again. Start out with the dance they learned today but after a few minutes let them improvise.

There are profound spiritual depths in the older sacred ceremonies [of the Plains tribes], with their constant theme that man's vocation is to live in harmony with the Creator and with Creation as a whole.   FATHER PETER J. POWELL, EPISCOPAL PRIEST

meeting area

- ingredients for making Indian Bread

Fried Indian Bread

4 cups flour
2 tablespoons lard
2 teaspoons salt
½ teaspoon baking powder
1½ cups lukewarm water

  Sift dry ingredients together, cut in lard, add water and knead. Let stand for 20 minutes or longer. Divide dough into 12 uniform size balls, stretch each one to about 5 inches in diameter. Deep fry at 425 degrees until golden brown. This recipe serves 12. These puff up as they fry leaving a central hollow into which honey can be poured.

- large bowls and mixing spoons
- electric fry pans
- oil for cooking
- paper towels
- spatula
- cups for each person
- honey
- margarine or butter
- natural tea (examples — leaves of fireweed or any herb tea. Mint tea is almost always available. Try to use a plant which grows locally)
- necessary utensils for making tea

ceremonial tepee area

- When the group enters the ceremonial area, each person will carry his give-away item: either fruit, nuts or leaves. Have a large wooden bowl just inside the entrance to put edible items in. Have sturdy jars or cans placed outside the circle area to put the leaves in. Have small rocks in the bottom of these so they are weighted and won't tip over easily when branches are placed in them
- sun poster
- braided sweet grass or other dried materials to use for smoke ceremony (Dry the grass and braid 3 strands together. Other pungent materials can be used such as eucalyptus leaves, sage, or pine needles)
- materials for shields:
    one piece of railroad board for each person. This is a 22 x 28 inch piece which must be cut into a circle 22 inches in diameter. This is precut before today's session
    watercolor felt pens
    natural items to be hung from the bottom of the shield — corn husks or dried leaves strung on thread (See cover of *Seven Arrows* for how this should look)
    punch for punching holes in the bottom of the shield
    thread and needle
    scissors
    sketch of a circle with W for winter at the top, S for summer at the bottom, A for autumn at the left and Sp for spring at the right
- rough textured squash
- smooth apple
- sage
- candle
- record player
- record: *American Indian Dances*, Folkways No. FD 6510 — side 1, "Apache Dance"
- books with designs which may be used for borders on the shields. Try to get as many of these as possible
    Decorative Art of the Southwestern Indians by Dorothy Smith Sides
    Pueblo Designs by H. P. Mera
    Your Symbol Book by F. Wallace and E. Kirby
    Indian Art of the Americas by Le Roy H. Appleton

The American Indian's view concerning nature is a most precious message for the modern world. The Indians, especially of the Plains, did not develop an articulate metaphysics, but nevertheless they possess the profoundest metaphysical doctrines expressed in the most concrete and primordial symbols. . . . Virgin nature was for the Indian the cathedral in which he lived and worshipped. His desperate struggle against the white man was not only for a living space but for a sanctuary. His civilization was so different from, and diametrically opposed to, that of the modern world that after living for thousands of years in nature, he left it in such a condition that today that very segment of nature must be turned into a national park in order to prevent it from becoming spoiled.

SEYYED HOSSEIN NASR, SPECIALIST ON ISLAM

There is something higher than ecology . . . And that's the native tradition of love and worship and appreciation of the environment that you live in as a manifestation of the living God. And you take care of your ecology because it's your flesh.

STEPHEN GASKIN

1 relationship with plants

Anybody here nine years old? Can you remember one really great fantastic thing which happened to you when you were nine? (discuss)

I'm going to tell you a legend about a Sioux Indian named Black Elk and what happened to him when he was nine years old.

The whitemen had built the railroad across the plains a few years before and already there had been some battles between the Indians and whitemen who were after the gold in the mountains. The railroad had cut the grazing grounds of the buffalo in half, so now there was a large herd north of the railroad and another herd south of the railroad. The herds moved with the seasons to find the best grazing. Black Elk's people were following the northern herd toward the Rocky Mountains.

One night they camped beside a small creek. An older friend had invited Black Elk to share his supper in his tepee. As Black Elk was eating he suddenly heard a loud voice calling his name.

"Black Elk! It is time; now they are calling you."[2]

Black Elk's friend did not hear the voice, but it continued to call to Black Elk. He started to get up to find out about the voice. Terrible pains shot through his thighs and he crumpled to the floor of the tepee. He became very ill during the night, and the next day when the tribe prepared to leave the camp, he had to be placed on a pony drag.

Several days later he was still very ill. His parents had set up camp so that he could rest. They were very worried about him. As he lay on the buffalo robe he could see through the opening of the tepee. Suddenly he saw two men coming from the clouds, head first like arrows coming down. Each carried a long spear and lightning flashed out from the points. They were calling, "Black Elk, it is time, it is time." He got up and went outside toward the men. Suddenly a little cloud came very fast out of the sky toward him, picked him up and carried him up into the air.

They rushed through the air toward a large tepee among the clouds which had a rainbow for a door. Inside were six very old wise grandfathers. Only later did Black Elk realize that they were the Powers of the World. The first was the Power of the West; the second was the Power of the North; the third, the Power of the East; and the fourth, the Power of the South. The fifth wise grandfather was the Power of the Sky and the Sixth was the Power of the Earth.

The voice called to him again, "Black Elk, look to the East for the special power gift of the Grandfather of the East."

Black Elk looked to the East and there he saw a sacred buffalo. Where he stood a sacred plant suddenly grew up. The single stem had four blossoms on it — blue, white, red and yellow and the light rays flashed out in a stream of light. It was the daybreakstar herb, the herb of understanding.

He saw a thin, sick old horse with all his bones showing. With the plant held high in his hand, Black Elk walked in a circle around the horse. The old horse neighed, rolled over on the ground and as he stood up he was a great shining black stallion.

Later the voice told him to drop the plant down to the earth. When he did that, he saw that it rooted and grew and flowered: four blossoms on one stem with rays of light streaming out in all directions.

The two men returned Black Elk to his tepee and to his father and mother. But when he spoke to his parents, they did not know that he had been far away. They thought he had been unconscious from illness. But now, he was well and they could hardly believe it. It had happened too suddenly.

Many years later Black Elk decided to try to find the plant which he had seen in his Vision. His people were having many problems and he hoped he could use the plant to help them. He rode to the area that he had seen in his Vision to hunt for the plant. From a distance he could see a place where many eagles were circling round and round. He came to the spot and saw that six dry gulches came together there. On the bank was the plant he had seen in his Vision. The root was as long as his arm but only as big around as his thumb. He offered a willow to the six Powers and made a prayer to the plant about how he and the

plant would go out and help sick men. That very evening he used the plant to help cure a boy who was about to die.

Black Elk became a very great medicine man and helped his people for many years.

✦ Discuss the story with the group.

Walk

 Today we are going to walk in the woods. We will look for plants which seem to give us some idea of the six Powers. Perhaps you will find a plant which has six lines running out from the center or maybe a design in each of the four corners of the leaf. Many lines running out from the center help to show us that all things are related through their relationship with "the Powers." We can learn many things from plants just as the Indians did.

Bring back any plants that seem to show any of these things or any plant which seems to be speaking to you especially. We can learn from our sisters, the plants. But remember an Indian never took a plant without praying to it. Black Elk told his plant what he needed it for and how it would help everyone.

One other thing to look for is to see how a plant gives-away to other things around it. A plant might give food for animals or shelter for some little animal or insect. Watch for that too.

✦ Discourage idle chatter and noise. If there are spider webs, there is an activity which will help concentrate attention so that everyone will be much more aware of patterns.

When someone finds a spider web let him or her spray it lightly with white spray paint. Then place a black piece of paper behind the web and lift the web off. This makes a very clear white web on the black paper. Be sure to have everyone check to see that there is no spider in the web when spraying.

Each person should be allowed only one web so that not too many webs are disturbed. By this time everybody will notice patterns easily and will begin to look for their plant.

Point out the patterns you come across. When the first person wants to pick a plant remind him or her to pray to the plant. In the first few cases you might even provide the words. Use any ritual words such as: "I need to pick you, little plant, that I might learn from

"In the life of the Indian," says Ohiyesa, the Sioux, "there was only one inevitable duty — the duty of prayer, the daily recognition of the Unseen and Eternal." His daily devotions were more necessary to him than daily food.

ERNEST THOMPSON SETON, ONE OF THE FOUNDERS OF THE BOY SCOUTS

Don Juan explained that a man who gathers plants must apologize every time for taking them and must assure them that someday his own body will serve as food for them.

CARLOS CASTANEDA

you." Remind everyone that plants know the give-away. They live to give-away to others. Only humans have trouble because they don't know the give-away.

During the walk help everyone to see how the plants give-away to others. Explain how much we learn when we begin to really see and how hard it is to see. Call attention to the changes in the plants due to decreasing sunlight as we move into autumn. When someone decides to cut a branch, help him or her select a branch which will help the tree. This would be a branch rubbing another or crossing over another. Say to the tree, "this will hurt you a bit but it will help you grow better by not scraping the other branches."

During the walk explain that the Indians used the native plants not only for food, clothing and shelter but also for dyes. The bark, roots, leaves and lichen found on trees and plants, when boiled, make a dye. Ask the group if anyone has ever had boiled beets to eat. The juice from beets makes a natural red dye. If possible, the area should be checked out beforehand for plants which can be used for dyes. See appendix for dye recipes that fit your locality. As the walk progresses, point out the dye plants and have everyone pick specimens to be used in making dyes the following week.

These should be collected at the end of the walk to keep until next week.

After returning from the walk, the group can copy the designs which they found using either pencil or crayons. Point out the directions which the designs give: north, south, east and west or the symmetry or how the design moves about a center. All of this leads up to mandala paintings later.

As they begin to finish their designs, bring out the book on Indian designs. Show how they are stylized from nature. Show how many designs are simplified and abstracted clouds, flowers or lightning. Encourage anyone who is interested to further simplify their pattern from nature so as to make it into a design. These ideas should be kept to use for borders around future Indian shields.

During the last part of the drawing time serve the natural tea and sunflower seeds and nuts as your give-away to the group after their walk.

only the meeting area is used this session

natural tea and utensils for making it	*Your Symbol Book* by F. Wallace and E. Kirby
cups	items to be used on the walk:
sunflower seeds and/or nuts	paper sack for each person to collect plants
honey	one can of white spray paint
one piece of drawing paper per person	one piece of 8 x 10 construction paper per person
soft pencil	pruning shears
crayons	

The shape of civilization, beyond what it has to extract from the earth, is evolved in the shade of the cliff, the heat of the plain, and its fiber and warp bent to the contour and sweep of the land around it. Even in the heart of cities brick is from clay, cement derived from the limy excess of antediluvian seas. In moments of hesitation or despair such knowledge can be a measure of sanity, a route to reality. The "natural" world is the world, and the productions of man extensions of it — always — even when seemingly obscene or tortuously remote. It helps to remember.
DAVID LEVESON

A truly ecological view of the world has religious overtones. . . . An ethical attitude in the scientific study of nature readily leads to a theology of the Earth.
RENE DUBOS

2 relationship with the earth

As everyone arrives, divide them into groups. Each group should have a pounding board and hammer, knives, pot and the natural leaves, stems and bark gathered last session. Using a hammer and the block, the bark is smashed. Using the proportions listed in the appendix, put the dyes on to boil while the session continues. The distinctive odor of the dyes will add an extra sense experience to the day's activities.

 Remember our thanksgiving to the earth which we recited at the Autumn Equinox Festival:

We give-away our thanks to the earth which gives us our home
We give-away our thanks to the rivers and lakes which give-away their water
We give-away our thanks to the sun who gives-away warmth and light to us

When we think about it, the entire earth is like Christmas all the time. Everything on earth is continually giving-away something to another kind of being on earth. Who gives us our food? (plants — animals give food too) Who gives the plant its food? (the sun — clouds give rain for water)

The plants can't live without soil. Who gives the plant its soil? Where does soil come from? Was it always there? The rocks of the primitive earth were broken up by lichens. Then other primitive plants could grow on that soil. Then earthworms, microbes and insects can live in it further enriching it. The thin soil gives-away to make a home for these creatures. In turn they enrich the soil — by what they eat passing through them and on out into the soil and by their dead bodies when they die. The soil gives a home for the earthworms but, in turn, he gives-away his body back to the soil to help make it better so it can give-away to plants.

Where do we get the oxygen we breathe? Was it always here? It was first released into the atmosphere by primitive organisms that lived more than 2 billion years ago. These give-away to the earth. Now it is being given to us by the plants and trees.

When we say all things on earth are in harmony or balance, this is what we mean. Each gives-away to another what the other needs and in return, gets what it needs. To upset this harmony or balance means that ultimately every living being on earth suffers to some degree. This is why the Indians were so careful never to upset the harmony of the earth any more than they needed to.

If an Indian had to cut a tree down to make a canoe he always said a prayer to the tree. If an Indian woman wanted to cut the roots of a young cedar tree to use to make a basket she prayed:

"Look at me, friend. I come to ask for your dress, for you have come to take pity on us; for there is nothing for which you cannot be used . . . you are really willing to give us your dress. . . . I pray, friend, not to feel angry with me on account of what I am going to do to you . . . Take care friend!"[3]

If an Indian had to kill something to eat it he always prayed to the plant or animal and said that he needed it, "that it may cause me to live."

In this way the Indian tried to remain in harmony with the earth. By thinking and talking to the tree or the animal as a fellow living being he would not be able to kill it needlessly.

What do you think about the way the white man treats the living beings of the earth? (discuss) What is this doing to the harmony of the earth and, ultimately, to us? (discuss) Do you see, now, why we have to learn how to live in harmony and balance with the other beings of the earth? The earth gives us everything. We must give-away to all the beings of the earth, and to the earth, itself, we must give praise and reverence and care.

Media show

We have some slides showing us the earth as we would see it if we were in outer space.

 Show the slides from NASA. Explain the slides as you show them and take all the time necessary to answer questions. Call attention to the patterns of the clouds if no one mentions them. Point out that they are spirals. When showing the slides which cover several countries, point out that there is no way to know where the boundary of a country ends — it's really all the same earth. These slides show that fact very clearly. As the last slide is still on recite:

"The earth was created by the assistance of the sun, and it should be left as it was. . . . The country was made without limits of demarcation, and it is no man's business to divide it." Chief Joseph[4]

When the astronauts were in space they looked back and saw the earth as a whole thing — almost like one living being. The earth has no boundary lines for countries on it. It is a circle — continuous — with no edges where one country stops and another starts. No part of the earth is cut off from any other part. The clouds move freely from the United States down to Mexico and even on down to South America. There is no stopping them. The rivers flow freely from the United States and on into Canada. All the land is joined together between the U.S., Canada and Mexico. It doesn't stop at one country's border. That's what Chief Joseph meant when he said, "and it is no man's business to divide it." The Indians thought of the earth as our mother because the earth gives us everything to keep us alive just as a mother does. One Indian named Smohalla said this to the white man:

"You ask me to plow the ground. Shall I take a knife and tear my mother's breast? You ask me to dig for stone. Shall I dig under her skin for her bones?"[5]

Remember, the first day we did a dance and chant with Indian names. Let's do another one now using only Indian names for rivers or mountains or other parts of the earth. Use Indian names from your local area for this.

Directions for milk light show. This is an unusual pattern show which moves in a similar manner to a regular light show. Divide the group so that there are an equal number at each place. Have them pour the milk into the glass pan to about one half inch deep. Three different individuals add a drop of each of the three colors to the dish. Then go along to each place and let one or two drops of the "magic ingredient" slide down the edge of the dish. Watch what happens. After the first excitement dies down explain that fresh colors may be added or another drop of the "magic ingredient." Later, they can gently stir the whole thing with a fork. This usually produces spirals. Point out the similarity to the clouds forming the storm patterns in the slides of the earth. Disturbance in the atmosphere produces the spiral patterns just as disturbing the milk produced spirals.

Mention that in the universe things are often the same pattern only on different scales. The cloud spirals and the spirals in the milk pattern are two examples of this. The round spirals of the cyclone clouds in the slides and the round spirals of our finger prints are two more examples. The human body has the same type of thing going on inside it as in the world. There is salt in the ocean and salt in our blood. (discuss) There is a saying, "As above; so below." This means that the same things go on in us as go on in the world as a whole. We are related to the earth and everything in it.

Black Elk, who had his vision when he was 9 years old, has given us a prayer for this relationship with the earth:

"Grandmother Earth, hear me! . . . The two-leggeds, the four-leggeds, the wingeds, and all that move upon You are Your children. With all beings and all things we shall be as relatives; just as we are related to You, O Mother."[6]

It is doubtful if American society can move very far or very significantly without a major revolution in theological concepts. . . . Within the traditions, beliefs, and customs of the American Indian people are the guidelines for mankind's future. . . .

There is a reason why shrines exist. . . . Mount Sinai, for example, has been a holy mountain for a considerable length of time, thus indicating that it has a religious existence over and above any temporary belief held by particular people. If this concept is true then economics cannot and should not be the sole determinant of land use. Unless the sacred places are discovered and protected and used as religious places, there is no possibility of a nation ever coming to grips with the land itself. Without this basic relationship, national stability is impossible. . . .

That a fundamental element of religion is an intimate relationship with the land on which the religion is practiced should be a major premise of future theological concern.

VINE DELORIA, JR.

How can the spirit of the earth like the White man? . . . Everywhere the White man has
touched it, it is sore.   AN OLD HOLY WINTU WOMAN

Finish the dying of the wool. Add one half skein white yarn to each pot of dye. Stir gently with a stick. When the yarn has colored to the desired shade, lift it out of the dye and place it in a pan or bowl. Take it outside or to an area where it can drip dry. Spread it out over a clothes rack or clothes line.

When the meeting is over gently squeeze out excess moisture and take the dyed yarn home to save for next week's meeting.

only the meeting area is used this session

- NASA color slides of the earth from space. Order from Finn Hill Arts. If you cannot afford the cost of the slides get from the library either of the following books:
  This Island Earth edited by Oran W. Nicks
  Exploring Space with a Camera edited by Edgar M. Cortright
- slide projector and screen
- materials for "light show." Divide everyone up into groups of four persons in each group. For each group provide:
  one flat bottom shallow pan such as a cake pan
  enough milk to cover the bottom of this pan to a depth of about ½ inch
  one fork
  one package vegetable dye. Use the type which has 4 colors in it
  "magic ingredient" — SweetHeart Lime dishwashing liquid made by Purex Corp.
- materials for the dyeing project:
  natural material for dyes. See dyeing recipes in appendix
  knives and chopping boards
  hammers
  stainless steel pots for boiling dyes
  hot plate or stove
  one half skein white yarn for each pot of dye
  stirring sticks
  plastic tarp or newspapers to protect floor

relationship

We are conscious that we have come to life in a universe that is both mysterious and formidable. We are not fully, or even mainly, masters of the situation in which we find ourselves. The ultimate mastery lies with powers, other than ourselves, with which we have to bring ourselves into harmony in order to make human life viable. ARNOLD TOYNBEE

He was about seven or eight years old, and I found by looking very close that he was a kind of rich kid, in a Blackfoot way. He had several horses and cattle in his name, and he owned a medicine bundle of particular value. Someone, a grown-up, turned up who wanted to buy the medicine bundle, which was the most valuable thing that he had. I learned from his father that what little Teddy did when he was made this offer — remember he was only seven years old — was to go into the wilderness by himself to meditate. He went away for about two or three days and nights, camping out, thinking for himself. He did not ask his father or his mother for advice, and they didn't tell him anything. He came back and announced his decision. I can just see us doing that with a seven-year-old kid. ABRAHAM MASLOW

3 relationship with "the powers"

Several times during these sessions we have mentioned "the Powers." Remember when Black Elk reached the tepee in the clouds he met the six wise grandfathers who represented the six Powers. Can you name any of these Powers? (discuss) We've learned some of the gifts each of these Powers gives us — the North gives us Wisdom, the South gives us innocence and trust, the West gives us the ability to look within, and the East gives us the gift of seeing far.

A Cheyenne Indian, Hyemeyohsts Storm, calls these Powers the Seven Teaching Arrows. Six of these we know about already: the four directions and Mother Earth and Father Sky but what is the seventh arrow? The seventh arrow is the Universal Harmony which holds all things together. Some people call this God.

Probably, the reason the Indians call these "teaching arrows" is because real learning is often painful but always exciting. For instance, when we fall out of a tree we learn a painful lesson from Mother Earth. We learn about gravity — that all things fall toward the earth. The Indians would say that we feel Mother Earth "turn an arrow in us, a teaching arrow." It hurts but we learn. We learn not only about gravity but about ourselves. We learn that we were not being really aware of the tree. If we had been totally aware of the tree we wouldn't have fallen. The reason we weren't aware was probably that we were either being proud or boastful by trying to show off and do something our body really wasn't ready to do. If we were totally aware of both the tree and our own body we would have been in harmony with both and we would never have fallen.

Teaching Arrows can turn in us from any of the four directions or from the sky or from Mother Earth below. These gifts from "the Powers" help us grow.

My give-away to you today is materials to make God's Eyes. From these God's Eyes we will learn more about "the Powers." Your give-away could be either to teach someone else how to make God's Eyes or to make one as a gift for a friend.

The God's Eye is more than just a fun craft. To the Huichol Indians of Mexico it is the symbol of children. The finished God's Eye represents the eye of God as seen by a child. When the Huichol child is born his umbilical cord is cut and then buried beneath an ancient tree. As the child grows he knows his tree and calls it "grandfather." When he is older

he takes two sticks from the tree and ties them together at the center. Using yarn that he has dyed he weaves in and out from stick to stick symbolizing the growth of his life. The colors of the four directions are used as well as those of the sky and Mother Earth. All these colors are used to form a pattern of "the Powers" in the child's life. They show a pattern of how the child moves through the medicine wheel. Sometimes only yarn dyed with natural dyes is used. These are all earth colors.

When the sticks have been covered by yarn, the God's Eye is tied to a branch of the "grandfather tree." From now on the wind will blow it and the rain will fall on it. Some birds might peck at it. Finally it will return to Mother Earth. The Medicine Teaching of the God's Eye tells of the child coming from the Tree of Life and returning to the Earth Mother.

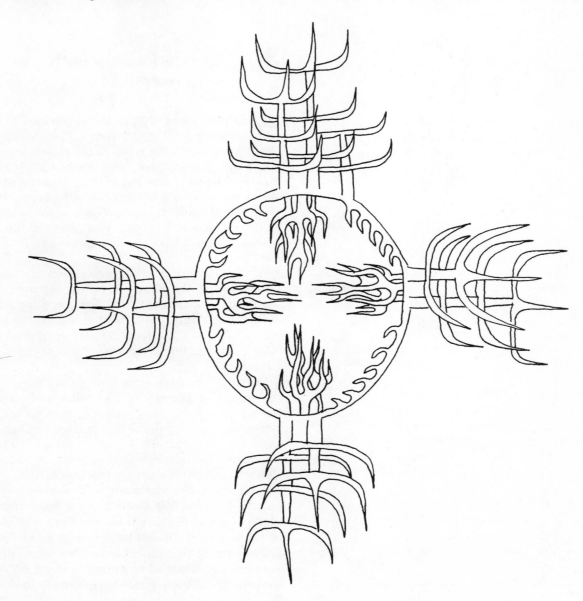

Reading and figuring are undoubtedly important (and, were it not for the culturally induced anxiety and dis-ease of our children, extremely easy to learn). But exercises in fundamental states of being, in something as basic as sensitivity to and union with others, in something as simple as merging identity with that of a tree (a familiar exercise in Tibetan mysticism), are far more important. GEORGE LEONARD

◆ Show a completed sample. Let everybody decide which of the directions are most important to them. Then they design a pattern using these colors. If someone wants to use only the natural dyed yarn he or she can make a pattern of one of the natural yarns followed by several wraps with black and then another natural dye. The black yarn helps set off the natural dyes. The natural dyed yarn from last session may be used for this. The natural yarns are nature's give-away to his God's Eye.

Directions
1. The two sticks are crossed at the center point to form right angles.
2. The sticks may be held in position with the left hand while weaving with the right. If dowels or branches are used, a niche may be carved at the crossing point. Flat sticks may be glued the day before the session so that the glue is set before the weaving is done.
3. Begin by tying the yarn close to the center. Carry the yarn around the stick and then bring it up over the stick.
4. The yarn is then carried under the next stick and around it to make a loop on the top side. The wrapping pattern is basically a figure 8.

5. After an inch or so has been wrapped, the pattern is reversed.
6. When the yarn is wound to cross on the top of the sticks, flat planes are formed. When it is reversed to cross on the underside of the sticks, the woven area is recessed.
7. When changing color, carefully tie a small knot joining the two colors. Snip off any tail. Keep all knots on the same side of the finished work — either the back or the front side.
8. To end the weaving, tie a double slip knot onto the wood. Snip the tail or back weave.

Suggested patterns:
1. Divide one of the sticks into 6 sections. Mark each section with a pencil. Wind the first section with one color. As you come to the next pencil mark, change colors etc.

continued

Real meditation is that quality of awareness where there is no separation between the observer and the observed. . . . Meditation never involves effort because that means something you want and that's future and that puts you back in time. JOEL KRAMER

---

continued

2. Begin with a small section of color woven around the center point where the sticks cross. As you add a color, make the next section larger. When you add a third color make that section larger still. This pattern causes the colors to grow outward from the center.

3. Tassels may be tied to the four end points. Each tassel could be the appropriate color for that direction.

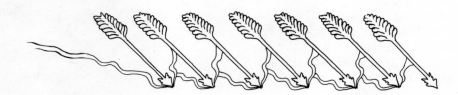

When the God's Eyes are finished have everyone gather in the ceremonial tepee area.

These designs, called God's Eyes, are for meditation. You can take yours in your hand now and try it for a few minutes. When you meditate you don't concentrate like when you study. Concentrating splits your mind up and makes things difficult because you aren't supposed to think of anything else but what you are studying. That makes it hard because, for that very reason dozens of other things come into your mind.

When you meditate you don't try to do anything. You just become very aware of the object you are looking at and you let it speak to you. You don't try to memorize it or analyze it. You really just look at it. You relax and you breathe deep and just become one with the object and then interesting things happen.

Hold your God's Eye up in front of your eye or place it at eye level and meditate for a few minutes in absolute silence. (Meditate for 2 or 3 minutes.)

That gives you an idea of how it goes. You can try it at home. This helps when you are angry or when too many demands have been made on you or things aren't going well. One of the things it does is help to put all the different parts of you back together and so it centers you in yourself.

---

meeting area	

materials for God's Eyes:
  2 sticks for each person. These can be either natural objects such as branches or wooden chopsticks or dowels. They should be about 12 inches long and the thickness of your small finger
	yarn: green, white, black and yellow for the four directions
	  brown for earth
	  blue for sky
	  natural dyed yarn from previous session
	fishline to hang the God's Eyes

ceremonial tepee area	
no special decoration needed here today	

A living body is not a fixed thing but a flowing event, like a flame or a whirlpool: the shape alone is stable, for the substance is a stream of energy going in at one end and out at the other. We are particular and temporarily identifiable wiggles in a stream that enters us in the form of light, heat, air, water, milk. . . . It goes out as gas and excrement — and also as semen, babies, talk, politics, war, poetry, and music.
ALAN WATTS

4  web of life

The wood from this tree could be hundreds of years old. Most of you have seen pictures of trees thousands of years old with the rings marked so that you can see how big the tree was when Columbus landed or at the time of the birth of Christ. (Show a picture of tree rings.) The sunlight and the nutrients from the air and soil are all stored in that tree from the time of its birth. Just think, sunlight stored over two thousand years! What do you think would happen if we burned a tree that old? Would those ancient atoms of water and nutrients be destroyed? (discuss) No, they would just change and be released back into the atmosphere through smoke. The ashes would go back into the soil.

Light the tiny pile of fragrant wood shavings. Let everyone breathe in the smoke.

Now each of us has inside us some of the atoms which were in the tree once and which came from the air of hundreds of years ago.

I have here a head of lettuce which was grown in California. (You could use a potato from Idaho or any vegetable from an area where you know the geologic background of the soil.) The lettuce fields of California lie in an area of ancient volcanoes. These erupted thousands of years ago spewing volcanic ash over the valleys. Rains and winds have washed the valleys, churning the ash and helping to reduce it to soil. As these fields are irrigated the young lettuce plant's roots suck up the molecules of ancient ash where these molecules become one with the lettuce plant. When we eat the lettuce it becomes one with us and so we have within us part of an ancient volcano. (Pass around leaves of lettuce for everyone to eat.)

We have just breathed some of the air of a long time past when I burned the shavings. We have just eaten part of a long dead volcano. We are now part of the earth from lòng ago. What is in us is eternal. We are only using these particles. From us they will pass on and on and on.

Gather in a tight circle with everyone putting his arms around the shoulders of the two people on either side. Close your eyes. Breathe deeply. Hold it and let it out. Breathe deeply again, hold it and let it

Straight or rational or "single vision" thinking has *a tendency to perceive differences rather than similarities between phenomena. A root function of the intellect is discrimination and classification — a function based upon the perception of differences in the appearances of things. This kind of intellectual activity has been very prominent in Western science. . . . By contrast, persons who forsake ego consciousness, even for a moment, often have an overwhelming sense of the essential similarity of all things; indeed, this direct perception of unity is the very heart of mystic experience. . . . The joy that invariably accompanies mystic experience (or any other kind of ego loss) is simply the natural emotion that wells up when this sense of fearful isolation ends.*   ANDREW WEIL

out. Breathe as deeply as you can, slowly exhale and sit down. Though you can't see it you have changed a little in the past few minutes. The oxygen which you breathed has been absorbed by your lungs. That oxygen may have been part of the oxygen given off by the plant. (Point to the growing plant.) The atoms of oxygen don't change as they go from plant to people. But the people change. With each breath we take and each morsel of food we eat we change to become more at one with Mother Earth and those people and creatures around us.

✦ Turn on the record player. Set the needle down on the place you have marked.

🔥 We have all eaten of the volcano when we ate the lettuce. Let's fold our bodies into the Mother Earth (have everyone sit down and clasp their arms around their knees with head bowed to touch knees). Feel the eruptions begin inside of you. (Jerk an arm or leg.) The eruptions are getting more violent. You are spewing lava, hot gasses and volcanic ash. You are regurgitating minerals and gasses from deep inside the earth. (Let everyone act out their violence for a few minutes.) You are calming down. As a volcano you are dying. You are quiet now but the ash you have spewed out covers the valley. (Have everyone lie down on their backs with arms and legs spread out wide.) Thousands of years pass. Feel the wind lift some of the ash from you. Feel the rain drops fall on you. Gradually you are broken up into small pieces. Plants send searching roots down through your cracks, sucking up particles that have waited thousands of years for them. A beetle crawls through the grasses eating leaves and absorbing the particles.

(Everyone imitates a beetle crawling because the particles are part of the beetle.) The beetle crawls out on a long grass stem. His weight becomes too much for the stem. It bends over. Splash! He falls into a stream. Snap! He has been eaten by a fish. (Become the fish, because now the particles are part of the fish.) The fish swims downstream to a quiet pond. Gulp! He has been swallowed by a duck! The duck, now full of food, flies away. Bang! A hunter has shot him. The duck is served for dinner and the particles are now part of YOU. Where will they go from here?

The Mother Earth gave to the grasses, the grasses gave food to the beetle, the beetle gave food to the fish, the fish gave food to the duck and the duck gave food to you. All have given-away.

We must learn to give-away too. We need not offer ourselves to be literally eaten by another in order to give-away. There are other ways to be involved in the give-away.

Everyone please look in your pockets or purse. Take one item out. Exchange one thing with someone else. Don't just exchange one time but several times. Pass on further the thing that you received the first time. If you have nothing in your pockets or purse use this paper to write an I.O.U. for some article, such as a stick of gum or a pencil, or a deed. For example you could write: "I'll write a poem for you." Or, "I'll help you do some type of work."

✦ Allow about 5 minutes or more for the give-away. Let them have plenty of time to exchange several times.

Food

 Everyone please sit in a circle. This is my give-away to you.

 Pass out cookies or fruit. Read the following poem while everyone is eating.

If we begin with the premise that man is an alien in the cosmos, then all we can do is strengthen the walls that keep us within our self-imposed prisons and learn to cope with loneliness. But true therapy consists in ridding ourselves of the illusion of individuality and dissolving our egocentrism in cosmic consciousness.   OSCAR ICHAZO

Song of the Taste

Eating the living germ of grasses
Eating the ova of large birds

the fleshy sweetness packed
around the sperm of swaying trees

The muscles of the flanks and thighs of
soft-voiced cows
the bounce in the lamb's leap
the swish in the ox's tail

Eating roots grown swoll
inside the soil

Drawing on life of living
clustered points of light spun
out of space
hidden in the grape.

Eating each other's seed
eating
ah, each other.

Kissing the lover in the mouth of bread:
lip to lip.

Gary Snyder[7]

"Web of life" game

✦ Go for a short walk in a nearby vacant area if possible. If there is no nearby area use a large colored picture of a familiar area in your locality. Using this picture, organisms present in the picture can be listed and then proceed with the game.

Provide each person with a card or paper. As you walk along each person writes down the name of anything he or she sees along the way. If they don't know the correct name for anything it doesn't matter. Just have them write a short description. Be sure they write each name on a separate line with space between.

Like the human body, the environment is an enormously complex system of interacting elements and processes — and most of the interactions are unknown. Disrupt this web of life with a random intervention: What is the probability that harm will not be done? It is surely vanishingly small. The conservative approach is, therefore, to make no change at all without an exhaustive investigation first.
GARRETT HARDIN

If it is a city area, animals may be hard to see so call attention to the signs that animals have been there: tracks of animals or droppings. Keep a close watch for marks on leaves which show insects have been there.

· Allow only about 10 or 15 minutes for this.

· When you return to the meeting area, have everybody sit in a circle. Have them cut their lists apart and arrange each item in front of them. Tape each item to the floor with masking tape.

· Beginning with the person who is sitting to the east, each person reads off his or her list. As the first person reads each name, others give out the names of whatever eats that organism or an organism which the first creature eats. If neither of these relationships is possible, then connect the organism with the sun or rain as almost every organism needs one or both of these. If the names of any man-made objects have been included give special attention to what effect this object has on the rest of the natural organisms.

· As each person calls out something that fits with the organism read out by the first person, have the one calling out the name, take a piece of string and tape one end to the first organism and the other end to the card it fits. For example: the first person reads *worm* from his list; another person calls out *robin*, because the robin eats the worm. The person calling out *robin* tapes a piece of string going from the card with *worm* written on it to the card with *robin* written on it. At the beginning of the game, the person calling out the word, *robin* will have to write it on the card. As the game progresses you will find that most of the things mentioned have already been written on a card.

· After the first person has finished, the rest of those present will understand how it works and they can all work it out together.

· Warn everyone to step carefully as they are constructing the web so that they don't disturb what is already in place.

· When all are finished there will be an intricate web of strings showing the interaction of all the beings in that area.

· Have someone suggest a natural or man-made disaster. This person should then give a quick light pull on the string connected with that disaster and see what happens to the "web of life." Let each person take turns suggesting changes which might occur. Let them discuss the implications of the term, "web of life," which was first used by Darwin.

Ecologists say we "can never do just one thing" because the web of life is so interconnected that when a human being thinks he is doing just one thing he is causing many other changes, which he is not always aware of, in the natural environment.

A Cheyenne Indian, Hyemeyohsts Storm, explains this when he says, "all things within this Universe Wheel know of their Harmony with every other thing, and know how to *Give-away* one to the other except man." But "loneliness is a teacher of giving" for man.[8]

During the next few weeks we will learn some games which will help us learn how to give-away to one another better.

Have everyone stand in a circle and repeat together the give-away thanksgiving from the Autumn Equinox Festival.

As everyone leaves remind them to bring some small item with them next week as a give-away. This can be something from nature such as an interesting rock or leaf or an item of food such as fruit or cookies.

---

only the meeting area is used this session

· picture of tree rings · piece of tree wood · wood shavings and match · green growing plant · lettuce or potato · record player · record: Gabor Szabo *Spellbinder* Impulse record AS 9123 Mark with masking tape the exact place on side 1, band 1 where the music seems best to fit the action called for at the end of the first discussion	· materials for game: ball of string pencil piece of stiff paper or cardboard for each person masking tape scissors optional: photo of a local outdoor area

RICHARD M. JONES

5  bone game

Last time we saw how we are a part of everything that exists on the earth. Everything in nature knows about the give-away and freely gives to one another. Human beings are the only ones who don't understand the give-away. But it is important they learn about it because, when human beings are not freely giving-away to one another, they are unbalanced and this can even ruin the balance and harmony of nature.

Today we are beginning our vision quest. The vision quest is a time in the life of an Indian when he tries to learn who he is. When we really try to learn who we are we learn about one another and about the whole world.

Each of us here has already learned that we belong to one of the four colors of the directions: North, South, East or West. Each person "upon the earth is a living fire of power and color . . . a Living, spinning Fire, a Medicine Wheel."[9] When we can get these different medicine wheels to work harmoniously together, then we get a lot of power and energy. You can just feel it happen.

Today and the next two sessions after that we are going to learn ways of getting these medicine wheels, each of us, to work harmoniously together so that we can get the energy going.

Today we will learn an Indian Game called the "bone game." Indians of many different tribes played it and all ages play it.

In one way the game is approached somewhat like the way the team acts in baseball. The *chatter* gives verbal support from the team members in the field to the pitcher. The more intense the level of chatter, the better the pitcher can pitch. In the bone game the "shooter" is much like the pitcher. He is backed up and reinforced by the various strategies of his team. It is this team involvement that generates the energy.

The bone game

 One team begins by hiding the bones. They choose two people to be the hiders. The two hiders stand in front of their own team; facing the opposing team. Each of the hiders has one set of bones. While their team chants or sings or whispers or shouts insults: both to support the hiders and confuse their opponents; each of the hiders goes through a bewildering series of motions designed to confuse the opposing team. The hider may throw the two bones into air, catch them, juggle with them, put his hands behind his back and exchange the bones between his two hands or twirl them around. Finally, with a bone hidden in each fist, he holds his two hands out toward his opponents.

The other team chooses a "shooter." It is his task to find the two bones with the leather wrapped round them. As the shooter is deciding where he feels the bones are hidden, the two teams use "strategy." Common strategies include cheering, chanting, singing, music making, casting spells, and dancing around. The shooter points to the hand which he feels has the leather wrapped bone in it.

There are four possible hands in which the bones can be hidden. When the shooter is ready to shoot, he faces the two hiders, shouts HO and points to the hand where he thinks the bone is hidden. After the shout the hider opens his fists showing the bones. This procedure is repeated with the second hider. A shooter can capture:

> no marked bones or
> one marked bone
> or two marked bones

Everytime the shooter fails to capture a marked

bone his team loses a marker stick; every time he succeeds, his team wins a marker stick. The shooter shoots until he has captured both marked bones or lost all of his team's marking sticks. When the shooter has captured both marked bones his team chooses two hiders and they hide the bones. The other team chooses a shooter. If a team wants to change shooters in the middle of a clash, they may.

Duration:
> A clash is over when the shooter has captured both marked bones.
> A round is over when one team has taken all the markers.
> A game is over when one team has won the agreed upon number of rounds.

The game is interesting because it deeply involves everyone, not just the hider and shooter. The game is really between the "spirit" of the two teams. Another interesting point is that, although, at first, the most popular are chosen for the hider and shooter; it soon becomes apparent that some people are much better psychically at this game and these latter are chosen more often. The team spirit seems to take almost automatic precedence over individuals.

Allow plenty of time for this game as it gets more intense the longer it is played.

When the game is over let everyone talk about it.

 Recite the balance chant while standing in a circle arms about one another.

NOTE: This session and the next two sessions give techniques for harmony and balance within the group. These techniques will only be given once but they should be used repeatedly throughout the ses-

sions whenever there is any disagreement or disharmony within the group. Use your discretion each time as to which of the three techniques will best restore harmony.

---

only the meeting area is used this session

4 magic bones
   Each bone must be small enough to be hidden easily in a closed fist. Two of the bones are marked by wrapping a thin leather thong around each of them and tying securely. Or you may just paint a thin line on them. Two bones: one marked and one unmarked, form a

set. You may use chicken or turkey bones.
marker sticks
   Each team begins with five marker sticks. Any kind of stick may be used.
prizes
   Use the give-away items brought from home by the participants.

Bali has one of the few living "steady-state" cultures remaining on earth. *The ordinary Balinese term for the period before the coming of the white man is "when the world was steady". . . . In sum it seems that the Balinese extend to human relationships attitudes based upon bodily balance, and that they generalize the idea that motion is essential to balance. This last point gives us, I believe, a partial answer to the question of why the society not only continues to function but functions rapidly and busily, continually undertaking ceremonial and artistic tasks which are not economically or competitively determined. This steady state is maintained by continual nonprogressive change.*

GREGORY BATESON

6  pillow game

Last week we learned an exciting way to balance a group so there is good energy. Today we will learn another, quieter way to achieve balance.

You know that when riding a bicycle you cannot lean too far to the right or too far to the left or you will fall over. You have to balance right and left.

Another example of balance is when you were younger and first learned to ride a teeter totter. It was fun to go up and down at first but even more exciting to balance the teeter perfectly so that you were in midair. To balance the teeter this way took awhile. You had to learn to do it.

We have to learn balance in the rest of our life. The game we will learn today, which is called the "pillow game," will help us balance many parts of our life.

Pass out paper and pencils to everybody so they can draw a pillow along with you. Using the real pillow, but at the same time drawing a pillow, so that they can follow you proceed.

Analysis

Side 1 — the problem — something is wrong.	we place the problem
Side 2 — the opposite — the right of it	we reverse it
Side 3 — wrong and right together	we include
Side 4 — neither wrong nor right	we surpass

I'm going to give you a couple of problems which I have made up. You follow along with your "pillow" until we solve the problems.

The problem is that Mrs. Smith's room wants to use the ball field. Mrs. Jon's room also wants to use the ball field.

Side one:
> We put the problem out in plain sight. Everybody fights over the use of the ball field.

Side two:
> On this side we reverse it. Nobody fights over the use of the ball field.

Side three:
  We now include both sides. Sometimes there are fights and sometimes there are not.
Side four:
  We go beyond both sides of the problem. We can take turns using the ball field or Mrs. Smith's room will be one team and play against a team from Mrs. Jon's room on the same field.

But here in the middle of the pillow we have the center. Draw two half circles here. This goes even beyond the solution to the problem. Remember in the session where we made the God's Eyes we talked about the seven teaching arrows or Powers of the Indians. There were the four directions and father sky and mother earth, which makes six. But what was the seventh arrow? The seventh arrow is the Universal Harmony which holds all things together. So, here in the center of the pillow is the place which represents the seventh arrow, Universal Harmony. We can't possibly see all of any problem as we are only human so we can't see how this problem fits into Universal Harmony. But we have already learned that each of the seven arrows can reflect back to us the emotion or feeling which we have. In this case the only answer can come from the two groups involved in the problem. These two groups can balance the situation for themselves so that they reflect the Universal Harmony.

In many problems you cannot say there is a right and a wrong. You can only say that two different people see the one thing from two different directions. They can fight about it but, then, no one wins or they can try to balance themselves within the total harmony of nature and then everyone wins. Such a learning is just as painful when you are going through it as falling out of a tree but you learn even more about yourself and others. So the teaching arrow turns within us again. There is no failure or success if we learn from it because if we learn we are just going through the turning of the medicine wheel and learning the other person's way of looking at it. The more ways we learn to look at something the more we

can reflect the seventh arrow, Universal Harmony.

If you hold your hands cupped in the center of your paper it will remind you of the totality of all in harmony.

As you've noticed many adults can no longer remember how to see beyond the winning and losing. They think that's the most important thing. But many children can see there are more important things.

I'll give you another example concerning baseball. Tom's team was the best in the league and he was their best catcher as well as being one of the best pitchers. The upper league needed three new players and they were going to draft three of the best players out of the lower league. The coaches were going to watch this game to pick the three players they wanted.

Tom had a real problem. He didn't want to go into the upper league because he couldn't play with his friends then. He thought to himself he had a choice: to play poorly and not get drafted (place your hand on side 1 of your drawing) or to play well and take a chance on being drafted (place your hand on side 2). He chose the first — to play poorly as they were all sure their team would win because the other team was one of the worst in the league. Well they lost. Tom really felt bad because he'd failed his team. He realized he should have played well and taken his chances. (Place your hands on side 3.) In fact he could have surpassed even this decision by just refusing to be drafted if they chose him. (Place your hand on side 4.) Anyway he realized that to feel good inside himself he must always do his best and not compromise. (Cup your hands in the center.) Here in the center he has learned a lifelong lesson. That for him to reflect the Universal Harmony he must do his best. If he doesn't do his best he can't reflect the Universal Harmony in his life.

 Ask the group for examples of problems. Have the group as a whole discuss the various steps.

Have everyone link arms and do a circle dance with the slide step. Ask for volunteers to make up the chant for today.

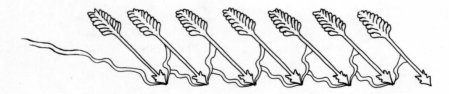

only the meeting area is used this session	
pillow	paper and pencil for each person

Dwellers in a wilderness . . . have a more intense awareness of the contrasting splendours and terrors of the universe than city dwellers pent within walls and living in cushioned ease; and, in Tibet especially, intimations of an all-encompassing glory are of almost daily occurrence, as when the sun god dances upon pinnacles of snow; or when the traveller, after fighting his way through blizzards howling amidst slippery crags and echoing caverns, crosses the pass and gazes down upon a lake flashing turquoise and emeralds amidst the shining rocks of the sunlit valley.

At those high altitudes and in that pure air, the richness of nature's colors is marvelously enhanced; so, also, man's perceptiveness.   JOHN BLOFIELD

7   tibet: an introduction to the mandala

We've been talking about the harmony and the balance of all things in nature. During the last two sessions we've learned two methods used by different people on earth to become more balanced in their own group so that they don't upset the balance of earth by their own lack of harmony. Today we're going to learn still another country's method of restoring balance among its people. It's a way which can help us when things are out of balance — inside us or all around us. This country is Tibet.

On the atlas or globe show where Tibet is in relation to our country. Point out the high altitude of the country by comparing the colors of the highest mountains in our country and the heighth of the mountains there.

Film

Show the film, "*Requiem for Tibet*". After it is over discuss it. Point out the Tibetan's way of showing great care for even the smallest creatures on earth — how they live in harmony with all their world. Be sure everyone sees the importance of living in balance with nature in such an extreme climate. If you don't have the film be sure to get picture books on Tibet from the library.

The Tibetans live among very rugged mountains with fierce storms but it is also a very beautiful country. The people have always tried to live a spiritual life so that they are not overcome by the big mountains, big glaciers and very cold temperatures. In such an overpowering area of mountains they worked out a special technique to help keep them centered so they wouldn't be afraid of nature or of their own problems inside. They call this technique making a mandala.

The idea for making the mandala comes from the structure of our eye. Seeing is very important. If everyone was completely capable of really seeing everything as it really is there would be no problems in the world. The problem comes because different people see things, differently, and then argue or fight about the difference. But to learn to really see takes most of our lifetime. In fact that's what living is really all about — learning to see — to see more, to see better and to see more different aspects of any one thing.

I'll give you an example. Suppose you like dogs and really want to have one but your mother doesn't like to clean up after a dog. She doesn't like dog hairs on the rugs and on the chairs and on clothes. Now, every time you see a dog you see a beautiful, lovable creature that you want to take home with you so you can play together. Your mother doesn't see that. She sees a messy, dirty animal which will cause her more work. The two of you argue about this. You can't see how she can resist the dog and she can't see the dog's beautiful eyes or his affection. All she sees is that he's covered with lots and lots of dog hair.

You see how complicated seeing is? You and your mother are looking at the same thing but you don't see the same thing do you? Who is wrong? (discuss) Your mother isn't wrong. The dog is covered with hairs. You aren't wrong either. It's just two different ways of seeing the same thing. Can anyone think of more examples of two different people seeing entirely different things when they are looking at the same thing?

Long ago the wise men in Tibet had figured out that people hardly ever see things the same. The Indian medicine wheel has the same idea. The buffalo person of the north can't be expected to see something the same way a mouse person of the south sees it can he? The wise men in Tibet knew that the more a person learned about the world and about what went on inside himself the more clearly he saw. He learned to see not only his own way clearly but he learned to see in the same way as all other types of people and even in the way that animals see. He learned to see

that all these ways of seeing are necessary in the world and one is not more right than another way. They are all necessary. Such a man does not disturb the balance of the world.

Remember, the Medicine Wheel doesn't turn either unless you learn to see from each of the four directions.

The mandala was developed as a way to help us see. It helps us see what is going on inside of us and outside at the same time because what is going on inside very often has an effect on what is going on outside you. The mandala helps to connect the two — inside and outside — and then the world is more harmonious.

I'm going to pass out magnifying glasses. Team up with another person and each of you take turns looking into the other person's eye. What do you see? (The iris which is coloured.) What is in the center of the iris? (A dark spot, the pupil, which is a dark circle.) On the outside of the iris is another circular rim and in between are rays or lines joining the center to the outer circle of the iris. The center circle is most important because that's where the light enters the human body.

All light comes from the rays of the round sun. (Point out the poster). The light of the sun is necessary for all life on the earth. The way this light enters the human body is through that tiny round place in the center of your eye. This center of the eye is very important because through it we see all the things going on in the world.

This form of your eye — the inner circle, the outer circle and the lines connecting the two — provide the basic form of the mandala. The word, *mandala*, means circle. We've already done some drawings in a circle, our shield drawings like the Indians make. We did a night and day shield and a season shield. The mandala is an even more powerful drawing.

We are going to do a mandala today. When we make a mandala it helps us to really see inside of ourselves. Both Indians and Tibetans know that when you are making a mandala it's a very sacred time because we are getting in touch with "the Powers" of the world. These Powers can help us through what we learn from the mandala. The Tibetans always make a mandala in concentrated silence. We can't do that this first time because I have to give you directions but we will light some pine incense to help us concentrate.

Everyone move apart so that you have room to work. (Pass out a dark felt pen or pencil to each person. Give everyone a large sheet of newsprint with the center point marked.) Stand on the center point of your newsprint and draw a big circle around yourself. We are going to mark the directions. North is this direction. (Point toward the north and have each person put the letter N in that section of their circle. Point out each of the other directions and have each person put the appropriate letter for each of these directions.) Do you remember which direction animal is yours?

Keep standing on the center point. Now extend your arms straight out. Turn completely round in a circle. Then point your right arm toward your direction. Put your arm down and walk in that direction until you stand on the letter marking your direction. Face toward the center of your circle. Now become very silent and meditate.

You are standing in your direction. You are wisdom if you are a north person, you are innocence and trust if you are a south person, you see far if east, and you look within if you are west. What else is inside of you? What good things are going on inside of you? Think on these things. See where they are in your circle. Are they to the right of you or to the left of you or in front? You are trying to put all of yourself in the circle — everything that is inside of you. What are you today — just today? Tomorrow you might be quite different. Now concentrate for a few minutes on what you see in your circle.

Mandala drawing

Give each person an 8 inch square piece of paper with the center point marked.

- Using the compass and pencil, first draw a big circle to cover most of the paper. This is like the big circle you just drew around yourself. Then, draw a small center circle in the middle of the big circle.
  Put a mark in the direction you were standing in. Now mark off all the other three directions. When you have marked all the four directions you are lined up with the earth.

- You can now draw designs or symbols or pictures of all the things you noticed going on inside of you while you meditated in your mandala circle. Leave the center empty for now. Just fill in the rest of the mandala. You can put lines to separate the different parts of your mandala if you want. These are similar to lines in your eye.

Meditation

Now we will prepare to do the center of our mandala, the most important place. Before we begin the center, each of us will look within. Sit quietly, close your eyes and become very still. Very still and quiet. Remember the center of the mandala is like the center of your eye — the place where all light enters you. Look within you and try to see the light rays which enter your head from the center of your eye. Be very silent and look.

- Now, open your eyes and put what you just saw in the center of your mandala.

continued

continued

 NOTE: If any person cannot think of what to put in the center of his or her mandala suggest that he or she stand and return to the big circle which was drawn on newsprint. Standing in the middle of the circle on the centerpoint, put the arms out and turn again as before. Eyes must be closed to facilitate remembering what was seen inside, before.

Finishing the drawing

Look over the whole mandala. It's important to fill in every part of a mandala with a design of some sort. You can use the design books for borders.

Does this mandala tell you how you feel just now? If you feel quiet does it show that? If it doesn't immediately feel right to you look inside yourself and see what you left out of your drawing. What is really inside you that you forgot about? Draw that in and then see if the mandala seems right to you.

We will put all the mandalas up on the wall where they can be seen because now we're going to do the "stamping out of demons." Look at your mandala. Keep in mind some of the things you thought of when we did the bone game or pillow game. Make a short list of the things you often find yourself doing which upset the harmony around you — things you really don't like when you find yourself doing them, again, even though you've tried to stop. Maybe you don't like it when you are sarcastic to someone so you would write down sarcasm as the demon you want to stamp out. Or, maybe you don't like it when you aren't patient with a younger brother. So you would write down patience. These are problems.

Then on the other side of the paper write down troubles which always seem to happen to you. For instance, some people think that others don't like them; so they would write down unpopular. Or, some people think their teachers are unfair so they would write down unfair.

Write down anything in you or which happens to you that you want to just throw out. We're going to do a Tibetan ritual which helps make these actions leave us.

When I pass among you with this paper bag just drop your list in it. Then I will shake it really well so they are all mixed up and no one can tell who wrote which list. So feel free to write down anything bothering you and no one will know. You'll have only three minutes to make the list.

The leader collects the lists. Then the leader makes 2 columns on the large piece of card-board. At the top of one column the word, *troubles*, is written; at the top of the other column, the word, *problems*. The leader writes each of the words from the list under one of these two columns.

All of these things I wrote here destroy our balance as a group. Have you ever seen a car going down the road with a flat tire? It doesn't move very well, does it? It's wheel is out of balance because it's not round anymore. Well, the medicine wheel of our life can get out of balance, too. Remember, we move through all four directions. We must stamp out what destroys our balance and prevents us moving. These things written here are problems which cause flat spots on the medicine wheel and we can't move well until we work on them. This dance for getting rid of demons helps us remove these problems.

Have everyone sit in a circle. Distribute ditto sheets of the "Dance of the Four Directions." Read it out loud as all follow by reading their own copy. Have someone choose two words from the list on the cardboard. These words fill the blanks marked *trouble* and *problem*. Choose a different person for each stanza. The leader writes the chosen words on a large cardboard to use during the dance. The chosen words should also be written on individual pieces of paper to be put on the floor in the center of the dancing area.

The basic theme of many Mandala rituals is the transformation of destructive energy through harmony of the opposites.
JOSÉ AND MIRIAM ARGÜELLES

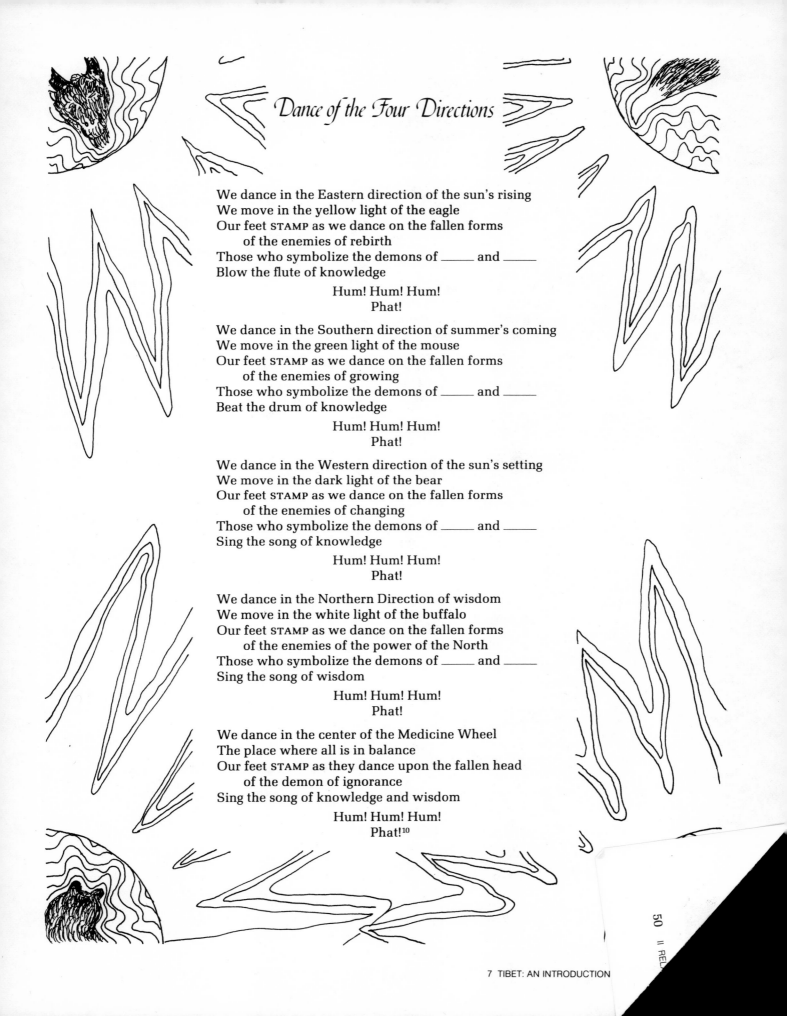

Dance of the Four Directions

We dance in the Eastern direction of the sun's rising
We move in the yellow light of the eagle
Our feet STAMP as we dance on the fallen forms
    of the enemies of rebirth
Those who symbolize the demons of _____ and _____
Blow the flute of knowledge

        Hum! Hum! Hum!
          Phat!

We dance in the Southern direction of summer's coming
We move in the green light of the mouse
Our feet STAMP as we dance on the fallen forms
    of the enemies of growing
Those who symbolize the demons of _____ and _____
Beat the drum of knowledge

        Hum! Hum! Hum!
          Phat!

We dance in the Western direction of the sun's setting
We move in the dark light of the bear
Our feet STAMP as we dance on the fallen forms
    of the enemies of changing
Those who symbolize the demons of _____ and _____
Sing the song of knowledge

        Hum! Hum! Hum!
          Phat!

We dance in the Northern Direction of wisdom
We move in the white light of the buffalo
Our feet STAMP as we dance on the fallen forms
    of the enemies of the power of the North
Those who symbolize the demons of _____ and _____
Sing the song of wisdom

        Hum! Hum! Hum!
          Phat!

We dance in the center of the Medicine Wheel
The place where all is in balance
Our feet STAMP as they dance upon the fallen head
    of the demon of ignorance
Sing the song of knowledge and wisdom

        Hum! Hum! Hum!
          Phat![10]

These inner motives spring from a deep source that is not made by consciousness and is not under its control. In the mythology of earlier times, these forces were called mana, or spirits, demons, and gods. They are as active today as they ever were. If they conform to our wishes, we call them happy hunches . . . and pat ourselves on the back. If they go against us, then we say that it is just bad luck, or that certain people are against us. . . . The one thing we refuse to admit is that we are dependent upon ''powers'' that are beyond our control.

C. G. JUNG

Dance

Move to the ceremonial tepee area. The group stands in a circle with each person holding the hands of those on either side. Use the basic Indian slide step which was learned for the Autumn Equinox Festival. As the leader recites the verse the circle turns using the slide step.

When the leader recites "hum, hum, hum" all raise the joined hands and march toward the center. One step is taken for each "hum." When the leader says, "Phat!" all stamp hard on the papers with the troubles and problems written on them. (These papers should be put in the center of the circle before the dance begins.)

Resume the circle slide step on the next verse and repeat as above on the refrain.

Choose one person to play each instrument called for in the dance. On the last verse everyone dances in the center.

Repeat the dance and chant as often as the group is interested. After the first few times let the group make up any words they wish to fit the blanks. Nonsense words are quite acceptable as often the content of the unconscious comes out better.

We've stamped out the problems which are unsettling us and we're really in balance. Let's chant the balance song as we do our circle dance. (Stamp the feet on phat!)

> All things that must be
> must be in balance
> And — *that* takes practice
>
> Hum! Hum! Hum!
> Phat!

As everyone leaves remind them to write down a dream which happens to them during the week. Bring it to the next session.

The person who has understood what is meant by psychic reality need have no fear that he has fallen back into primitive demonology. If indeed the unconscious figures are not taken seriously as spontaneously active factors, we become victims of a one-sided faith in the conscious mind, which finally leads to a state of over-tension. Catastrophes are then bound to occur, because, despite all our consciousness, the dark psychic powers have been overlooked. It is not we who personify them; they have a personal nature from the very beginning. Only when this is thoroughly recognized can we think of depersonalizing them.

C. G. JUNG

The oldest mandala drawing known to me is a palaeolithic so-called "sun wheel", recently discovered in Rhodesia. It also is based on the principle of four. Things reaching so far back in human history naturally touch upon the deepest layers of the unconscious and affect the latter where conscious speech shows itself to be quite impotent. . . . The early Middle Ages are especially rich in Christian mandalas, and for the most part show Christ in the centre, with the four evangelists, or their symbols, at the cardinal points.

C. G. JUNG

About the structure of the eye and the mandala

One of the sources of the power of the mandala is due to its relationship to the neurophysiology of the eye. Gerald Oster, during his study of moire patterns and the structure of the eye, made a circular figure transparency. This consisted of equispaced concentric circles of spacing with black lines twice as wide as that of the clear, transparent lines. When this circular figure was held in front of the eyes and a scene was viewed through it, the observer saw the same effects as when using LSD. From this and other experiments Oster concluded that "all vision has a circular pattern superimposed on it and LSD reveals the presence of this screen via the moire effect."[11]

The fovea, the point of fixation on the retina of the eye, is made up of cones. Each of these cones "is connected by individual nerves which lead to the optic center via the 'blind spot' of the eyeball. The nerves lie in front of the cones, i.e., the light received is intercepted by a layer of nerve fibers. These nerve fibers would be expected to curve out and around the fovea to produce a screen consisting of curved lines."[12]

The mandala duplicates the structure of the eye, with the center of the mandala in the position of the foveal "blind spot." As Ralph Metzner points out, "Since this 'blind spot' is the exit from the eye to the visual system of the brain, by going 'out' through the center you are going *in* to the brain."[13]

Mandalas . . . are all based on the squaring of a circle. Their basic motif is the premonition of a centre of personality, a kind of central point within the psyche, to which everything is related, by which everything is arranged, and which is itself a source of energy. The energy of the central point is manifested in the almost irresistible compulsion and urge to become what one is, just as every organism is driven to assume the form that is characteristic of its nature, no matter what the circumstances.   C. G. JUNG

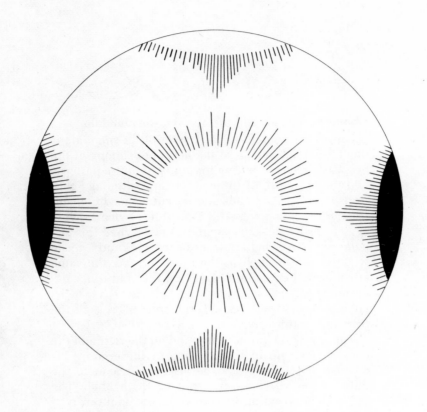

meeting area	

• movie projector and screen
• film — *Requiem for Tibet*
• one magnifying glass for every two people
• an atlas of the world showing altitudes of mountains in color
• sun poster
• pine incense and matches
• several sets of watercolor felt pens
• books of Indian designs (see Cycle I, Session 3)
• one paper bag
• compass — this will be needed from now on
	every time a mandala is constructed
	• small slips of paper
	• for each person:
	  1 large sheet of newsprint with center point marked
	  1 eight inch square of drawing paper with center point marked
	  1 pencil or dark felt pen
	  1 ditto sheet of the Dance of the Four Directions

ceremonial tepee area	
• ditto sheets of the Dance • drum	• whistle or flute

8 dream mandala

Last session we made a mandala. Mandalas and medicine wheels line us up with the world. They are a way of being together in harmony with everything else which lives on the earth.

Today I am going to tell you an Indian legend which will help you to learn more about the four directions of the medicine wheel and the mandala.

Story

Once, when a tribe of Indian people were very hungry because there had not been good hunting, the Coyote of Learning, the Trickster, visited two children and gave them two coyote robes of understanding. He told the children to give the Gifts to the tribe and tell the people to put them on and they would not be hungry any more.

But when the children offered the robes to the people, the people just laughed at the children and said, "We can't eat these robes. We need buffalo meat to eat."

The two children were very sad and ashamed because everyone laughed at them. But, finally, two people came up to them and put their arms around the children and said they would wear the robes. When they put the robes on they were very surprised because now they could see buffalo everywhere whereas before they could not see any buffalo at all.

"There are Buffalo to the North and to the South," the Man said to the People, because now he could See them.

"And there are Buffalo to the West and to the East" the Woman said, because now she too could see them.

The People all became excited, because Suddenly they too could See the Buffalo.

"Let us Hunt them in the North," some of the People said.

"No," Others Quickly Shouted. *"The Buffalo are much fatter in the South."*

"No! No!" the Rest of the People said Angrily. *"The best ones of All are to the East."*

"Please! Please! Do not Fight Among yourselves," the Man, Woman, Little Boy and Little Girl pleaded. *"You are Only Tricking yourselves. Put On the Coyote Robes and you will Understand."*

But the People were very Angry, and they would not Come Together in a Circle to Counsel.

"Kill these Trouble Makers," the People shouted. And they rushed in All Together Upon these Four who were

sitting in the middle of the Camp Circle. But when they reached the Center of the Camp Circle, they Discovered that the Little Boy and the Little Girl had Become a Flowering Forked Tree. They Quickly Looked for the Man and the Woman who had Adopted the Two Children, but All they Found of them were their Tracks. They were the Tracks of Two Mountain Lions. These tracks were leading to the north. The People were so angry they struck at the flowering tree.

"Let us follow the two lions and kill them," the people then decided together. They followed the tracks to the north to find them. They ran and ran, until suddenly the tracks of the two lions became the tracks of four lions. These led the people in a great circle back to the flowering tree.

The people sat down together around the tree because they were so tired, and they began to talk to one another.

"Why are we doing this?" Some of them asked the others.

"We do not really wish to hurt or kill anything," said some others.

"Then why were you running?" asked still others.

"We were only following you," those spoken to said in amazement. And they all began to laugh.

Then the people all heard singing, and they looked up. There, sitting in the north, they saw a white coyote and he was singing. Then they looked to the south, and sitting there was a green coyote. She too was singing. Then they looked to the west, and sitting there was a black coyote and he was singing. Finally they looked to the east, and sitting there was a gold coyote and she was singing.

The people sat there quietly all together and learned these four beautiful songs. They were the songs of four lions. Then the people looked all around and saw that each of them was wearing a coyote robe. They put their arms around each other and began to dance toward the flowering tree together in a great circle. The people were very happy."[14]

Explanation

This is the end of the story as the Indians tell it. There are some things in it which puzzle us aren't there? And we don't quite understand it. That is because it's a teaching story which was told so that people could learn more about the medicine wheel and its directions. After the wise old Indian told the story then he usually explained its meaning. And so will I.

You know all along we have been trying to learn to see inside ourselves — to see whether we are a person of the North or West or of the East or South. Well before this story begins the two children had already learned to see inside themselves and therefore they understood themselves but no one else in the tribe had learned how to do this. That is why the Coyote of Learning gives the children the robes.

The rest of the people of the tribe are hungry for understanding. That is why they are unhappy and fighting among themselves. They were no longer in balance so they were unable to talk to one another. The coyote robes which the children are to give to the people are really gifts which would help the people to see inside themselves so they could understand. The Coyote of Learning wants to give-away these robes to the people so they will no longer be starving for understanding.

But the people don't understand and they reject them. The two kind people who finally put the robes on immediately understand and explain to the others about the gifts. When the man says "There are buffalo to the North and to the South." What does he really mean? What gifts of understanding come from those directions? What does North stand for? And South? (north — wisdom; south — trust and innocence) And the woman says "There are buffalo to the West and to the East." What are those gifts? When the people in the story hear about these buffalo they are excited. Remember they said let's hunt these and then they began to argue about which direction was the best way to hunt for the gifts.

"Let us hunt these Gifts of Wisdom," some of the People say. "No," others quickly shout. "These Gifts of Trust and Innocence are more healing."

"No! No!" still others of the People argue. "There are bigger Gifts of Introspection to the West."

"No! No!" the rest of the People reply angrily. "The best gifts of all are to be found to the East within Illumination."[15]

What do you think about this argument about which gift is best? (discuss) We'll see what the people learned. While they were arguing they saw the tracks of two mountain lions. The mountain lion is the symbol of complete balance, of wholeness. The mountain lion tracks go toward the north, the place of wisdom. The people want to follow the tracks of the two balances and kill them. But, remember, they are following the tracks toward the north so they are really going toward the place of wisdom, the north aren't they?

So the people run and run following the balance tracks. When they get to the north, the place of wisdom, they discover wisdom itself. What wisdom do they discover? They "discover that they have run in a Great Circle and have come back to themselves." They are very angry at first because they've been tricked by the Coyote Teacher but by tricking them he's got them together as a Whole People and because of that they can now discover their balance within the four directions. They are tired so they sit down to rest and because they are balanced now they can talk to one another and one asks:

"*Why are we doing this?*"
"*We do not want to hurt or kill anything,*" two others say.
"*Then why were you running?*" ask still others.
"*We were only following you.*"[16]

And then everybody laughs. They hear singing which is the sound of harmony. Then they see to the north a white coyote and he is in harmony with the people. To the south what do they see? (Let the group tell what is seen in each of the other directions.) The people learn from the four harmonies of balance from the coyotes of the four directions.

When they learn this harmony they suddenly see that they are all teachers. We are all teachers of one another in the song of harmony. The people all put their arms around one another and dance toward the flowering tree together. Each person's way of seeing has been changed. "As we learn we always change, and so does our way of seeing. This changed seeing then becomes a new Teacher inside each of us."

"Our first Teacher is our own heart." The other teachers are called the seven Arrows. Four of these arrows are the four directions. Can you think what are the other two arrows? (Mother Earth and Father Sky) And the seventh arrow is the Great Spirit — the Universal Harmony which holds all things together.

Dance

 Let's dance the dance of the four harmonies which make balance.

✦ Move to the ceremonial area. Do the Dance of the Four Directions as given in the previous session. Then return to the meeting area.

At the beginning of our story today the two children were the only ones in the whole tribe of people who had learned to see inside themselves so that they had understanding. How do you suppose they had learned to see inside of themselves? They had learned because they listened to that powerful person who lives within each of us. That person is our true "self." Each of us has deep within him his true "self" which really knows what to do at all times but we don't listen to our "self" because we are too busy to listen.

Many times our own "self", deep within us, can't reach us because we just won't listen and then our "self" has to talk to us through our dreams. Remember the Senoi Indian story earlier this fall. The Senoi Indians thought that when the spirits called you in a dream you should bring back a gift for the others in the tribe from what you learn in your dream. If we really pay attention to our dreams we, too, can bring back a gift of understanding to others just as the children in our story today brought the gift of understanding to their People. (discuss)

Today we are going to make dream mandalas which will help each of us to have the gift of understanding. We will use them for our Winter Solstice Festival.

◆ Distribute the necessary materials.

• First, have everyone draw an 18 inch circle.

• Next, draw a 3 in. diameter circle in the center. Explain that the center circle is each "self" as it is in the middle of the dream. The large outer circle is the dream.

• Have them design the center circle. They may use the colors and their direction animal from the medicine wheel for this center.

• If they wish, they may run spokes from the center circle toward the edge. This makes divisions in their dream world. This is optional.

• In the outer circle, they should have complete freedom to express their *feelings* about the dream. Suggestions can be given as listed below but make sure that they understand that these suggestions are merely to stimulate their thinking but they are free to do their own interpretations.

Suggestions for designing the outer circle

1. The dream world may be drawn like a cartoon with different events drawn cartoon fashion around the circle. Words may be included.

2. If the dream caused feelings but left no real memory of a sequential story they may wish to draw designs which express those feelings: happy, sad, empty, afraid, overwhelmed, or joy. Some people may want to express their feelings with color only.

3. Perhaps someone brought back from his or her dream a song or poem. This could be written in the outer circle.

4. As a result of the dream someone may decide to take some action. The cause and effect could be drawn.

When the mandalas are finished collect them for use in the Winter Solstice Festival.

Peeling sticks for next session

When some people have finished their mandalas bring out the tree branches. Explain that these will be used next session to make the Indian singing sticks. They must be peeled today so that they will be dry enough to paint next session. When they are all peeled collect them to keep until next session.

Show the group the shield in the frontispiece of *Seven Arrows*. Talk about the forked tree with them and let them discuss what they see in the shield.

meeting area	
• each person needs: 18 inch square of drawing paper compass pencil one straight tree branch about 12 in. long and ¾ to 1 inch thick. Use any type of wood which splits easily. If no tree branches are available	use the leftover branches which have been trimmed off Christmas trees • Materials all can use: watercolor felt pen crayons colored pencils chisels and knives

ceremonial tepee area
this area does not need any special preparation

He must be introduced to the universal law of coexisting opposites. He has to realize that completeness consists in opposites co-operating through conflict, and that harmony is essentially a resolution of irreducible tensions . . . the pattern of existence is woven of antagonistic co-operation, alternations of ascendancy and decline, that is built of bright and dark, day and night.
HEINRICH ZIMMER

9 preparation for winter solstice

Last session we learned of the seven teaching arrows. Another way to describe these arrows is to think of them as mirrors because each of these teaching arrows shows us a little more of ourselves. These seven arrows reflect some of each of you but these reflections don't stop there because people can reflect emotions back to one another too.

Let everyone see the cover shield on the book, *Seven Arrows.*

This is an Indian Medicine shield which shows how the reflections are many and make up the medicine wheel. (Then show the frontispiece shield of the forked branch.)

Remember last week the time we heard the legend where the boy and girl had become a flowering forked tree and this forked tree reflected back the people's own emotions. At first, when the people were angry, they attacked the forked tree. Later, when the people had discovered wisdom, they found that they were again back at the forked tree but this time, because the people had learned and were changed, they liked the forked tree and danced around it.

The forked tree is another way of showing that each of us has different aspects of "the Powers" in us. Take a look at this forked branch (showing one of the forked twigs.) Each branch mirrors the other doesn't it — like a twin image.

An Indian named Yellow Robe explained it this way:

> "There is a twinness about man. A twinness of his nature. And there have always existed the twin parts of the People. It is always the Other Man who does not understand, or the Other Man who is the one at fault. This Other Man is represented by the Forked Tree, the Center Pole of the Sun Dance. It is Forked, but both parts of this are One Thing. Leaves are left upon the Forked Tree as a Sign to the People that these things of twinness mirror twinness again within the People. The two Forks look exactly the same. And each Fork branches into many leaves that are exactly the same. But the question is always, which reflection is which? Which one am I? Or am I both? It is a great Teaching."[17]

So you see one half of you can love; the other half may hate sometimes. But you are still the same person. Yellow Robe explains:

"This is the Forked Medicine Pole of Man. The clever thing the Medicine has taught us here is this. One half of you must understand the other half or you will tear yourself apart. It is the same with the other half of any People who live together. One must understand the other, or they will destroy each other. But remember! Both halves must try to understand. Even within yourself it is hard to know which of the Forks is which. 'Now why did I do that?, one half of you asks the other half. You do things quite often which you do not mean to say or do, sometimes to yourself and sometimes to others. But you would not kill yourself for these mistakes, would you? I am quite certain that you would not. Yet there are those who have done this, who have killed either themselves or others. These are men who have not learned. An entire People can be like this. These People and men are not Full, they are not Whole."[18]

It's sort of like the people in the legend we told last session. They were fighting over which of the Gifts of Understanding is the best.

Some people think we should be happy all the time and never sad. Or, maybe they think we should be excited all the time and never feeling low or blue. But you can't separate these things. They are found in the same Forked tree. If we have a forked tree where one half is sad; the other happy and one of these halves tries to split itself from the other half the tree will become broken, won't it, and may die.

 While saying this, break off one side of the forked branch you have been using in the demonstration above. Distribute a forked twig to each person.

Take a look at your forked twigs. Think about two aspects inside of you — one which you like and one which you don't like. Call one side of the twig the part of you which you like to be. Let's say, you like the part of you which is excited — full of enthusiasm. Call the other side of the twig something you think might not be so good — like when you are feeling low or sad. Now you have different names for the two sides but do they look different? No, they look the same because they still are the same, really. Can you separate them and still have a whole well-formed twig? No. Neither can you do that to yourself.

Everyone of us is a mirror to others. If you decide you don't like the low or blue part of yourself and try to get rid of it then you begin to hate the feeling low part of everyone else because it mirrors the part of you which you don't like. You refuse to accept the feeling low part of people. That is because other people mirror your thoughts back to you. So soon things get very bad and you hate more and more people. But if you stop trying to split yourself and accept the excited or enthusiastic part and the feeling low part of you then you will see enthusiastic people and sad people all around you and you realize that both emotions are necessary. All the reflections or mirrors which we see in the world are our teachers too because everything and everyone can teach us about ourselves if we only learn to see.

Another example of this problem is when someone is up to bat and strikes out. Others tease him or her not so much because the "out" will affect the game,

We haven't yet comprehended, as have the Indians, the psychical ecology underlying physical ecology . . . As I see it, we must graduate to this belief, to attune ourselves to both the inner and outer realities of life if we are to close the widening rupture between our minds and hearts. By rupture, I mean this. In ruthlessly destroying nature, man, who is also part of nature, ruptures his own inner self. We set ourselves apart not only from the earth, but from the dark maternal unconscious, its psychic counterpart. For man's unconscious is equated to and rooted in nature. And by our destructive and materialistic rationalism, we have alienated our conscious self from the earthy substratum of our essential being. In subduing nature we also fought to subdue the forces of nature within ourselves — the secret and sinful desires of natural man, all of the instincts so incompatible to the mores of rational man. Our own bodies became the battleground of reason versus instinct, the conscious versus the unconscious. This split in the wholeness of the psyche C.G. Jung views as the tragedy of overcivilized man. So it seems to me we've got to learn from the Indians. We've got to listen to the voice of the secret and invisible spirit of the land itself. FRANK WATERS

but because they hate themselves when they strike out. They can project this feeling onto another person even if they cannot accept it in themselves.

 Show the slingshot.

We need both sides to make a slingshot. The power in the slingshot comes from the fact that both sides are there. We have to develop both sides in ourselves, too. If one side is weaker it will break off and that will throw the sling shot off balance. We need both sides of an emotion or feeling in us, too, in order to have power.

Note to adults

Parents and other adults often cause more trouble to the child who exhibits qualities similar to the adult especially if those qualities are ones which the adult dislikes in himself (shyness, fear of water, aggressiveness or lack of aggressiveness etc.)

Everything has both sides: happy and sad, enthusiastic or low, night and day, cold and hot, summer and winter. Next session we come to one of the most important times of the year. The sun has been giving less and less light for months now and next week we have the shortest day of the year so that is the beginning of winter. We call this the winter solstice.

The Hopi Indians say that every year at the time of the winter solstice in December the sun leaves his winter house and starts travelling to his summer house which he reaches in June. The Hopi Indians and many other Indians believe that we must help the sun make this turn around so he doesn't stay in his winter house and then spring would never come. At first, it may seem strange to think of helping the sun

but let's discuss it. Even when the sun is out bright and there are no clouds sometimes in the city we don't see the sun or else we see it very dimly. What is wrong? (pollution) Who causes pollution? So we can damage the effects of the sun in this way so maybe the Indians are right and we need to help the sun in its work. That's what the Winter Solstice Festival is all about. During this festival, human beings give their energy to help the sun in its work.

The Plains Indians danced the sun dance to give energy to the sun. The Hopis also dance to give energy to the sun during their winter solstice ceremony. For this dance they make sun shields. That is what we will do now so we can use them for the festival at the next session.

 Directions for sun shields

• Using the marked center point draw a circle as big as possible with the compass. Cut this out for the shield.

• For the handle, tie the ends of two plastic bags together. Braid the two bags together and then tie the other end. Staple this to the shield as a handle. The side of the shield which has the marked center point is the front. Staple the handle to the back. Make sure that the staples are outside the center three inch circle as they should not protrude on to the front side where the mirror will be glued.

• Glue the 2 in. mirror in the center of the shield with contact glue. This is glued on the front side of the shield, where the center mark is located.

• Paint a border around this mirror about ½ inch wide with gold tempera paint. Each person draws the sun around this center with the mirror as the center. Each person may use his own ideas or copy from a picture of the sun or the sun poster.

• The sun may be colored with felt pens or yellow latex paint. Leave a border ½ inch wide at the bottom of the shield for putting the fringe on later.

• Allow to dry, while the singing sticks are made.

Directions for making singing sticks

• "Singing sticks" were used by the Indians to accompany them when they sang songs or performed rituals.

• Spread newspapers several layers deep in the painting area.

• Punch holes in the bottom of the egg cartons. When the sticks are painted, one end will be placed in a hole to hold it upright while it dries.

• The sticks, which were peeled at the previous session, should be about 12 in. long. Make a mark 8 inches along the stick. The stick is split in half down to this mark. Then split each of these pieces in half again. This provides a completed singing stick with a 4 in. handle and 4 thin sections of wood which rattle together when shaken or hit.

• Take the stick to the painting area. Paint the handle of the stick red as this is the Cheyenne color for life. Paint the tip ends of each of the four sections blue to symbolize the sky. Paint one of the cut portions black, one yellow, one green, one white to symbolize the four directions of the medicine wheel.

• While it is drying wash hands. Be sure they are dried well to facilitate handling the feathers.

• Tie the four white feathers (one for each direction) onto the string.

• When the sticks have dried, tie the string to the handle of the stick.

• Tie the end of the sticks together when not in use so they will not break or warp.

Finishing the sun shields

When the shields have dried, the fringe along the bottom of the shield is attached. (See the shield on the cover of *Seven Arrows* which has feathers for a fringe.) Listed below are three suggestions for a special winter solstice fringe.

1. Gold icicles from Christmas tree decorations may be glued along the bottom edge of the shield. Gold is for the sun and these items are available this time of year.

2. Pine twigs may be tied together with strong thread to make long strings. Using the punch, make holes in the bottom edge of the shield, and tie strings of twigs on the shield. Green is the sign of returning life which the sun will bring.

3. Tiny god's eyes made of toothpicks and yarn may be used. Tie a string to one of the points of a finished god's eye. Then tie it through the holes punched on the bottom edge of the shield.

The group forms couples facing one another. Each person holds his completed shield toward the person facing him.

Now make a sad face. Look at your face reflected in the mirror of the other person's shield. When you see a sad face like that, how does it make you feel? You don't feel good when you see a sad face like that do you? You feel much better when you see a smiling face. So, think of how a person coming toward you feels when he sees your sad face.

Remember we learned that "the Powers" reflect back to us what we feel. If you feel fear "the Powers" reflect fear back to you. If you feel joy "the Powers" reflect joy back to you. This same thing is true of people. People very often reflect back to you the emotion you feel.

The Indians held festivals like the one we are having next session so that they could get themselves in harmony to reflect the Universal Harmony.

Encourage everyone to experiment with making faces to the shields and reflecting lights off the mirror.

Note for next week's session: If you have access to a wooded area the group as a whole can go out together sometime during the week to choose a large forked branch for next week's Winter Solstice Festival. The branch should be five or six feet tall. The two forks of the branch should be as nearly alike as possible. Try to get a branch from a deciduous tree but if this is impossible, use a double top Christmas tree.

The right side of the cortex primarily controls the left side of the body, and the left side of the cortex largely controls the right side of the body. The structure and the function of these two "half-brains" influence the two modes of consciousness. The left hemisphere is predominantly involved with analytic thinking, especially language and logic. This hemisphere seems to process information sequentially, which is necessary for logical thought since logic depends on sequence and order.

The right hemisphere, by contrast, appears to be primarily responsible for our orientation in space, artistic talents, body awareness, and recognition of faces. It processes information more diffusely than the left hemisphere does, and integrates material in a simultaneous, rather than linear fashion.
ROBERT E. ORNSTEIN

About the right and left hemispheres of the brain

Just as the left hemisphere of the brain learns through thinking and reading, the right hemisphere learns through the creation of arts and crafts and through performing ritual. To reach the whole person both kinds of learning must occur. This session, though not specifically based on right/left brain research, is an introduction to the fact that there are two different sides of a human being. Further sessions delve more specifically into right/left brain differences.

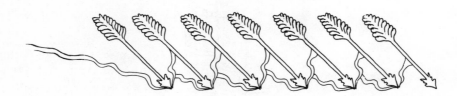

---

only the meeting area is used this session

- one forked twig for each person
- one slingshot made from a forked branch
- *Seven Arrows* book
- sun poster
- pictures of the sun: Blake type sun, Toltec sun, and photos

materials for making sun shields
- each person needs:
    - 1 piece (22 x 28 in.) railroad board with center point marked
    - 2 plastic bread bags
    - 1 mirror (2 inches in diameter). Order from Grey Owl Mfg. They are cheaper by the dozen
- they share:
    - contact glue
    - bright yellow latex paint
    - brushes
    - watercolor felt pens
    - needles
    - thread

stapler
gold icicles (Christmas tree decorations) or strips of gold paper
pine twigs
gold tempera paint
brushes
optional: material for making tiny god's eyes — toothpicks and yarn

materials for making singing sticks
- each person needs:
    - 1 peeled tree branch from last session
    - 1 knife
    - 4 white feathers
    - one foot of fishing line, strong cord, or string
- they share:
    - brushes
    - newspapers to protect work surface
    - clean up water and towels
    - several egg cartons
    - latex paint in bright green, white, yellow, blue and red

Man's very survival as a species has been placed in grave jeopardy by our repression of the human celebrative and imaginative faculties. . . .

Man is by his very nature a creature who not only works and thinks but who sings, dances, prays, tell stories, and celebrates. He is homo festivus. *. . .*

Man inhabits a world of constant change, and in such a world both festival and fantasy are indispensable for survival. . . . Festivity by breaking routine and opening man to the past, enlarges his experience and reduces his provincialism. Fantasy opens doors that merely empirical calculation ignores. It widens the possibilities for innovation. Together, festivity and fantasy enable man to experience his present in a richer, more joyful, more creative way. Without them he may go the way of the diplodocus and the tyranosaurus. . . . Without social imagaination no one will be able to think up fundamentally new ways to relate to the rest of the world. Unless the industrialized world recovers its sense of festivity and fantasy, it will die or be destroyed. HARVEY COX

10 ✦ winter solstice festival

Upon arriving, each person cuts up cedar to begin boiling for the ceremony later. The pots are put on the fire now.

Our last festival was the Autumn Equinox. At the time of the Autumn Equinox there was exactly the same amount of light and dark. During the months following that time we gradually got more and more darkness. At the time of the Autumn Equinox we talked about how important it is for us to remain in balance; to even change a little, so that we can remain in balance as the light changes around us and we get more and more darkness. All through the weeks since then we learned ways of staying in balance — inside ourselves — and ways of restoring balance in the group. We learned the pillow game, the bone game and mandalas. We learned how people must remain balanced inside themselves so they don't upset the greater balance of nature.

Now, today we celebrate an even more important festival — the Winter Solstice. (See appendix for full explanation of the solstices.) This is the darkest time during the year. The sun has reached its winter house and it will begin the return journey to its summer house, which it will reach in June. This is a very important time when the sun turns around and begins its journey toward summer. For this important change we must contribute our energy too. That's because everything in the universe is in relationship to everything else so we are in relationship to the sun. The Hopi Indians say that although we have human parents, our real parents are Mother Earth and Father Sun, "the one who gives life to all the universe." So you have an earthly family but you also have a cosmic family too.

But the original and the only source of food is sun, however packaged and arranged on the supermarket shelves and in whatever variety, no matter how late the market is open. . . .

How much food is there? How much sun poured on the earth, stored in golden jellies beneath the surface of the land . . . and how much sun is there left?

RICHARD GROSSINGER

What one thing gives us practically every thing that we need to live? (Discuss the sun which gives us life because it gives us food and light. End the discussion with this phrase:)

"every creature feeds on sun . . . and builds its home out of stored sunlight."[19]

People must help the sun just as it helps us and gives us life. This is our give-away to the sun.

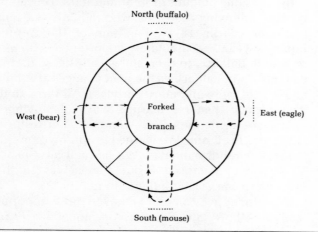

Group Mandala Painting

The first thing we are going to do for the festival is to draw a mandala on the floor so we know where to dance.

Divide everyone into four groups: those who are buffalo people, those who are bear people, those who are eagle people and those who are mouse people.

- The center of the mandala is the forked branch. Put this forked branch in the center of the room. Around this center draw a circle almost as large as the room. Then draw lines out from the center toward each compass point as shown above.
- Each of the four groups works on the section of the large circle which is their direction. Instruct them to draw a large picture of the animal of their direction: buffalo, bear, eagle or mouse. Then each person in the group is free to draw any symbol which is important to them: god's eyes, the sun, patterns from the milk light show or patterns from nature, etc.
- Draw a short line outside the mandala circle at each of the four compass points, shown above by the dotted lines.
- When the group mandala painting is finished, take the boiling cedar water off the fire and cool it by adding cold water until it is lukewarm. Keep until later in the ceremony.

 *Painting the Dancers*

As this is a sun ceremony, a sun should be painted on each person's forehead. Have everyone pair up and paint one another. When this is finished the leader asks this question.

Remember we have found that we always need two different aspects of something to make the whole. The sun causes things to grow but what else

do growing things need? (water) The Indians believe that the moon causes moisture so we need a moon. Paint a moon on your two hands — one can be a full moon and one, a half moon or quarter moon.

Yellow paint is used for the sun and white for the moon.

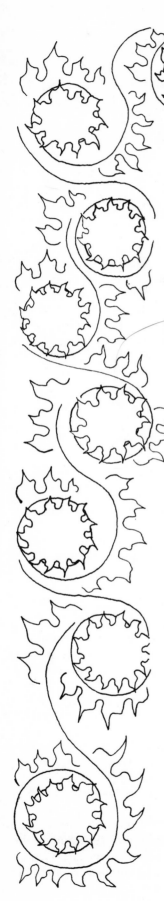

Celebration

✦ Have everyone go to their own direction and put their shields and singing sticks behind the line. Each person stands behind this line. The ceremony begins with each person picking up his singing sticks and lining up in single file at the eastern part of the mandala.

· The leader leads them in a circle of the entire mandala before entering from the eastern direction — where the sun rises.

· All walk to the center area and gather around the center tree where everyone shakes his singing stick in rhythm while the leader says:

The sun is the center of the earth's medicine wheel. During the year the earth goes through all the seasons and so makes a complete turn of the cosmic medicine wheel. We are going to help turn the medicine wheel by dancing and chanting. (The leader reads the following chant. The refrain will be used later in the dancing.)

Sun's Give-away Chant

You, who move in the sky, you are the sun of millions of years ago.

You gave-away food to the giant fern forests where the dinosaurs roamed.

The forests died and fell down and were pressed into the earth. Now they give-away coal and oil to keep us warm.

We keep warm from the stored sunlight given-away by the sun.

Give-away to the sun — push the sun along its path.

You, who move in the sky, you are the sun of a few hundred years ago giving food to trees. We cut these trees to build our houses.

We are sheltered by the stored sunlight given-away by the sun.

Give-away to the sun — turn the sun along its path.

You, who move in the sky, you are the sun now, sending out light to make food for us.

Give-away to the sun — help the sun turn back from its winter house.

✦ All leave by the eastern direction and pile their singing sticks behind the line in their own direction. They pick up their shields and hold them in front by means of the arm loop.

Dance

✦ All gather again in the center by the forked tree. The Indian dance record is played and everyone dances using a stomping step. Begin the chanting by repeating the phrases: "Push the sun along its path, turn the sun along its path, help the sun turn back." The group will pick this up and chant variations on it.

1. From the center of the mandala move toward the east twirling or pushing the sun shields. Follow the dotted arrows on the diagram.

2. When the edge of the circle is reached, stop and dance backward toward the forked tree.
3. Now, turn toward the south and repeat the movement in steps number 1 and 2 above.
4. Do this same movement toward the west and north.
5. At the end of the dance place the shields in a corner and each group returns to its own direction and stands behind the line.

Race

◉ The race begins with those who are of the eagle of the east because the sun rises in the east. This is a relay race so it is not one person against another or one group against another group; instead, it is the entire group in the fastest possible time so we develop a lot of energy. I will explain how the race goes as I walk through it.

• Eagle people, standing outside the circle to the east, pick up their singing sticks, run into the circle toward the forked tree and circle it once.

They run out the circle toward the south, then run back into the circle to the center and circle the forked tree twice.

They run out the circle toward the west and then run back in and circle the tree three times.

Then they run out the south and hand the singing sticks to the group at the south. These mouse people of the south cannot start until the last eagle person hands his stick to the mouse person.

• The mouse people of the south run in, circle the tree once and then repeat the same pattern. At the end of their pattern they give the sticks to the bear people of the west.

• The bear people run in, circle the tree once and then repeat the same pattern, ending up by giving the sticks to the northern people.

• The buffalo people of the north repeat the pattern ending up by running out to the east and thus back to the starting point.

Remember, the next group cannot begin to race until all the sticks have been given to them by the preceding group.

The first time in, the tree is circled once; second time in, the tree is circled twice; third time, the tree is circled three times.

✦ Be sure the eagle people have the same amount of sticks as people in the largest group or you will run short. The race begins as the eagle people of the east begin to run.

After the race is finished, instruct everyone to take up their singing sticks and return to the forked tree. Bring the bowl of cedar water into the center. Using the very ends of their sticks they dip them in the bowl and throw cedar water toward the forked tree. (Water is the sign of life.) Then they throw water at one another using the sticks. This will be a joyous free occasion.

The leader ends the water throwing by telling everyone that at the end of special ceremonies the mandala is destroyed because its power has been all used up. Then all wipe up the mandala or remove the tape.

Feast

Tortilla recipe

At a specialty food or Mexican food store you may be able to buy Masa-Hrina, a fine corn meal. For 12 tortillas mix:

2   cups cornmeal
1¼   cups water

Mix thoroughly. Knead for about 10 minutes. Shape into 12 balls. Pat each ball out by hand to make a 6 inch circle. Bake on a hot lightly greased griddle until light brown on both sides.

If you cannot find Masa-Hrina use any cornmeal with the following recipe:

2   cups cornmeal
1½   cups water
1   teaspoon salt
1   teaspoon baking powder

Follow the above directions for making the tortillas. The tortillas are eaten with honey and butter. Serve the natural tea.

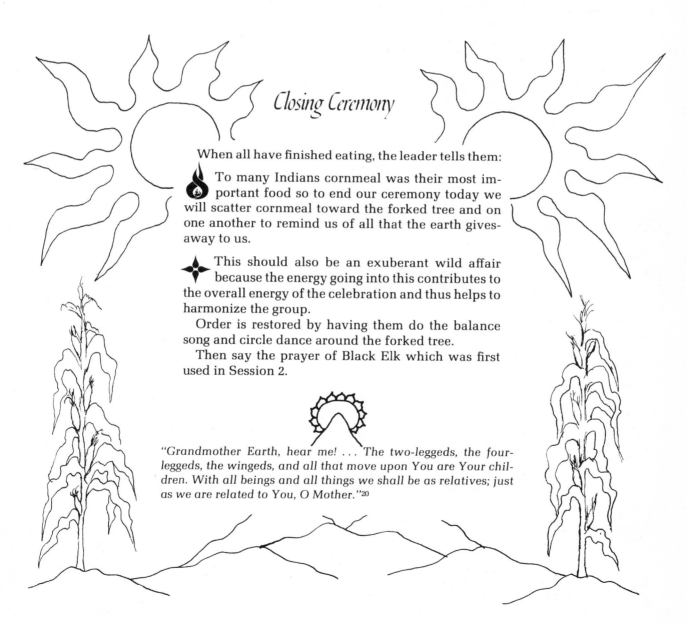

Closing Ceremony

When all have finished eating, the leader tells them:

To many Indians cornmeal was their most important food so to end our ceremony today we will scatter cornmeal toward the forked tree and on one another to remind us of all that the earth gives-away to us.

This should also be an exuberant wild affair because the energy going into this contributes to the overall energy of the celebration and thus helps to harmonize the group.

Order is restored by having them do the balance song and circle dance around the forked tree.

Then say the prayer of Black Elk which was first used in Session 2.

"Grandmother Earth, hear me! ... The two-leggeds, the four-leggeds, the wingeds, and all that move upon You are Your children. With all beings and all things we shall be as relatives; just as we are related to You, O Mother."[20]

ceremonial tepee area

- large forked branch (5 or 6 ft. tall) tied to a tether ball stand or placed in a large bucket filled with sand as a counterweight. A deciduous tree is best but if this is impossible, select a double top Christmas tree. Strip off some of the branches so that the double top is clearly seen
- the area should not have a rug because a floor painting will be done today. The area should be clean and dry
- dream mandalas from session 8 should be arranged along the wall
- cedar branches. In most neighborhoods there is usually a house with ornamental cedars or low-lying juniper plants. If these are not available use any natural plant in your locality which has a strong fragrance when boiled. Birch is one example
- watercolor felt pens for the floor mandala. If your area has a rug which cannot be removed use colored tape which can be pulled off, for the lines of the mandala. For an area with a rug, drawings should be done on paper and taped to the floor
- materials for washing the floor
- record — *American Indian Dances* Folkways No. FD 6510. Use any dance which appeals to your group
- record player
- hot plate or stove
- pans for boiling water
- "singing sticks" which were made last session
- sun shields from last session
- sun poster
- body paint: Mix together ½ cup liquid soap (Crystal brand is the best), ½ cup liquid starch (Vano brand) and 1 tablespoon tempera paint. Two colors are needed: white and yellow. This paint will wash off easily

meeting area

- tortilla ingredients (see recipe given in the session)
- natural tea and materials to make it
- cups
- honey
- butter
- extra cornmeal

There is a form of consciousness which was defined by Meister Eckhart as ''when he sees all in all . . .'' *In this form of consciousness, then, the ordinary distinctions between self and other vanish, as do distinctions between one object and another. All is seen as one whole, wherein not only is everything part of everything else; everything is everything else. . . . From a higher level of consciousness . . . it is apparent that we and our environment are an interwoven fabric, in which every strand crosses every other. When we corrupt it, we corrupt ourselves, because in reality the two cannot be separated.* BRENN STILLEY

It is a fact that symbols, by their very nature, can so unite the opposites that these no longer diverge or clash, but mutually supplement one another and give meaningful shape to life.
C. G. JUNG

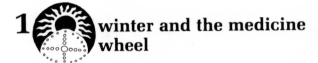

1 winter and the medicine wheel

Last time we were together we celebrated the Winter Solstice. Now winter is here. What do you suppose Indians did in the winter time? In most parts of the country, winter was a time of cold, snow and ice, or wind and rain. The days had shortened and the animals had hibernated. The food which the Indians needed had been stored inside. What do you suppose they did with their time?

In January, the Iroquois Indians held a festival of dreams and they told stories. Both men and women in many different tribes used this time to decorate their clothing and make ceremonial garb — masks, head-dresses, jewelry and vests.

Other Indians told stories too — often about the teachings of the medicine wheel.

Since the most important thing in the lives of the Indians was to live in harmony with nature, they used the time they had in winter to prepare everything they needed for their nature rituals and to prepare themselves by trying to understand more about what was inside them. This is why the Iroquois had a festival of dreams and this is why other Indians told teaching stories about the medicine wheel.

We learned that in the medicine wheel the buffalo is the animal of the north and is also the sign for winter. The color is white.

I've made a medicine wheel which is a little different from others we've seen. Actually, it is a wheel inside of a wheel. The inner wheel and the outer wheel are both marked into four sections. Each section is designated with a season, animal, color and characteristic. Let's start out by lining up the winter section of the small wheel and the winter section of the large wheel. We'll put this wire pointer on the winter section to show which section we are talking about. Now let's slide the inner circle a few inches to the left. What has happened? Part of the fall inner circle goes into the winter outer circle. Part of the winter inner circle slides over into the spring outer circle. Let's talk about it together and see if we can find what this shows us.

In the fall, all nature prepares for the winter. Can you think of examples? (discuss) How about the tulip bulbs which you plants in the fall? They have to go through winter in order to bloom in the spring. How about all the moisture which arrives in the winter. (discuss)

You can slide the inner circle even further until it is in line with the outer circle for summer. Even in winter the earth is preparing for summer. Out of the cold of winter comes the snow which gives the life-giving water of summer. (discuss)

(With the winter inner circle lined up with the summer outer circle move the wire pointer to line up the spring inner circle and fall outer circle.) Now we have lined up spring and fall. How does what hap-

pens in the spring relate to what happens in the fall? (discuss)

(Move the pointer to the inner summer and outer winter sections.)

How does what happens in the summer relate to the winter? (discuss)

(Move the pointer to inner fall and outer spring.)

How does what happens in the fall effect the spring?

Even though we give different names to the seasons they are all part of the same medicine wheel of the earth. It is the same with us. Although last summer you might have been a mouse, seeing only things close to you, this winter you may really have become wiser and no longer only see things which are near to you. But both these things are within you now — the mouse and the buffalo. You are neither one nor the other. You are both and the medicine wheel teaches us that we must develop *all* that is within us as we travel along the medicine wheel.

Even in the middle of winter it is already starting to become summer. The sun has reached its farthest away point at the winter solstice and now the sun is beginning to return to its summer house. So, although it is cold, summer is on the way.

The wheel will be available for you to look and to use later on today. But most of our time, today, we are going to do as the Indians did in the winter and work on a ceremonial vest to use in future festivals and other ceremonies.

Because some of you have never sewn before, I am going to demonstrate the process for everyone, and then you will be free to create your own designs to decorate the vest.

Directions for the ceremonial vest

Two-third yard of 36 in. material is needed for each vest. This is enough material for any size up to size 12. The Grey Owl buckskin finish cloth or suede cloth is best. If you do not want to send away for the material, felt is a possible substitute or one of the new polyester knits which do not have to be hemmed. The fabric should not have a pattern.

Pattern: The pattern is set up on a grid. Each square on the grid is equal to a three inch square. To expand the pattern to a size 12, lay

out a piece of paper that is at least 1 yd. square. Using a yardstick, mark the paper off in three inch squares length and width so that your paper is covered with three inch squares. By noting the angle of the pattern line in each square and copying it onto the corresponding square on your pattern you can explode the diagram in the book into a size 12 pattern on your paper. If you have an overhead projector lay the pattern on the projector, tape the grid to the wall and project the pattern onto it. Draw in the lines.

continued

continued

Preparations for group sewing:

1. Have everybody lay out their patterns. Be sure to check that the correct sides of the fabric are together if you are using fabric with a right and wrong side.
2. Pass out the packages with the needles and pins.
3. Caution everybody to pin their vests completely together before they begin sewing. It is very important that they match the corners of the bottom edge of the side seam first and then the edges of the seam on the bottom of the arm hole.
4. When the vests are pinned together correctly, let them begin sewing the seams. Caution everybody to sew good strong knots at the end of the seam so that the seam will not come apart after the vest is worn.
5. After the vest is sewn, place *all* the pins and needles and extra thread into the little bags.

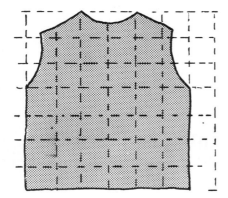
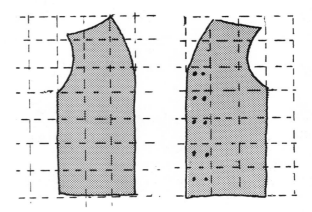

Decorating the vests:

Turn the vest right side out. There should be various techniques available from which the group can choose. Decoration should be open-ended, so that as time progresses, various things may be added to the vest. To prevent restlessness from too much demonstration, choose one or two of the methods given, demonstrate quickly, and let everybody experiment. Plan to introduce other methods at other sessions if there is time. Some may want to work on their vests at home.

1. Punch a series of two holes in the vest along the front openings and/or the bottom edge. Tie leather thongs through the holes. They can be left to dangle loose or objects may be tied to them.
   a) Bones. Lamb bones are the best. They should be drilled with a hole while they are still fresh; otherwise they become brittle and crack when drilled. After the drilling, boil them to clean. For white bones bleach them in a solution of clorox; for darker bones darken them with a solution of strong tea.
   b) Seeds of various types. They must be drilled through so they can be tied on.
   c) Beads may be used but it is best to use natural materials.
2. Buttons, beads, bones or seeds may be sewn on in designs.
3. Designs may be embroidered. Patterns can be put on the vest by carbon paper or by using an overhead projector.
4. Applique:
   a) Various colors of iron-on patches may be cut into designs and then ironed on. Or, after the patches are ironed on, various designs could be done on them with the coloring dye pens.
   b) "Stitch-witchery" bonding material is available at most fabric stores. It can be used to bond many things onto fabric. If you are unfamiliar with this product ask the salesperson to show you how to use it.

The vests may be kept at the meeting area to work on whenever time permits. They may also

continued

continued

be taken home for further designing at this time. However they should be brought back for the next session as more decorating will be done and the vests will be used for the first time. The double medicine wheel should be kept at the meeting area from now on for the group to work with. Many interesting concepts develop with repeated use.

NOTE: Directions for making the double medicine wheel

1. Cut a circle 20 inches in diameter from white railroad board.
2. Cut a circle 10 inches in diameter from white railroad board.
3. Punch a hole in the center of each circle.
4. Straighten out a paper clip so that only one end is bent.
5. Place the small wheel on the large wheel, lining up the holes.
6. Place a metal washer so its hole is lined up with the two circle holes.
7. Place the tines of a brad (paper fastener) through the hole in the bent end of the paper clip, on through the washer, and through both circles. At the back of the larger circle bend the tines of the brad back to secure the brad. The brad should be bent so that both the paper clip and the small circle move freely.
8. With a ruler, divide the circles into fourths.
9. Design each quarter as pictured in the drawing.

meeting area only

double medicine wheel
   This is made by the leader before the session begins. For directions see note at the end of the session
materials for making ceremonial vests:
- Two-third yd. of 36 in. wide fabric for each child. These vests were made from deerskin by the Indians; today, however it is more ecologically valid that these be made from cloth. Grey Owl Indian Craft Mfg. Co. sells two types of cloth which resemble buckskin: Buckskin finish cloth is cheaper than suede cloth. Send 25¢ for Grey Owl's Catalog of Indian Craft Supplies. Write:

   Grey Owl Indian Craft Mfg. Co.
   150-02 Beaver Road
   Jamaica Queens, N.Y. 11433

- leather punch
- several sets of coloring dye pens for use on leather

   Order from Grey Owl

- water color felt pens
- small lamb bones for decorations
- any kinds of seeds or shells for decoration. You can order any type of beads, bells, etc. to decorate in Indian fashion from Grey Owl but it is much better if you use natural objects which can be found in the environment. Seeds can be secured from many types of vegetables and fruits which can be bought at any produce store
- materials necessary for applique or embroidering if desired — see directions for decorating the vest

Historically, the Chinese and many of the Far Eastern people conceived the entire universe, developed from Tai Chi or Tao, as activated by two principles, the Yin and the Yang, the negative and the positive, and they considered that nothing that exists, either animate or inanimate, does so except by virtue of ceaseless interplay of these two forces. Matter and Energy, Yang and Yin, Heaven and Earth are conceived as essentially one, or as two co-existent poles of one indivisible whole. In this "One Law": "Yin activity and Yang activity attract one another. Nothing is wholly Yin nor wholly Yang."

With this truism in view, Chungtzu, the chief follower of Laotze, said, "Heaven and Earth and I are of the same root, the ten thousand things and I are of the one substance. . ."

But it must be pointed out that the underlying principle in nature's unique law between the pair of opposites — Yin and Yang — is harmony, balance or equilibrium, or more exactly, the Vital Centre. Where one of the poles predominates the Vital Centre is lacking. Extremism is not correct because there exists no axis around which the bipolar whole harmoniously revolves. The wrong form which lacks the centre, has no equilibrium. . . . To gain awareness of this Oneness — the Way of the "Mean" — is precisely man's raison d'etre.

WEN-SHAN HUANG

2 yin and yang

Remember, in December we told the Indian legend about the forked tree. Then at our Winter Solstice celebration we danced around a forked tree. We talked about how the two sides of the forked branch stand for two different parts inside us.

Use the forked branch for demonstration during the following section.

For instance, one part of you is excited about things and that's this part of the branch. The other part of you feels low or depressed and that's this other part of the branch. Sometimes you are very excited about things. It's as if we are seeing only the left side of the branch. Other times, you are a bit depressed. Then we are seeing the right side of the branch. But it's still the same you, just as the two different parts of the branch are still the same branch.

This is true, not only for individuals, but for everything in the world. There is nothing without its opposite.

Let's look at nature and the seasons. Last session, we talked about how summer needs winter and cold has its opposite, warmth. We know that when a snowflake falls it is very cold and separate from the other falling flakes. Then they land near one another and begin to stick together. Soon there is a solid blanket of snow formed by all these snowflakes melting a bit together. These thick blankets of snow in the high mountains hold water in storage for the summer months. In the summer this snow melts and the water runs down to make the rivers which water our crops. Solid snow becomes liquid water; winter becomes summer. There is nothing without its opposite. There is nothing that does not change or move in order to exist.

Plants begin to grow from seed, they bloom and make new seeds and then die. The new seed begins the same movement again. It starts to grow, blooms, makes new seeds and dies. Day changes into night and night returns to day. Winter changes gradually into spring and then becomes summer. Summer begins to turn into autumn and then it's winter again.

Can anyone think of any other movements like this — where things change and then return as they were in the beginning and then change again? (discuss)

The ancient Chinese thought that this was the basic movement in life so they made a symbol for it.

Does anyone know the name of this symbol? (Show the yin/yang symbol at the end of this session.) It's the yin-yang symbol. The dark side is called yin. Winter is yin, women are yin, the earth is yin. The light side is called yang. The sun is yang, men are yang, so is fire. But notice the two dots. What do these mean? There's a tiny dark dot on the light side and a light dot on the dark side. This means that, though something might be yin right now (dark), it has already got within it a bit of yang (light) and might eventually become yang.

As an example of this let's think about our lungs. What do the lungs do? (discuss) That's right. They breathe in and out; expand and contract. Now suppose your lung said, "I'm tired of doing all that. I'm only going to breathe out." What would happen?

(discuss) That's right, for a lung to exist at all it must both expand and contract. Its movement means life. If it fails to move it dies. Every living thing must move or change to live.

The lungs both expand and contract continuously. The year doesn't stay the same. Winter turns into spring. But it's very difficult to say just the exact moment when winter stops and spring begins. It's winter now. Let's say winter is yin — dark. (Show the dark side of the symbol.) Yet, look, here is a small light point. Although it's winter now, summer is already on the way. The warmth of spring is already beginning to come. How can that be? Remember, the sun has turned around from its farthest away point and is already beginning the journey to his summer house. We can't feel the warmth, yet, but it's on the way. The same thing with day and night. Day gradually becomes night but who can say at just what moment it is night?

In human life it's the same. If we were happy all the time how could we know we were happy. We need sadness too.

The interesting thing is that everything does change or move. Supposing you don't like the weather today, if you wait long enough the weather will be what you want. This is easy to understand when we are talking about weather. That's easy to do — to wait for a sunny day. But in our own lives, to wait is difficult. But all wise men tell us this is the real secret of living. The Indian medicine men teach that this is the secret of living in harmony with nature —

not to force nature but to wait until things are already moving in the direction we want and then no effort on our parts is necessary to do what we want to do.

The same yin/yang movement goes on within people. Let's take a look at the forked branch. Suppose I'm very happy and outgoing for days. Things are really going well. I begin to wonder. Things are going too good. Maybe they might change. With this tiny doubt there is already within me a bit of sadness — like the tiny dot in the yin/yang symbol; so already I am on the way to being sad and the tiny dot of sadness may become bigger.

Yin/yang symbol for the ceremonial vest

1. Pass out to each person a 6 in. square of pellon and the paper. Do the following steps on paper first. Then it is copied on the pellon.

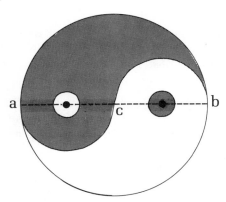

2. Using the compass, draw a 6 in. circle and cut it out.
3. Then with a pencil draw a very faint horizontal line (a - b) dividing the circle in half.
4. Place the compass point half way between the center point c and point a. Swing an arc to the left between a and c.
5. Place the compass point half way between c and point b and swing an arc to the right finishing the curve.
6. One side should be colored with a dark color — black or red; the other side a light color.
7. On the dark segment place a light dot halfway between a and c.
8. On the light segment place a dark dot halfway between c and b.
9. When it is finished, either sew, glue with Elmer's glue or use "stitch witchery" to attach it to the ceremonial vest. The yin-/yang symbol may be put anywhere on the vest except the middle of the back. Save this place for the vibration mandala which will be made in session 5.

Food

Serve two different kinds of food — yin and yang — so everyone can begin to get some idea of the difference.

Even food is yin or yang. Yin foods are acid so they are generally sharper tasting. Most fruits are yin: fruits such as oranges and peaches. Yang foods are alkaline. Some yang foods are fish, grains, goat cheese, pumpkins and eggs. One yang fruit is the apple. Sometimes, when you are feeling very restless it might be you are too yang and you need a yin food to make you a little yin and restore your balance.

Today, we've practiced a little more how to be in balance in our own bodies. We've learned that we can eat or drink certain foods which help keep the balance within our bodies and that's the first step to keeping in balance with the world.

We can put on our ceremonial vests with the yin/yang symbol we made today. We will chant and dance the balance chant. Use the same basic Indian step.

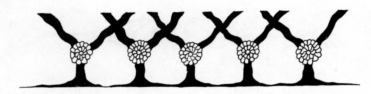

About wild food

"The spicy teas and tasty delicacies I prepare from wild ingredients are the bread and wine in which I have communion and fellowship with nature, and with the Author of that nature."[21]

EUELL GIBBONS

To establish the closest communion with nature it is important that you use the natural foods of each region as far as possible; therefore, ideas for food and drink will no longer be listed for each session. The following books will provide sufficient information to enable you to locate and prepare edible natural foods in your own environment.

1. *Stalking the Wild Asparagus* and *Stalking the Blue-eyed Scallop* by Euell Gibbons. Good recipes.

2. *The Weed Cookbook* by Adrienne Crowhurst. Good recipes.

3. *The Edible Wild* by Berndt Berglund and C. Bolsby.

Although adequate for most of the country, the books listed above provide little help for certain western states. The books, listed below provide information for specific areas in the west.

1. *Some Useful Wild Plants* by David Manning, Dan and Nancy Jason. It deals specifically with the plants of British Columbia and Washington state.

2. *Western Edible Wild Plants* by H. D. Harrington. This covers western states such as Nevada, Arizona, Utah and Colorado.

meeting area	

• one forked branch or twig of a tree
• materials for yin/yang symbol
    one 6 inch square of pellon fabric for each
        person. Purchase at a fabric store
    one piece of paper for each person
    compass
	pencils
	felt pens
	materials to attach the symbol to the vest:
	    Elmer's glue, "stitch witchery", or needle
	    and thread. Use the one which best fits
	    your needs

There is a relationship between what we think *is out there in the world and what we experience as being out there. There is a way in which the energy of thought and the energy of matter modify each other and interrelate. A kind of rough mirroring takes place between our mind and our reality. . . . Reality is not a fixed entity. It is a contingent interlocking of moving events. And events do not just happen to us. We are an integral part of every event.*   JOSEPH CHILTON PEARCE

3 mirroring of the medicine wheel

✦ Make the room as dark as possible. Be sure there is no direct light leaking through. The room does not have to be black but it must be uniformly dim.

Have everyone sit in a circle. Distribute the small pocket mirrors. Then turn on a flashlight. Encourage everyone to play around with reflecting the light with their mirrors.

After a few minutes, stop the general activity and explain the experiment. One person is to catch the light from the flashlight with his mirror. When another person can see the light in the first mirror, he tries to pick it up with his mirror. When a third person sees the light in the second mirror, he tries to pick it up with his mirror. Continue in this manner with each person passing the reflection on to someone opposite him. See how far the one light beam can go.

◉ It was only one light but almost everyone in the room eventually caught the light. Each person reflected the other person's light. This shows us something else about the medicine wheel. I'll tell you a teaching story to explain this, but first we'll collect the mirrors. Have you ever walked around your yard or in a park or a vacant lot on a beautiful warm summer night with a full moon? Everything is quiet and peaceful. Smells are stronger at night. The earth smell is good. Flowers are very powerful. You feel very peaceful as you watch the moon and the complicated shadows it makes.

Then, suddenly, you hear a strange noise — a weird groaning. It groans but it also shrieks — not loud but very scary. Immediately fear comes over you and suddenly all the beauty is gone. You can't see what is making the noise and so EVERYTHING is scary. That shadowy shape looks like a monster. You realize right away — no, it's that lilac bush I saw a minute ago. But, wait, what's that over there? It's moving. It's reaching out its tentacles to grab you. You jump back in terror and realize it was only the tendrils of a vine. But before you calm down you feel something clutching at your back and you panic and run for home with your heart pounding. You feel relieved and safe when you slam the door behind you.

Next morning, when you walk out to that area, you see clearly that the lilac bush was only a bush; that the vine had some extra long tentacles hanging down and the monster that clutched at you was only a blackberry bush. And, just then a bit of wind comes up and there's the weird groaning sound. It's just two branches of a tree rubbing together in the wind. Your fear of the night before seems so stupid to you now. You would never ever tell anybody how scared you had been.

Why do you suppose it's possible to get so scared over nothing? (discuss) The truth is that everything around us mirrors our own emotions. If we are peaceful, the world is peaceful. If we have fear in our hearts, the world becomes fearful. This is hard to believe but if you learn to watch carefully you'll see this happening over and over.

The medicine wheel teaches us this. Look at this medicine wheel in our *Seven Arrows* book (p. 213). In the middle of the wheel there are 7 stones. They are the 7 arrows. They are also the 7 natures of man and the Universe.

"Man is mirrored within these 7. Two of the 7 can be love and fear. The rest we must search out for ourselves because this is part of our learning. Seven Arrows always reflects what we truly are."[22]

This shield on the cover of our *Seven Arrows* book shows this mirroring. Remember we had mirrors on the sun shield we made for the Winter Solstice to remind us of this.

Because each of us mirrors the emotions of everyone else, an emotion such as unhappiness can be passed around just as we passed the light. To see how this works I will tell you about something which happened to Johnny.

The alarm clock didn't ring at Johnny's house so everybody is late. Dad is late for work and mother has to give all her attention to helping him get off to work. She had promised Johnny that she would help him finish up a project he had to take to school that very day and she hasn't time now. So Johnny goes off to school cross and angry. Nobody loves him; nobody will help him. Everybody else is more important to mother than he is.

Johnny is grumping along when his friend, Mike, comes along. Mike is cheerful and happy to see Johnny. He wants to tell him something important, but Johnny just grunts in reply. Mike is hurt. He begins to mirror Johnny's emotion in himself. Something is wrong. Maybe Johnny is mad at him. What did he do yesterday to make Johnny mad at him? Mike becomes unhappy. Nobody likes him. By the time the two boys get to school they are so low they can pull a whole group of other friends down with them.

This is how we mirror one another. We can pass on an emotion until it grows and grows and then the whole world seems bad to us — or good to us if it's a positive emotion. That makes us responsible for the

world in a way doesn't it? If I don't like the world I can change it by changing myself and then the world reflects or mirrors back to me my changed self.

Remember, last time we talked about how each branch of a forked twig can be different (yin or yang) yet they are part of the same twig. Not only is there some yin and some yang in each of us, but each of us can mirror the yin or the yang in another person. If there's one part of us we don't like and someone else reflects or mirrors that part back to us, we find we can't stand that person. This is the reason for much hate and fights. Yet we must learn to understand that part of us we don't like when it is mirrored by another person. We must learn to recognize that the reason we don't like that person is because he mirrors something in us we don't like. Yet, that person has other things in him which we might like if we learned to understand him.

Last fall we learned some games to help us change our world. One was the bone game and another was the pillow game. These are both ways to get back to the Universal Harmony. Today we are going to try something else. This will help us see how we reflect back to others.

The Ojibway Indians have a special way of drawing which shows how emotions move between people. Here is a book done by an Ojibway Indian named Morrisseau.

In order that we can understand the pictures better I want to play a record for you first. I'm going to put the record player here in the center of the floor and I want you to lie so that your head is in the direction of the record player. Be sure you are spread out enough so that you have enough room to be comfortable.

NOTE: Do not explain what the record is about or how the music is made. Have the volume turned up fairly high. When everyone is settled on the floor with eyes closed, put the record on side A and play the Drumbeat to Summon Deities. Then play about 3 minutes of the chant. Stop the record so that the group can talk about it. Be prepared for laughter or other verbalization about the "strange" sound. The record will be explained more in the next session so just tell them it's Tibetan chanting which causes vibrations. Then have everyone sit facing the speakers, close their eyes and listen and FEEL. Play side B for about 7 to 10 minutes.

Ask if they can feel the vibrations in their hands. Or feet. Or stomachs. See if they feel vibrations in any other part of their body. Connect this feeling with the vibrations of hate or anger or good feelings one feels from another person.

Then show the pictures in the Windigo book. Begin with the picture on the frontispiece of the Windigo eating the beaver people. Then go through the book looking at the pictures and telling names of the characters in the pictures. (These are printed in small type in the lower right hand corner of the picture). Talk about lines drawn to show the interchange of energies. This is an important visual experience which provides necessary background for the next step. When you have looked at all the pictures, ask everybody to lie down again and close their eyes. Play side B, softly, in the background as you read to them.

Story

Read "Grandfather Potan and the Bear" pages 8 and 9. Then, read either "The Forbidden Mountain" on page 12 or "Whiskey Jack" on page 33. When the story is finished let the group remain lying with eyes closed for a few moments.

Think of a time when you were the most angry you have ever been in your life. Who else would be in the picture in your mind? If you were to draw lines, like you saw in the book, what kinds of lines would you draw? Make a picture in your mind of this situation and put in the energy lines.

Now think of a time when you were the most frightened you have ever been. Make a picture of it in your mind. Draw in the energy lines.

Now think of the time when you were very, very happy. Make a picture of it in your mind and draw in the energy lines.

Choose one of the three experiences and think about it. Try to relive it in your mind.

(While the group is doing this, check to see that you have about five minutes playing time left on the record. Then lay out for each person, paper and a black, a red, and a blue crayon or felt pen.)

Before you open your eyes I want you to draw a picture in your mind of your event. Make it in line drawings, like a cartoon in the comics. When you open your eyes you will have paper and crayons to make a picture of your event. Try to make it say everything by using lines and not words.

Give plenty of time for drawing. Continue to let the record play in the background. At first do not permit talking as it disturbs the thought patterns. As the pictures are nearing completion talking is permitted as many will want to share their pictures and talk about what others have drawn. This can be done as a group activity or spontaneously.

We saw, today, that a perfectly natural blackberry bush may turn into a monster that clutches at us. What turned it into a monster? (our own minds, our own thoughts or fear) Long ago, the Tibetans realized this. One of their wise men wrote a little book to help people understand this. Some of the short parts of the book, which we can call "power sayings", can be memorized so that you can say them to yourself when you are afraid and it will help you to realize that all that fear and terror is really created by your own mind.

In these "power sayings" the wise man is usually speaking directly to you. He calls you, nobly-born. Although we usually think of kings or lords when we hear the word *noble*, the wise man really means us. Within each of us is a person just as great as a king. This is your true "self." So the wise man calls you nobly-born to make you realize that within you is your true "self" trying to become whole. This true "self" is not fully showing in any of us but it is there. The wise man talks directly to that true "self" not to our frightened self at the moment we are afraid.

Here is one of these "power sayings" for you to remember when you are frightened:

O nobly-born when such thought-forms come to you be not afraid, nor terrified; they are coming from your own mind.

By thought-forms the wise man is trying to tell you that the monster you see in the bush at night isn't really there at all. It is just something formed in your head which you then think you see. This "power saying" really helps because as soon as you say this to yourself you begin to realize that *you* are the one who is afraid — fear is not out there it is within you so if it's in you, you can stop it at any time.

At the end of the session, explain that tie-dying will be done at the next session. Each person should bring an all-cotton T-shirt. (Be sure it does not have polyester in with the cotton, as it does not absorb the dye.) They should also wear old clothes and bring an apron to cover their clothes while working.

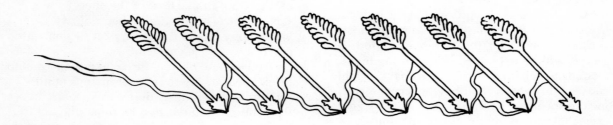

meeting area only is used this session	

one flashlight
one small mirror for each person
Windigo and Other Tales of the Ojibways illustrated by Norval Morrisseau and told by Herbert T. Schwarz
record player of good quality which can clearly reproduce very low notes
	record: *The Music of Tibet, the Tantric Rituals* recorded by Huston Smith
	each person needs:
	  one piece of drawing paper
	  black, red and blue felt pens or crayons

energy

By studying the speeds of vibrations I realized that everything in the universe is vibration, and the only difference between phenomena is the varying speeds of vibration. Material objects vibrate at slower speeds than invisible phenomena like sound and light. . . . There is no one key or scale for any particular person or entity. All scales are contained within all entities, and when all sounds combine they equal silence, which is the total sound of the universe. Just as clear light is the source of all colors, silence is the source of sound.

EDGAR STANISTREET

4 energy and vibration — I

Last time we talked about how trees and bushes and other people can mirror our emotions. Today, we are going to go a little deeper into this. To do this we are going to listen to the Tibetan chant record again.

We talked about Tibet last fall and we learned how to make mandalas. On this record Tibetan monks chant and play some strange instruments. When you listen to this kind of chanting you listen with more than your ears. You listen with your entire body.

Record

Everyone move so that you face the speakers. Take your shoes off so you can hear with your feet too. As you know, this chanting is like nothing you've ever heard before but just keep listening quietly with your whole body. First, we'll hear the drumbeat to summon "the power" and then we'll hear the chanting. (Play the record.)

How did you feel? Where did you feel it? In what different parts of your body? (discuss) Can you see these vibrations? (No, but they are there, aren't they?)

Each of the musical instruments is not playing a melody as we do in our music. Instead, the instrument is giving us a sound of a fundamental part of nature. The Tibetans try to make the deepest vibrations that an instrument or the human voice can produce. Some sounds seem to come from the very deepest part of the earth — maybe a deep deep cave. Other sounds seem to come from the sky like rolling thunder. Remember, the Tibetans live very close to nature at its most powerful. They believe that the human voice is only one of the many vibrations that make up the universe. Everything gives off its own vibration.

Strike a gong.

You can feel those vibrations as well as hear them can't you. Everything in the universe gives off its own particular vibration.

All kinds of things on earth have different vibration

Before Clerk Maxwell, people conceived of physical reality — insofar as it is supposed to represent events in nature — as material points, whose changes consist exclusively of motions. . . . After Maxwell they conceived physical reality as represented by continuous fields, not mechanically explicable. . . . This change in the conception of reality is the most profound and fruitful one that has come to physics since Newton. ALBERT EINSTEIN

rates. In us, different emotions produce variations in our vibrations.

That's why our emotions can influence animals. When we are afraid, we send fear vibrations out around us and dogs know this.

Some things have slower vibrations than others. (Try hitting metal objects of various kinds and getting the different vibrations.) We can hear the vibrations of all those things. Some things have much faster vibrations — so fast that we can't even hear them.

Everything in the universe is just different vibrations of energy. Many years ago people used to think that the universe was made up of hard little round bits of matter — the smallest of which was the atom. They thought that one bit of matter hit another bit and this caused all the actions of the universe. This was called the "billiard ball theory." But now we know this isn't what is going on at all. Now, the scientists think that everything has different vibrations of energy — even things which we think of as solid.

To us, this chair seems solid. We can even sit on it. But is it? (Discuss) No, it's made up of whirling atoms and molecules all vibrating with enormous spaces between them. If you were a very tiny creature you could see all those whirling atoms with huge spaces between them. But we are big so all we see is the overall pattern which they make and we call that a chair. These whirling masses of atoms make us feel that the chair is solid because we are too big to get even a finger between the spaces in the atoms of the molecules. But let's think of an atom that was as big as a baseball. In such an atom, the nucleus would be smaller than a period at the end of a sentence. The rest of that space as big as a baseball is mostly empty space with a few electrons whirling around. The atoms in the chair are smaller but there's a similar amount of space around each of the nuclei of the atoms so that, really, the chair is mostly space.

Everything is a pattern of energy. One of the basic laws of the universe is that energy can neither be created nor destroyed. It just changes — from one pattern of energy to another. Our body is one pattern of energy but we can't live for a minute without other patterns of energy. Some of these we will call animals, some we call plants, some, rocks. Yes, even rocks are just patterns of energy but they give off vibrations beyond our ability to sense them.

Different emotions in us give off different vibrations. What kinds of emotional messages do you think you are sending out to others? Are your vibrations changing any one else's emotions? It's hard to see or feel our own vibrations but, today, we'll get some idea of this process by capturing some of those emotional vibrations on a shirt. At first you won't see what effect your work has on the shirt just as we often don't see the effect our emotions have on others. You will think you haven't changed the shirt at all but when the process is finished, you'll have a real surprise.

Directions for process of tie-dying:
1. Distribute all necessary materials.
2. Lay the damp shirt on a flat surface, front side up. The design should be in the middle of the front.

continued

The physicist and the mystic follow different paths: they have different technical goals in view; they use different tools and methods; their attitudes are not the same. However, in the world-picture they are led to by these different roads they perceive the same basic structure, the same reality. LAWRENCE LeSHAN

continued

3. Pick up the fabric in the center of the front side only.

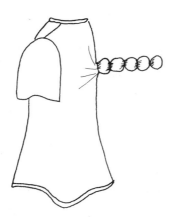

4. Pinch the fabric into a puff about 1½ inches high.
5. While holding the puff with one hand, wrap it with a rubber band very tightly.
6. Slide your hand down another 1½ inches. Secure a rubber band here, very tightly.
7. For a mandala sunburst effect, band puffs 8 or 9 times. The more bands you use, the more rings will result in the finished design.
8. Repeat this banding of puffs on the back of the T-shirt and on each sleeve.

9. With the squirt bottle, force the pointed nozzle under a rubber band. Squeeze un-

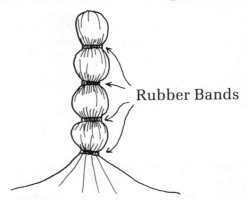

Rubber Bands

til the dye is forced into the material under the rubber band.
10. Use a different color under each rubber band. The rubber band will protect the dye and fabric under it so that when the shirt dyeing is completed there will be a ring of color on the shirt where each rubber band has been secured.
11. Any rubber banded areas which do not have colored dye squirted under them will remain white.
12. When all banded areas have been squirted, immerse the shirt into the pot of simmering blue dye.

Miso experiment

✦ While the shirts are simmering, proceed with the following:

☀ There's something we can do to make the movement of the patterns of energy clearer. Someone fill this bowl with hot water.

✦ Let the water sit until the sloshing dies down. Let everyone look in and see that the water is quiet.

☀ It looks like the water is sitting there with no movement. But that's not necessarily true. One of you pour this into the bowl and stir it. Now, look what's happening.

✦ The miso particles show the convection currents of the water. These currents will continue for some time.

☀ The water molecules are continually moving. Ordinarily, we can't see them but when we add something which has very tiny particles in it, they are carried along by the motion. Molecules move freely in gases and liquids. Molecules move very slowly in rocks. They are also moving in this chair.

Each one of us is a fountain of energy, each one of us is like a valve from which universal life energy is metered into the world. . . . The energy is free, from in front . . . inexhaustible, eternal, can't run out of it. . . . Here's the thing about energy, you can't store it. We're not batteries. We can handle a lot more energy as conduits than we can as capacitors. So to flow it through.
STEPHEN GASKIN

Wakonda of the Dakota Indians, oki of the Iroquois, Manitu of the Algonquin, churinga of the Australian aborigine, and the mana of the Melanesian refer to a concept of energy.

In the case of mana, *as with the other concepts, we are dealing with a concept of energy which alone enables us to explain the remarkable fact of these primitve ideas. This is not to suggest that the primitive has an abstract idea of energy, but there can be no doubt that his concept is the preliminary concretistic stage of the abstract idea. . . .*

[These] concepts are not primarily names for the "supernormal" . . . but rather for the efficacious, the powerful, the productive. The concept in question really concerns the idea of a diffused substance or energy upon the possession of which all exceptional power or ability or fecundity depends. . . . For us mana *would be a psychological concept of energy, but for the primitive it is a psychic phenomenon that is perceived as something inseparable from the object.*

C. G. JUNG

Remember the web of life game we played last fall. When we think of the world as many patterns of energy, the web of life becomes even more interesting.

There is only energy. Where do we get our energy? (discuss) Does energy stay with us once we've got some? Where does food go? Breath energy? What happens if we try to hold onto energy? (We lose it anyway.) This is what the Indians mean by the give-away.

The energy in our body is the same energy as the universe. If we think about yin and yang it will help us here. This same basic energy of the universe sometimes expands (yin) and other times contracts (yang). When it contracts it's matter — solid things like chairs. All things have varying mixtures of yin and yang. Some things seem solid to us — such as chairs. Other things we can't see at all. Electricity is one of these. Electricity in our house wiring vibrates at 60 cycles per second. We can't see it but we can get

a shock if we touch bare wire. Light has a vibration frequency of billions of cycles per second. We can see it and feel it. We feel the light energy of the sun as heat. We have a certain vibration in our brains, called an alpha wave, which vibrates at 10 cycles per second. Our heart beats 72 times a minute.

Let's take a specific example of this energy change going on. We have to eat to live. Right? A chicken is a certain pattern of energy. We have to kill this pattern of energy to eat it. Actually, we are changing the pattern of energy labelled *chicken* into a pattern of energy which is a human being. This pattern of energy, a human being, creates other patterns of energy: art, houses, gardens, etc. This is another aspect of the "give-away."

You see energy changes and gives form to something else. Everything is a kind of energy in the process of changing into another kind of energy.

Now it's time to take a look at the pattern of energy which the simmering process has given us.

The leader puts on the rubber gloves and, using the spoon or stick, lifts the shirts carefully into a bucket. The shirts are carried outside where they can be placed on a sheet of plastic. Let everyone take turns hosing them until they are cool and water runs clear. Then let everybody find their own shirts. (This is impossible to do unless their names were put on with a plastic label maker.) Cut the rubber bands with scissors. Rinse the shirts again with clear water.

You may want to dip them in vinegar water (1 cup vinegar to one gallon of water.) This helps to set the dye. Hang the shirts to drip dry.

If the dye has spilled on counters or floor, wipe up, immediately, with a cloth soaked in a weak solution of bleach. If it is impossible to do the rinsing outside, it can be done in the bath tub but more care must be taken not to drip the dye all over. It is more fun to do it outside.

The dye solution in the pot may be saved in a bleach jug and used again at a later date.

All forms of life and being are simply variations on a single theme . . . all these myriad I-centers are yourself — not, indeed, your personal and superficial conscious ego, but what Hindus call the . . . Self of all selves. As the retina enables us to see countless pulses of energy as a single light, so the mystical experience shows us innumerable individuals as a single Self. . . . [This] awareness of eternal energy [is] often in the form of intense white light, which seems to be both the current in your nerves and that mysterious e which equals mc^2. This may sound like megalomania or delusion of grandeur — but one sees quite clearly that all existence is a single energy, and that this energy is one's own being.

ALAN WATTS

A great man, Alan Watts, said that art is "playful patterns of energy." You see we have all different kinds of patterns on our shirts. They are different playful patterns of energy. Which is better? Which is worse? You can't really say. They are just all different patterns of energy.

Perhaps the human organism may be considered analogous to a symphony orchestra, consisting of a multitude of energies and vibrations. However, under ordinary conditions of living, the organism is seldom properly tuned, integrated, organized, and it operates in a rather random, erratic fashion. Meditation, chanting, ritual dancing, and other specialized exercises are designed to tune the organism.

BURYL PAYNE

- record: *The Music of Tibet, the Tantric Rituals* recorded by Huston Smith
- gong or large stainless steel mixing bowl as a substitute
- wooden implement to hit the gong
- instant miso soup which can be bought at a Japanese grocery or regular miso which can be bought at health food stores. The instant miso dissolves as soon as stirred into water. The regular miso must first be mixed with a little water in a separate container and then added to the hot water. Add a heaping teaspoon of miso to 1 cup water
- a bowl which holds about a pint of water

About tie-dyeing

Note: After the shirts have been boiled in the dye they will need to be rinsed. It is best to take them outside and hose them down with running water. If you can put up a rope clothesline outside you can hang the shirts up to dry where the dripping dye will do no harm. If you dry them inside they will have to be hung over a bathtub or drain area.

Background information and hints on dyeing

- Make all knots on wet fabric which has been laid on a flat surface
- Be sure the rubber bands are wrapped on very tightly
- The shirts will become dyed in 10 to 15 minutes; however, if possible, simmer the shirts up to one hour to set the dye
- When the shirts are laundered at home, they should be washed separately in cool water as the dye may run the first few times they are washed. If necessary, send notes home to inform the mothers of this fact.
- The shirts will be more attractive if they are ironed while damp. The rubber band process leaves lots of wrinkles:
- Each person's name should be made on a label maker and stapled to the hem before the dyeing process begins. Without the name on the shirt there is no way for anyone to find his or her own shirt as the designs always turn out different than expected. If you cannot borrow a label maker buy a laundry marking pen.

Materials needed for dyeing

- white all-cotton T-shirt for each person. If they are new, they should be washed to remove the sizing
- rubber bands — have several different widths for each person. Wide bands produce heavy stripes; thin bands create fine, cobwebby lines
- dye. Use a royal blue for the pan in which the shirts will be dyed. It takes 1 qt. of water for each shirt. Use ¼ cup of liquid dye for each quart of water. For making the patterns, liquid dye is put into the squirt bottles. There should be at least four colors: red, yellow, green and orange
- vinegar (optional to set dye)

Implements needed

- pans. glass, metal or enamel. Never use a teflon-lined pan. The pans should be large enough to hold a completely immersed T-shirt without crowding. A canning kettle (3 to 5 gallons) is large enough for about 8 to 10 T-shirts
- stove or hot plate. Dyeing can be done on a camping stove but it takes a lot longer to get the water hot enough to simmer with the shirts in it. The dye solution should be kept simmering throughout the dyeing process but never allowed to boil
- one pair of rubber or plastic gloves
- one very long handled spoon or stick measuring about 2 feet
  This will be used to stir the dye bath
- one squirt bottle for each four people. These plastic bottles are found in the drug store in the section where they sell hair-dye kits. They hold about ½ cup liquid and have a pointed nozzle through which to squirt the liquid
- scissors — one pair for each four persons
- one bucket or dishpan for every four persons. This is used to carry the dyed shirts outside

For protection and clean-up:

- large plastic garbage bag for each person. Make slits for the head and arms and wear to protect clothing
- plenty of newspapers to cover the floor and counters
- one plastic bag for each person to carry the damp shirt home
- bleach for clean up
- paper towels for clean up

At this latitude [that of Virginia] I'm spinning 836 miles an hour round the earth's axis. . . . I feel my sweeping fall as a breakneck arc like the dive of dolphins, and the hollow rushing of wind raises the hairs on my neck and the side of my face. In orbit around the sun I'm moving 64,800 miles an hour. The solar system as a whole, like a merry-go-round unhinged, spins, bobs, and blinks at the speed of 43,000 miles an hour along a course set east of Hercules.

ANNIE DILLARD

Our present state of knowledge about man's potential is at about the same level as that of man's first attempt, two hundred years ago, to understand the "mysterious" phenomena of electricity, forces which we now control with the flick of a switch, and which are available to nearly every man, not to just a few isolated scientists. . . . I think science is on the verge of discovering a new type of energy which may be as useful to the development of men's lives as electricity has been to the development of men's machines. This type of energy may be manifest now, but only in the strange and feeble way that electricity and magnetism were known before the nineteenth century.

BURYL PAYNE

5 energy and vibration — II

Begin by duplicating the miso experiment which was done in the previous session. Let everyone watch quietly.

What is going on? What does it make you think of? How do you feel when you think that that sort of movement is going on all around us? It's going on in the air and in lakes and in the ocean. (Let the discussion continue as long as necessary to let everyone express their ideas.)

All kinds of energies are hitting us each moment. The air carries light waves to us. These bits of energy are hitting our eyes. Other energies, which we can't even see or feel, are bombarding us. X-rays and radio waves are all around us. We only see the results of x-rays when the doctor takes an x-ray of a broken bone. We never see the rays themselves. We don't see radio waves either but when we turn on a special machine, which we call a radio, we tune into the radio waves which bring us music from far away. The air around us vibrates, also. This is how sound travels to our ear.

We have another whole set of energies from the earth. The constant energy of gravity pulls us down toward the ground. Air presses on our bodies. Air molecules are hitting us all the time but, ordinarily, we don't notice it because the air inside our body is hitting against us just as hard as the air outside our body so it's equal and we don't feel it. But sometimes we *can* feel it. When you are going up in an airplane or driving up in a car from lower to higher altitude, you can feel the difference in air pressure.

Do you not see how logical thinking, in order to even function, must limit to a specific, and that this specific is then the only apparent reality — and how this fragmented form of thinking then orients quite naturally around the notion of scarcity, the idea that in order to have we must take from and deprive others, since only a limited amount can be seen? Do you not see that fragmented thinking turns all others into potential enemies. . . . Can you not see that opening to the whole mind must open to a constant yield always sufficient, always ample? The cause of the need is the cause of the fulfillment of the need. Our universe is not a fixed and frozen machine grinding out in entropy. It can always be what we have need of it to be. The eternal mental life of God and Man has enough to go around — eternally round and round — by moving for and not against.

JOSEPH CHILTON PEARCE

In addition to these energies from the natural world there are other vibrations of energy which cause us to feel the emotions of other people. Remember when we discussed how fear can be reflected back to us from other people?

There is still another kind of energy which the Indians knew about. They were aware that there was a "Power" which gave them energy. They called it by different names. Some called it Wakonda. The Algonquin Indians called it Manitu. The Indian knew that when he lived in harmony with nature and other men, the energy flowed through him from "the Powers." He knew, also, that he could lose this energy, too, if he didn't remain in harmony or if he blocked the energy flow.

What were the names of "the Powers" in the medicine wheel? (north, south, east and west) We can use the energy which comes from "the Powers" but if we try to stop the flow of energy we lose it. You have to give-away the energy to other creatures and then it keeps flowing through you.

Children have lots more energy than most adults don't they? Why? Part of the reason is you are younger so you don't get physically so tired but there are other reasons. Can you think of any? Well, one good reason is that adults often block energy flow. They try to hold on to it and then they lose it. I'll give you an example of this.

Story

For months Father had been planning for his son's birthday. It had taken a lot of effort but he had saved the amount needed to buy a good 10-speed bike. He knew that Jack would be really surprised because he had been told many times that the bike was just too expensive.

When the morning finally arrived he felt a great glow of anticipation while Jack read the note that lay on his breakfast plate: "Look in the carport storage shed. You will find a big box. Open it."

Jack ran out with his father close behind him. Father wanted to be with Jack when he opened the box.

What do you think happened when the box was opened? How do you think Jack felt? How do you think his father felt? (discuss) What kind of energy was flowing? (discuss)

Jack rode the bike down the driveway toward the street but the chain slipped off. Father ran out to help fix it. It was pretty complicated. He went in to get his tool box. When he came back outside, the bike lay forgotten on the curb and Jack and a friend were playing inside the box, which the bike had come in. The sight of the bike lying, forgotten, and the laughter from the box made father feel angry.

What do you think happened next? How did Jack and his father feel? What kinds of energy do you think flowed now? (discuss)

In your own life you've noticed that on some days you have lots of energy. Things go well. You have all the energy you need to do all the things you want — run, ride your bike, play ball and still have some left over to help out at home. You are letting energy flow through you and out to others. The Indians think that at those times one is vibrating in harmony with "the Powers" and so has unlimited energy.

The Hopi Indians believe that our bodies and the earth, itself, have a similar structure. The earth has an axis running through the center of it and our bodies have an axis, the backbone. The earth has vibrations coming out from its center. We, too, have vibration

Energy is a confusing term. I try to make it clear that it is not nervous tension and not phony mental wishing. It is subtle and powerful, and circulates continuously in one's mental-physical self. Acupuncture meridians show the paths of this ch'i energy. . . . Energy is open, free-moving, unburdened, basically undefinable. It is life-force unforced, which then becomes forceful and powerful.

AL CHUNG-LIANG HUANG

[Om], the symbol for an urge of liberation . . . based upon the understanding that all beings and things are inseperably connected and interwoven with each other, so that all discrimination of "own" and "other" is illusion.　　　LAMA GOVINDA

centers along our backbone which tune us into all the universe. In our body, one center is at the top of the head. This is the same place which is soft in young babies. You can see it vibrating in babies. Another vibration center is in the brain.

The third vibration center is in the throat. It is attuned to the universal vibration of all creation. By making certain vibration sounds you can put yourself back in harmony with "the Powers" so that you can renew the abundant flow of energy.

Remember, we felt the vibration of the Tibetan chants when we played the record. Today we will begin to learn a Tibetan chant which helps us get in harmony with the vibrations around us.

Learning the chant

The first word which we are going to learn is the one which the Tibetans believe is the sound made by the rotation of the planets around the sun. If you put all the sounds of all the vibrations of the universe together it would sound like this.

The *A* sound starts at the back of your throat with your mouth open. Then without stopping the sound you slowly close your mouth, rounding your lips until you make a tiny hole. Then you gently close your lips. Last of all put the front teeth together so that the sound vibrates the bones of your skull. Continue the sound for awhile until it dies away. This makes the sound, Aum. However, the word is spelled Om.

Everyone practice for a few minutes. Then all stand in a circle either holding hands or linking arms. Do the Om chant with eyes closed for some minutes to feel the power.

This meditation is to help prepare everyone to draw a vibration mandala.

One of the most powerful energies, which continually vibrates around us, is light energy. Light energy enables our eyes to see. There is another place in the body, which light energy reaches. The pineal gland registers light in some way not fully understood. The pineal gland is located deep in the middle of the brain behind the spot just above and between your eyes. This is what the Tibetans call the third eye — right between our eyebrows.

Today we will meditate on light.

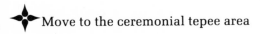Move to the ceremonial tepee area

Setting up the meditation
- Darken the room
- Put a candle on a very low table or in a candle holder on the floor.

Leading the meditation

Everyone is to form a circle around the candle. When the Indians were doing an important ritual they, first, found the place where "the Power" could most easily come to them. This isn't necessarily your direction on the medicine wheel because, some days, you have moved in a different direction on the medicine wheel. Everyone move around the circle until you have found your "place of power", a place which feels right to you. Then sit down there with the soles of your feet toward the candle. You can move to another place if the first one doesn't feel right to you. (After each person has found his place, go on to the next step.)

Relaxing exercise:
- Close your eyes as tightly as you can and count up to 10 in your mind. Now relax.
- Now pull every muscle in your face as tightly as you can. Hold it while you count to 10. Relax.
- Clench your eyes, face, hands as hard as you can. Count to 10. Relax.
- This time clench your eyes, face, hands, arms and stomach as hard as you can. Count to 10. Relax.
- Clench your eyes, face, arms, stomach and legs to the count of 10. Relax
- Clench your whole body. Pull every muscle as hard as you can. Hold it while you count, slowly, to 10 in your mind. Now totally relax.

Meditation
- Look at the candle. Look deep into the flame and watch the pattern it makes. Just sit quietly and look steadily into the flame for a minute.
- Now close your eyes and look up inside your head to the place of the third eye between your eyebrows. Visualize the light in your third eye. Concentrate on the light there.
- Now, open your eyes and focus on the candle. Breathe slowly in and out. Breathe in and out. Notice how the light gets brighter when you breathe in. (Wait for a minute or two of silence)
- Now, let the light start down your backbone and through all the nerves of your arms and legs to the bottoms of your feet. Some of the atoms and

Recent scientific discoveries suggest that (as Einstein predicted in 1916) magnetic fields are wave phenomena, much like light and electricity. The distance between crests of the magnetic waves appears to be 100 miles, making them the product of very long-wave broadcasting indeed.

This discovery has led to the further suggestion that the Milky Way, with its 100 billion stars acting as molecules, forms a lens that focuses magnetic energy that is generated "somewhere else." Where "somewhere else" may be is not given. Perhaps it is another dimension. Perhaps it is a projection of human thought. Either way, out there or in here, there are pulsations of energy from somewhere.

We do not, as yet, know the source of this energy, but bit by bit we develop the instruments to detect it and, in time, may produce the kinds of human minds that can state the theoretical basis for it. The discovery and exploration of new forms of energy may be the most exciting human adventure of the next thirty years.   KATHY HYLAND

molecules of your nervous system are electrically charged. They are a source of electrical energy in your body. Feel the light and electricity flowing through your body. We are connected by these electrical forces to the sun and the stars. These powerful centers of energy whirling through space, are sending out great quantities of energy. All we have to do is tune in the vibrations of energy in our body with these powerful energy sources — the sun and the stars. Just like when we tune a radio into radio waves, we can now tune into Father Sun. The energy coming from the sun floods us with light. We are filled up with light.

- We begin to glow. We feel the golden light filling us and flowing around us. We begin to feel warm. We begin to tune our vibrations with the sun and the stars.
- Feel the vibration, while you quietly breathe in and out.
- Feel the energy flow through your body. Continue to quietly breathe in and out.
- Now, feel the light build up in your head. Imagine it building up into a great force and then flashing out to the candle flame and then flowing back toward you and through the soles of your feet.
- Now — feel the flash. It leaps out from your head to the flame and then back into your feet and through you and out through the vibratory center in the top of your head and back to the candle. Make a circle of light from your head to the flame and back through your feet. Feel it. Continue breathing, deeply, in and out as you feel this circle of light.
- Now, we enter into the light of the candle and become the light ourselves. We become one with the light and energy and vibration. Our breath carries the pulsating light through us. We breathe in the pure energy of the universe. It fills us and then we breathe it out. We give it away.
- Our own breath becomes the same as the vibrating energy of the universe. We are filled with energy from "the Powers." Feel the energy flow as you breathe in and out, in and out. Feel the warm golden glow grow around you. You are filled with peace, filled with energy.
- (Then, very gently, say) Take one last deep breath. Open your eyes and look at the candle. You felt all that power and energy flow through you. All you have to do to get all the energy you need is to tune into it. It's always there. We lose it so often because we block the flow. When you focus your mind on your problems and your fears, you block the flow of energy and you get tired. But if you focus your mind on the universal energy of "the Powers" the energy flows through you all the time and you don't have as many pains or sicknesses or worries. You become a strong glowing center.

Vibration Mandala

While everyone is still seated pass out the materials.

In the small center circle of this mandala make a picture of how you felt just now, when all the golden energy of the sun was flowing through you. Sketch this on the paper now.

When most have finished this sketch, blow out the candle and let everyone move and arrange themselves any way that is most comfortable in order to finish the mandala.

Copy the sketch you just made onto your pellon circle, using felt pens. This is going to be a vibration mandala. In the center is you — filled with energy and light. All around you, draw the vibrations of the things in your life. Put in the good things and the bad things if you want — whatever you feel is important to you. You can draw the actual objects which make you feel good. Draw the vibration lines coming down into you from them. You can use some of the lines, which we used when we drew the pictures similar to those in the *Windigo* book. Or you can draw colors which make you feel good.

• If something is bothering you, some bad vibration, you can draw it and put a strong golden line around your center for protection. If your own center is in harmony with all the energy of the sun, what can hurt you?

• You can sketch these things on the piece of paper, first, to get your ideas in order and then copy them onto your circle of pellon, using felt pens.

When everybody finishes the mandalas, they attach them to their ceremonial vests using any of the methods used before: Elmer's glue, "stitch witchery" or sewing. This mandala goes in the center of the back of the vest.

Do you see what we have done today? We have taken part in a different kind of give-away. We have used the energy we got from our food and the breathing energy we got from the air and the special energy we got from "the Powers" in our meditation. We've used all these different kinds of energies and converted them into a mandala. Human beings can do this. They can take all different kinds of energies and through the use of their human mind convert these energies into "playful patterns of energy."

Sometime when you are feeling low or tired you can meditate on the mandala and you will feel energy

Mathematical formulas make possible the strategic arrangement of magnets and wires in the powerhouse so that . . . force is manifested in the way we call an electric current. . . . But the mathematics used in such a case is a specialized formula-language, contrived for making available a specialized type of force manifestation through metallic bodies only, namely, electricity as we today define what we call by that name. The mantric formula-language is specialized in a different way, in order to make available a different type of force manifestation, by repatterning states in the nervous system and glands — or again rather in the subtle "electronic" or "etheric" forces in and around those physical bodies. Those parts of the organism, until such strategic patterning has been effected are . . . as incapable of dynamic power as loose magnets and loose wires, but in the proper pattern they are something else again — not to be understood from the properties of the unpatterned parts, and able to amplify and activate latent forces. BENJAMIN LEE WHORF

flowing back into you. A mandala can begin the flow of energy from "the Powers" for us. That's what the Tibetans use them for.

 After putting on their ceremonial vests, everybody forms a circle to do the *Om* chant.

 We are going to chant Om. The Om is the first word of a mantra. That's what the Tibetans call these chants. We will learn more of it in the next few weeks. Mantras help us concentrate all the energies from "the Powers." A mantra acts like a magnifying glass. You know how a magnifying glass concentrates the rays of the sun so they become strong enough to burn paper. This mantra, we are learning, concentrates the energies in the same way so that we are filled with energy and become very strong.

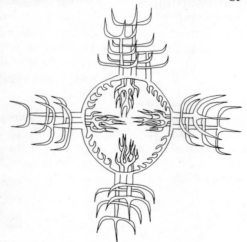

meeting area
instant miso or regular miso
ceremonial tepee area

• candle on a very low table or in a candle holder on the floor
• each person must have his ceremonial vest
• materials needed for vibration mandala:
    each person needs:
      6 inch circle of pellon fabric. A 2-inch diameter circle should be outlined in the center of this larger circle
 	
    piece of ordinary paper to sketch the design
    pencil
to be shared:
    felt pens
    material to attach the mandala to the vest:
      Elmer's glue, "stitch witchery" or needle and thread

Trance experience is a disengagement from ordinary reality orientation. It is a suspension of the ordinary critera, or common consensus. . . . There are many forms of trance-thinking. . . . Sometimes this state is only a temporary lowering of the threshold of the logical mind to incorporate a new experience not available to logic. Recall Hans Selye's observation that every great scientific postulate-illumination had happened to the scientist in a hypnagogic state.
JOSEPH CHILTON PEARCE

6 sidewinder

Last session we did a light meditation. This is one way to tune ourselves into the energy from "the Powers." Indians used many ways to get in touch with this kind of energy. They smoked a ceremonial pipe or sang songs or danced without stopping to the rhythms of drums. Other times, an Indian would find a particular place in nature where he could feel an unseen presence. Sometimes this was by a great waterfall or on top of a high mountain or in a desert.

Have any of you ever experienced being in a special place where you really felt one with everything that was around you? Perhaps it was near a waterfall and the sound drowned out all other sounds and completely enveloped you in its roar. Or maybe it was a quiet spot in the woods where you glimpsed the flash of a squirrel tail and then tried to melt into the trees in hopes that he would return?

Even a crowded summer beach could provide such an experience, sometimes. Have you ever had someone cover you with hot sand and then drowsily close your eyes and absorb into the mound leaving your real self free? Or, you can swim under water, turn yourself upside down, close your eyes and dissolve into the water. That's another way to get that feeling.

Still another way is to roll over and over down a grassy hill with the world flying upside down around you and become one with the universe. (discuss)

You cannot always be in the woods or desert or at the beach but there are other ways of getting in touch with "the Powers." One of these ways is special music. Today we are going to try this.

Everyone moves to the ceremonial tepee area.

The Indians knew that it was important to sort of tune their body, first, before they tried to get in touch with this energy. To do this they needed to adjust their inner tensions. We're going to accomplish this by doing the exercise which we did last week before we did the light meditation.

Everyone lie down. Spread out so that you are not touching anyone. Either your head or your feet must be pointing toward the speakers.

✦ Follow the directions in session 5 for the relaxing exercise. At the end of the relaxing exercise, say:

"Keep your eyes closed and don't move. Listen to the music." Put on the record, *Sidewinder,* side 2. Let it play completely through. After the record has finished, let everybody tell about what they experienced as they heard the music.

NOTE: Children experience such things as floating about, floating like a feather, floating horizontally up into space, and spinning down. These and other movements are also experienced by adults. The in-teresting thing is that children seem to meet monsters and other things which frighten them but the monsters cannot hurt them or don't want to hurt them in that space. This seems to really surprise the children. Be sure you do not program the group as to what it will experience ahead of time.

✦ When they have finished telling of their experiences, have them close their eyes and visualize how they felt, just now, during the music meditation. What shapes do they see or feel like? What colors do they see or what colors most show how they feel?

Then have them open their eyes and sketch on paper what they saw or felt.

✦ Move back to the meeting area. Everyone transfers the sketch onto the felt or pellon. Several ideas are given below:

· To make a design of the emotions which were felt, cut out free-forms from the felt fabric. Use the color which most goes with that feeling.

· Draw any pictures or designs directly onto the pellon.

· Use the designs which they saw as a repeating border down the front of the vest or around the armholes or along the bottom edge.

· Neither the felt nor pellon forms need be circular. They may use any form which best expresses what they felt.

· The finished design is glued or sewed or bonded onto the vest.

Summarizing Hilgard's research on trance states, Pearce states: *As children, all those capable of deep trance as adults had shared in fantasy play and imaginative ventures of some sort with their parents. Their parents had read to them a great deal, entering with them into the "inner space travel" that reading brings about. Or their parents told them tales, ghostly stories, saw giant-castles in the clouds with them . . . listened to the children's fantasies with respect. And, not incidentally at all, always brought them back to reality of the norm with "enough of that now, back we come," back to the world of real people. . . .*

Having found that he can let go of reality adjustment in favor of other experiences, confident in his ability to return to the world, he has a favorable background for acceptance of novelty. On this background new experience can be grafted. Without this uncritical spirit of adventure, however, this faculty of mind is repressed until it atrophies, rather as speech in a child missing the formative elements in language development. . . .

This background gives the temperament capable of deep religious experience, empathy, compassion, ability to see from a different world view, willingness to agree quickly with the adversary, and other marks of a flexible tolerance that does not feel threatened by strangeness.

JOSEPH CHILTON PEARCE

Last session we began to learn the Tibetan chant. We learned the first word, Om. Let's chant Om for a few minutes.

The next word is mani which means jewel. (The a is pronounced like the a in the word, *all*; ni rhymes with knee.) This precious jewel is our true "self" deep within our consciousness. We don't often realize this "self" is in us because we let our minds get all muddied up with our desires such as: "I want some candy" or "I want to go to the movie." Sometimes fears cover up our real self. "I'm afraid he won't like me" or "I'm afraid I can't do that." So the clear "self" within us rarely has a chance to exist. This "self" is the same one which really knows what is best for us if we take the time to listen to it. This "self" is the part of us which can tune into all the energies of "the Powers." Can anyone give me an idea of why we call this "self" a jewel? (discuss)

Padme is the next word (pronounced to rhyme with pay-may). It means lotus flower. The lotus flower grows in India and, sometimes, you can see it in pools in this country. It's like a water lily. The lotus plant grows straight up from the mud toward the light of the sun. When it reaches the surface of the water, the flower unfolds its petals layer by layer as it starts to bloom, until finally the innermost center is revealed.

In this chant, the meaning of padme is that if we keep working so that we don't let our minds muddy things up with passing desires and dreams or hatred and fears our consciousness rises above the mud of all these things and gradually unfolds just like a lotus, layer by layer until finally our true "self" is revealed — the shining jewel in each of us. The true "self" then, can give off good energies and vibrations because it is in tune with the Universe. All around this jewel "self" things are peaceful and harmonious.

Practice the chant

The simplest form is to chant the two new words on the same note as the last part of the Om. It makes no difference what note this is — just continue with it.

Depending on the leader's experience with chanting, any combination of notes may be used. Practice the new words several times.

Return to the ceremonial tepee area.

Everyone puts on their ceremonial vests. Standing in a circle chant "Om mani padme" for as long as the energy continues.

He who possesses this shining jewel overcomes death and rebirth and gains liberation. But this jewel cannot be found anywhere except in the lotus of one's own heart.

LAMA GOVINDA

meeting area	
felt fabric of various colors pellon watercolor felt pens ball point pens	scissors materials to attach designs to vest: Elmer's glue, needle and thread or "stitch witchery"
ceremonial tepee area	
stereo record player record: *Sidewinder* by Morton Subotnick, Columbia N30683	pencil and paper for each person

7 spirals

Do the milk "light show." See session 2 of the Relationship cycle. After the original patterns form and diminish a bit, put a drop of red food coloring on one side of the pan and a drop of blue or green on the other side. Slowly draw a fork across the bottom of the pan between these two drops. Spirals will form all over the pan. Point out that when two different colors meet they begin spiralling and spiral together tighter and tighter. The movement of the different layers of liquid coming together create a form which we call a spiral.

Slide show

Explain that these are the slides of the earth, taken from space, which were shown last fall. During the showing point out that there are spirals of clouds similar to what was seen in the "light show." Explain that the meeting of warm air and cold air on a rotating earth cause these spirals to form.

Pass out papers, felt pens, and pencils. Explain that these materials are for doodling any design they wish as the discussion continues.

We've seen the spiral patterns in our milk "light show" and in the clouds as seen from space. Where else can we see spirals? (See if anyone can give examples.)

Look at your fingertips. What do you see there? A spiral growing smaller and smaller as it gets to the center of your fingertip. Look at the back of someone's head. What do you see? The hair grows in a spiral form.

Seashells are often spirals. A snail's shell is a spiral. The horns of most animals make a spiral form as they grow. Many plants grow in spirals. Ferns unfold from a spiral. Twigs grow out from the branch in a spiral form. First, one twig grows on one side and then a twig grows on the other side and on up in a spiral helix.

A spiral helix is a spiral stretched out and up as we see in the screw. (Display the screw.)

As you know, our earth is part of the solar system but the solar system is part of a galaxy 75 billion light years across. This galaxy is a spiral too. This is the largest thing we know about and can see. Of course, we only see a part of it.

Inside us, the most important molecule is the DNA molecule. The DNA molecule makes us who we are. All the things we inherit from our parents such as eye color, hair color, etc. are coded in this molecule. The DNA molecule is a spiral helix also.

If the pattern of the largest thing we know about, our galaxy, and one of the smallest things we know about, the DNA molecule, are spirals and all the other plants and animals we talked about are spirals, there must be something special about spirals. The Indians thought so, too. They used spirals to decorate all kinds of utensils. The Hopi Indians believed that when man first emerged onto this earth he was told to travel in a big spiral before he finally settled down in the Hopi country.

We will take a short break here so that you can make your own fingerprints and see the spiral form they have.

Distribute the ink pads. Allow only 3 or 4 minutes for this activity. Then explain that you will continue to talk about spirals and they may continue to doodle the designs which come to them as you talk or they may make their own fingerprints.

The spiral form is often produced from the meeting of two different things as we saw in our "light show." The motion of the fork through the two substances, milk and detergent, produced spirals which we could see because of the food coloring. When warm and cold air meets, it spirals. Remember, a few weeks ago we talked about how thousands of years ago the people of ancient China and Japan believed that everything in the universe is continuously changing. They drew the yin yang sign for this idea. Everyone could draw a yin/yang symbol on your paper as we go on. Something may begin as a little bit yin and it becomes more and more yin. When it becomes just as yin as possible there's still a tiny bit of yang in it and then the yang begins growing and it becomes more yang until the whole thing reverses. Summer begins to get a little cooler and then it's autumn. It becomes colder still and it's winter. Everything is in a process of gradual change.

The yin and yang emerge continuously from the source of energy which never stops. Indians call that "the Powers." One way to think of it is to think of our milk "light show." We only put one or two drops of magic in it but it keeps going and going. That's something like the energy of the universe. As the yin and yang emerge from the universal energy they begin to combine and interact and the different ways they combine and interact make all the things in the world. Just now we saw the two different colored streams of liquid combine and make a spiral so the yin and yang combine and make different patterns. Some of these patterns we call solid matter like a chair and some we call energy like heat or light energy. Some we call animals and people.

During the last few weeks we've learned that we don't really live in a world of solid unchanging things like we thought we did. Everything can interact and change. We live in a world of whirling energy in many different forms. Some of these forms of energy are vibrations — expanded (yin). Other forms of this energy is matter — compacted (yang). But it's all energy — just different patterns of energy. This is much easier for children to understand than for adults. When most adults went to school they were still being taught the old kind of science which is called Newtonian. The new science had been discovered by Einstein but no one really understood much of it.

Einstein wrote this famous equation which you've all seen:

$$E = mc^2 \text{ (write this out for all to see)}$$

In this equation E stands for energy, m stands for mass, meaning the amount or form of matter, and c stands for the velocity of light. This shows that matter can be transformed into energy. The discovery of the atom bomb came from this fact. All the energy of the atom bomb comes from matter. But equations can be reversed, too. So it should be possible to reverse this and make matter come out of energy. Recently at the University of California they succeeded in, actually, doing this. A photograph of this process showed the newly created bits of matter creating a spiral as they were formed.

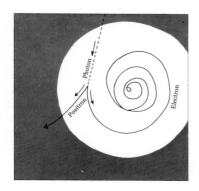

What this really means is that someday maybe another idea from science fiction may come true. That's the idea of having a ray gun which will change something like a truckload of furniture into energy so that you can store it in your pocket and when you get to your new house change it back again into matter or furniture. But, again, we discover that there's a spiral involved — the newly created bits of matter form a spiral. So it's no wonder that the Indians thought life takes the form of a spiral. Take a look at this shield on p. 328 of our "Seven Arrows" book (paperback, p. 310). What do you see? Spirals, again, that's right. It shows spirals of energy coming into your center (the center circle) from "the Powers." We'll talk more about this shield next session. But now we'd better continue with spirals.

The spiral gives us a design which shows us how everything can change from yin to yang and back again.

Using your doodle paper let's draw a spiral showing hot and cold.

For this the leader draws on a large cardboard or blackboard while the group draws with him.

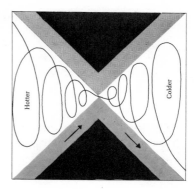

Heat is a yang form like the sun — compressed and dense. Cold is a dispersed form. So we start at the outside of our spiral with cold, and, as the spiral gets tighter, things become more compact and then we have heat. It's hot here at the center. But nothing stays the same forever and soon a heat loss begins and we start moving out along the transformed spiral. We draw a dotted line to show the new spiral. Things begin to cool off as it's more dispersed or spread out and soon it's cold again.

We can use the same idea for energy in us. Let's say you are really peaceful and calm walking along. A friend comes out of the side street (throw a ball to someone who is really paying attention so that he can catch it) and throws a ball at you. You catch it and throw it back and soon you are in a game of catch. You are further along in the spiral. The energy exchange gets more intense as you reach the center of the spiral. But you don't stay at that intense level. You begin to tire or be bored with the game and you start moving out of the spiral into less action and soon you and your friend sit down and rest on the grass and you are out into yin again. So you see the spiral is a good way to see how you use energy.

Let's talk about energy systems in us using the idea of a spiral. (Pass out the sun flower seeds or nuts.) We eat something and get food energy in us. Our body starts to work on that energy. The mouth chews and digests it and sends it down to the stomach. The stomach and intestines draw out the rest of the energy. So we have all that energy inside us. We are at the center of the spiral. Now, if we want to stay in harmony with nature, we have to give-away that food energy in some form to others. At home, after eating, we might use some of the food energy to help wash the dishes and we start moving out the spiral. Some of the energy we share with friends while playing. Maybe, later on in the day, we work on a design we've been making. You give this design to your mother and the energy you put into it flows out to her and makes her happy. So she decides to make you some cookies and her spiral begins of using energy for the cookies. But when they are finished, she gives them to you and

If we're all energy sources, how come some people seem to have a lot more energy than other people. One of the heaviest reasons for that is holes in your bucket. . . . The holes in your bucket are like selfishness, thinking about yourself, thinking about how things might have been . . . you know, going back over your memory tapes and re-writing them so they'll look better when you remember them.   STEPHEN GASKIN

others in the family so you see the energy spirals go on and on if someone doesn't stop the energy, the energy will keep on flowing.

We can't really see the spirals of energy in our interactions with other people but we can feel them. However, in nature, we can actually see the spirals at work. When warm and cold air meet we have a storm front and it begins spiralling on our spinning earth and that's what makes the wind that comes just before a storm.

 Project one of the slides from space which shows a spiralling storm.

Sometimes, when you are sitting by the fire-place, you will see a little hot spark break off from the wood and get caught in the hot flame and it will spiral up and sometimes leap out on the rug. That shows us another energy spiral. The energy produced by the hot fire causes a spiral eddy in the air.

Have you ever watched a hawk riding the warm air currents in summer? He never moves a wing but he rises up and up just riding the spiral of warm air. If we learn to feel nature and the energy around us we can get things done just that easily. It doesn't take much energy to just flow with things. This is what being in harmony with nature means for the Indian. The Indians always tried to pay attention to the flow of energy and go along with it.

 Today we will make spiral patterns which can show various patterns of energy.

 Pass out the materials including the precut circles — one to each person.

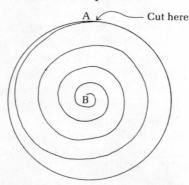

For the demonstration
· Using the large circle, draw a spiral from point A to B. The width between the lines of the spiral diminish as the line nears the center point.
· Then cut from point A to point B along the spiral line until the center is reached.
· Holding the center point, let the spiral hang down. It is now actually a helix. This center point will be attached to fishing line or thread so it can hang.
· Explain that the spirals must be designed before they are cut. Give several suggestions for designs and let them choose two — one for each side of their spirals.

Suggestions for design:
  1. A personal time line
     At the center point, have everybody write the date they were born, the city and any-thing else about the birth which is of in-

continued

continued

terest. Working outward on the spiral have them write words or draw cartoon pictures of important events in their life. If they wish, the last spiral in the circle can be an idea of what they project for their life in the future.

2. Designs of any type they wish — Indian designs, floral, plants, animals, etc.

3. A give-away
Encourage everybody to think about an object — either one which they have been given or one they have given away. On the center of the spiral, draw the object. Fol-low the adventures of the object as it is repeatedly given away.

4. Ecology interactions
Follow the energy cycle of photosynthesis, plant, animal, etc. Follow one atom of oxy-gen through its travels.

5. Energy spiral
From the discussions today, draw cartoon pictures of energy as it flows from person to person. The group could make use of the techniques learned in the Windigo draw-ing in Session 3.

• Attach fish line or heavy thread to the center point of each spiral.

When the spirals are finished, move to the cer-emonial area. Hang the spirals up using the fish line or thread which has been attached. Put on cer-emonial vests. Do the Om chant — Om mani padme. First, do the chant with arms linked in a circle. Then try it with eyes closed so as to feel the vibrations. Then try facing the spirals which are hanging in the air so they can watch the moving patterns of the spirals.

---

meeting area

• materials for milk "light show" — see Session 2 of the Relationship cycle
• materials for demonstration:
  a screw   *Seven Arrows* book
  a ball
  sunflower seeds or nuts
• space slides — see Session 2 of the Relation-ship cycle
• projector and screen
• one paper for each person to doodle on so they can more easily visualize the concepts
• several ink pads
• felt pens
• pictures or books showing spiral designs used by Indians on pottery, masks, etc.
• (optional) A picture of spiral galaxies would be most helpful but not an absolute necessity. Hale Observatories has an excellent montage photo of six spiral galaxies. The cost is only a little over a dollar for an 8 x 10 print. Write for free Hale Observatory catalog from California Institute of Technology Bookstore, 1201 East California Blvd., Pasadena, Calif. 91109. The catalog number for the "montage of six Gal-laxies" is 138

• materials for activity:
  1. 8 in. precut circles cut from various kinds of paper:
     heavy construction paper in various colors
     typing paper
     textured paper
     There should be one for each person with a few extra ones for those who wish to make more spirals. They should be precut because today's discussion is such a long one they will need more time here
  2. fishing line or heavy thread to use to hang the spirals
  3. scissors for each person
  4. crayons, pencils, felt pens
  5. a large circle already made by the leader for demonstration

continued

ceremonial tepee area

Provide places at eye level or above for the group to hang their finished spirals. If this area could be located near or above a heating vent so that they move all the better.

By opening ourselves, surrendering ourselves, we may know the reality, or spirits, of many things . . . . As we bring ourselves in resonance with these spirits, align our own centers with them; they may talk to us, teach us, guide us, protect us, help us, and endow us with The Power as it is manifested in them.

A thing of power is given its power through our recognition in it of the Power that flows through everything — it is given its holy power through the power of our consciousness, which is not ours, but of the Great Spirit.
GAYLE HIGH PINE

8 star water

The last few sessions we've been learning about energy and vibrations in the world. All these energies and vibrations are part of the medicine wheel. I want to tell you an Indian legend concerning these gifts of the medicine wheel.

Read "Star Water," p. 210 and 211, from *Seven Arrows.*

This is a beautiful story but kind of hard to understand isn't it? Remember, in December I told you the Indian legend about the Flowering Forked Tree. It came to mean much more to us after we thought about it and talked about it. That's the interesting thing about Teaching stories. They always have so many levels of meaning.

The Star Water in our story are signs of energy which come from "the Powers." These signs are understanding, kindness, love, truth, joy, and compassion. There are many others too. But when we get angry at someone or feel afraid we want to throw all these good energies away and go off and hide. These are the people in our story who threw the star water away and lived underground. They felt safer underground because they thought that if no one knew how they felt no one could hurt them. When you are angry at someone and feel they have hurt your feelings, your first thought is to hide away from them so they can't hurt you anymore or make you cry. But this really only makes the disagreement worse because, then, there can be no understanding. You have to be brave enough to show your signs of understanding and compassion to the other person and then the other person has a chance to show his signs and you will both find out many new truths about the relationship. You will find, often, that you said something which the other person took in the wrong way and was hurt by it and that he or she only hurt you to get back at you. And when you explain what you really meant, both of you are so relieved everything is happy in the world again.

The Star Water is also like a mirror. Remember, when we talked about how even objects like trees and bushes can mirror our emotions. These mirrors are the Forked Medicine Poles that make the Circle of the Great Lodge. "The Medicine has made it this way that man might learn."

Make a medicine wheel of stones.

The medicine wheel is the sign of the universe. Everything in the universe is represented by a stone in the medicine wheel. You and I are one of the stones in the wheel. All the vibrations of the dance of energy, which we've been talking about, are shown by one of the stones here. In the center of the wheel there is a circle of 7 stones. They are the 7 arrows. They are also the 7 natures of man and the universe. "Man is mirrored within these 7. Two of the seven can be love and fear. The rest we must search out for ourselves because this is part of our learning. Seven Arrows always reflects what we truly are."[23]

The medicine wheel also gives us the four great directions. Let's look again at the shield on p. 328 (paperback, p. 310) of *Seven Arrows* which we saw last session. What do you think it is telling you? (discuss) It shows the teaching arrows of the four directions coming from "the Powers" into your center. As they enter your center, they form spirals of energy if you are clear and do not block what you learn from the four directions of the medicine wheel. The swirling clouds in the center are the energy generated there by these gifts from "the Powers." The bows are shooting the energy into us from "the Powers." The golden ring around the center protects and encloses our center so no real harm can reach us if we allow the gifts from "the Powers" to penetrate us. These arrows stand for the 4 ways we learn as we come out into the open and show our signs clearly. North is what? (buffalo, wisdom) That's one way of learning. But often people are confused about true wisdom. In our story, some of the people who had gone north to learn wisdom came back to steal the Star Water from the Elk. That isn't true wisdom is it?

South is what? (mouse, innocence) But innocence can also be confused. The people who went south came back to trick the Elk to get the Star Water.

West is what? (bear, looks-within) But the people who went West tried to take the Star Water by force.

The people who went East never returned because they found that they could see far and they didn't need to steal the star water.

There are four ways of learning. But there is a fifth way — here in the center (point to the center of the stone medicine wheel) is Mother Earth herself. Remember the Star Water fell to the earth to begin with and Mother Earth gave it to us.

The Sixth way is the stars where the star water came from.

The seventh way is the Medicine itself. It is truth. This is the greatest but also the hardest way. It's strange that truth is such a hard way. The thing we are often most afraid of is to tell someone the truth about how we feel. So each of us hides in our lodge underground and never lets the Star Water of truth show to any other person. No wonder people have trouble understanding one another. What happens when you don't tell someone how you feel? Can anyone give an example?

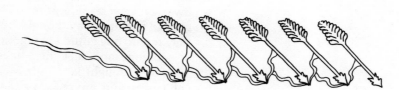

Game

There's a game we can play. We'll call it the Star Water game.

The reason we don't tell another person the truth is because we are afraid he or she won't like us or he or she would be disgusted with us and never speak to us again. This Star Water game is a chance to write down a real secret about yourself that you would never tell anyone. You write it down and we mix all the secrets up so no one knows whose secret is whose. Then, these are read out loud and you get a chance to see what happens.

Each of you take a piece of identical paper and go off and write down a secret that you really are afraid to have anyone know — about yourself. Then fold it up and drop it in this box. I will shake the box so that the secrets are all mixed up so there's no way of telling which secret belongs to you. When you write down your secret try to be specific. If you are afraid of boys say, "I'm afraid of boys because they push me around" or whatever else your secret is.

Write the secrets. Wait until everyone is finished before proceeding.

The first volunteer to read the secrets should reach into the box and pick up one piece of paper. Open it up and read it as if you were that person telling your own secret. Say, "My secret is that . . . " After he or she reads it, the rest of you, each in turn, say how you feel toward this person who has just revealed "his" or "her" secret. It won't really be the secret of the person who read the secret but he or she will act as if it were. What would you say to him or her?

✦ Then take turns reading the secrets. When all are done discuss the "whole experience."

◉ Did you find out that others had the same secret as you had? Then why continue hiding your secret when you've discovered, now, that others have the very same secret?

Hiding secrets is one of the ways we block the energy flow. The energy can't flow through us and out to others if we are hiding something. Energy must flow or move. If we block it we lose it.

In the last part of our Indian legend today, the Elk went to the East taking the girl and the star water with him. "And now if you want to find the Morning Star, you must go to where the Elk is." Have you ever wondered why Indians have the name, Morning Star, and also often name their horses Morning Star? The Morning Star is the Toltec symbol of the spiritual energy of truth. Remember when Black Elk was nine years old and first saw the 4-rayed daybreak star herb which was a healing herb. Daybreak star is another name for the Morning Star. Many of the Indians in our country got their spiritual ideas from the Toltec Indians who lived in Mexico long ago. The Toltec ideas came up from Mexico to the Southwestern Indians and the Southeastern Indians and then on up the Mississippi River to the Sioux and the Cheyenne Indians. The Morning Star is very important to all these Indians. The Morning Star rises in the east and our name for it is Venus. (See appendix)

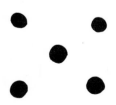

The Toltec Indian symbol for Venus is this. At the center is one circle. This center means your own true self which always knows what to do, which is filled with energy from living in harmony with "the Powers." Into this self come 4 streams of energy from the four different directions of "the Powers," and from this real self come four streams of energy going out to the four directions, shown by the four circles around the center, influencing all the people, animals and plants in all these four directions.

This symbol for Venus is called the "movement symbol" because of this movement of eternal energy. You can see this movement in these examples of the "movement symbol."

Eternal energy moves into our center, and if we are clear and don't block the energy, it moves out to all the beings in the four directions so that they live in harmony.

The interesting thing is that the basic structure of the Toltec "movement symbol," the one with the 5 circles, is the same as a Tibetan symbol.

The Tibetans usually draw lines through here.

Yes, it's sort of like a swastika; but slightly different. The Tibetan symbol deals with good energy. The Nazis reversed it because their swastika was concerned with hate energy.

The arms of the Tibetan symbol go through the center and show that the energy of the center is the same as that of the four directions. It is all the same energy in the world.

The Hopi Indians have a similar symbol too.

The "movement symbol" is very powerful because of the energy in it. Notice how each of the symbols takes the energy of the four directions and centers this energy either in a circle or by twisting it about a center and then sends it out again to the four directions. This is just what happens in us. (Point to the various components of the movement symbols as you continue this discussion.

If we always tell the truth, we become very clear and unmuddied. We live clear. Then all the energy of the universe can pour through us into our center (point to the center of the symbol). And, because we are clear, we don't block the energy so the energy can move out to all the beings in all the four directions. We are going to move to our ceremonial tepee and do a ritual dance which moves the energy out from our center and back into it. We will become moving movement symbols.

◆ The group moves to the ceremonial tepee area.

✦ Directions for movement dance:

If your group really enjoyed the different dances in the program, choose the one that they have come to like the best. If you have a group which has not become involved in the dancing with enthusiasm, use the "Hoky Poky" for the first record. This can be

found on almost any record of collections of songs for children. For the second part of the experience, use any currently popular record which is loud, has lots of rhythm, and different moods. This experience should be a ritual of movement, music and media which really moves everyone. As this is the age in which many children become self conscious about their bodies you have to begin with the "Hoky Poky" to get them started easily.

1. Have the record player turned up quite loud.
2. Have everyone put on their ceremonial vests and stand in a circle.
3. Give everyone four streamers — black, green, white and yellow — two go in each hand.
4. The "Hoky Poky" or a favorite chant and dance should be done first.
5. Encourage everyone to really fling the streamers around to the beat of the music.
6. As the first dance finishes, immediately put on the second record — a popular song with lots of rhythm. Encourage everyone to go wild and loose with movement using the streamers. Do not be hassled if things get wild as this is what is wanted here. Total involvement with the music and movement is the goal.
7. Use several records with different moods.

◆ Return to the meeting area. Again show to the group the various types of movement symbols. Point out to them how in the dance they just did they were the center, the circle or place which the energies twist, and their streamers of the four directions were the energy moving out (as shown in the movement symbols by the patterns of lines moving away from the center in each direction). The activity, today,

consists in making movement symbols to put on their ceremonial vests.

1. Using felt scraps, copy any of the movement symbols given above. This may be done with pencil first if necessary, then redone with coloring dye pens or felt pens.
2. Cut them out.
3. Glue onto ceremonial vests.

◆ Return to the ceremonial tepee area.

🕯 Today we learn the last word of our Tibetan chant. Remember last fall we learned the dance of the Four Directions and chanted "hum, hum, hum phat." This *hum* is the last word of our chant. It stands for the good energies and vibrations which our true "self", the jewel, gives off when it is clearly shining. This energy is the same energy which comes to us from "the Powers" so that when we have our

minds clear and no desires or fears or hatreds in our consciousness we are a clear channel of energy. All the energy from "the Powers" is pouring through us and on out to all of creation — not only to other people but to animals and plants. We are truly in harmony with the earth. We felt some of this in our energy dance just now, and we have our energy symbols on our vests too.

Last fall we just said *hum* as it is spelled but ac-

*In the Om we open ourselves, in the Hum, we give ourselves. Om is the door of knowledge
. . . hum is a sacrificial sound. The Sanskrit syllable "hu" means "to sacrifice, to perform a
sacrificial act or rite." The sole sacrifice, however, that the Buddha recognizes, is the
sacrifice of one's own self.* LAMA GOVINDA

tually the Tibetans pronounce it more like a nasal —
hung.

The (ng) vibrates for a long time until you can feel
the vibrations in your teeth and head. Then you close
your lips which makes it become an m sound.

The *hung* is chanted on the same note as mani
padme. This note just continues on as you chant
hung.

 Practice the entire chant, "Om mani padme
hung" a few times. Remind everyone to notice

the vibrations moving through their head and out and
back into their center as they chant the syllable, *hung.*

This is the energy moving into us and through us
and out to all the four directions just as our
movement symbol shows. When we say the *hum* we
are giving away our self — sending our energy from
our center. And when we do this we automatically
receive a give-away of energy back to us from "the
Powers." The vibrations away from us and back to us
put us in harmony with everything.

Then, when everyone has learned it, put on the
ceremonial vests and do the entire chant
standing in a circle, arms linked, for as long as they
wish.

You can see the streams of energy shot into us
by "the Powers" which is shown in the
"movement symbol" in this shield on p. 328 (p. 310,
paperback).

All Wisdoms are fused into one by the flame of an all-embracing feeling of solidarity (we may call it love, sympathy, benevolence . . .) and the urge to act for the benefit of all living beings. . . . Thus hum unites both sides of reality: the living, pulsating presence of individual existence and the supra-individual timelessness beyond all dualities.

LAMA GOVINDA

NOTE concerning next cycle:

It is necessary to have a supply of pollen for the activity in Session 2 of the Vegetation cycle which comes next. It is also needed for the festival in Session 3. If you have a very cold climate and no pollen is produced naturally this early in spring, you should gather willow branches for forcing it this week. Scrub willow grows as a weed along most small streams and in many city parks. Look for those with the more swollen buds. Cut these and keep them in water in a sunny window. Soon the pussy willows will come out. A few days later, pollen grains can be seen on the individual hairs of the pussy willow. This will occur in a week or two after putting them in water. Each pussy willow comes out at a different time so some should be producing pollen when needed for Session 2.

About the swastika

It is important to clarify the true meaning of this symbol. Children are very attracted to the swastika, using it for doodles and drawing it on walls and sidewalks. Adults frequently worry about this practice and waste energy condemning it. Actually, referring as it does to the four cardinal directions and the centering of this energy, the swastika is a very basic symbol for the human race. Primitive humans were using this symbol for thousands of years before Nazi misuse so it is completely natural for children to continue using it; however, it is about time that children be helped to understand more clearly their natural attraction to it.

meeting area	
• identical pieces of paper for each person — any size or type but they must be identical in every way • pencils • *Seven Arrows* book • 31 small round rocks to make a medicine wheel • ceremonial vests • crepe paper streamers • 1½ to 2 in. wide. One each of black, green, yellow and white for each person	• record player and records. See actual session for type of records. *Hoky Poky* is on a Capital record No. 6026, *Ray Anthony*, a 45 single • materials for activity: Elmer's glue felt scraps scissors pencils and felt pens Grey Owl coloring dye pens
ceremonial tepee area no special directions for here today	

Behold, my brothers, the spring has come; the earth has received the embraces of the sun and we shall soon see the results of that love!

Every seed is awakened and so has all the animal life. It is through this mysterious power that we too have our being and we therefore yield to our neighbors, even our animal neighbors, the same right as ourselves, to inhabit this land. SITTING BULL

1  spring

Refer to the double medicine wheel during the following discussion.

We have moved to another place on the earth's medicine wheel. When we began these sessions it was autumn — west, the sign of the bear. Then we moved into winter — north, the sign of the buffalo and now we are in spring — east, the sign of the eagle. We are moving on the way toward summer. In winter the earth was covered with the white of snow and the waters were frozen. In the spring the snow melts, the water flows freely and the world turns green — the color of south and summer. The earth's medicine wheel turns for us.

Last autumn, the seeds fell into the ground where they lay all winter waiting for the warmth of spring. Now, spring has come; the sun gives-away its warmth to the earth and the seeds begin to push up through the earth toward the sun.

Today, we will walk so that we can feel the earth's medicine wheel turning — bringing us warmth and new life. Look for "good medicine" plants. Mother Earth provides plants to cure almost every physical sickness man can get. She also provides plants to help us feel better when we are sad. That is the kind of plant we are looking for today. We don't quite know how this works but having plants around does help us feel better. This is why, for every great festival, the Indians always went out and collected plants to make a ritual object for the festival. The Indian took the energy of the plant and combined that with his own energy to make a "playful pattern of energy", or work of art, to help him get in a harmonious state with nature.

We will look for parts of plants to help us make such a work of art. Today, it will be a plant wall hanging. So find parts of plants which appeal to you because of color or feel and which can be woven into the design — branches, cattails, large leaves, ferns, dried weeds left over from last autumn.

Also, if you find something which seems to you to have special power pick it up and save it, separately, because you can use it for a special project next session. This could be a seed or a feather or a strange shaped twig or rock.

Walk

✦ At the beginning of the walk, you should remind everyone of the care they should give the earth.

🔥 Walk softly on the earth as new life is beginning under it in spring. Tender young plants may be killed if one steps carelessly. The Indians thought of the earth as their mother. Remember Smohalla said, "You ask me to plow the ground. Shall I take a knife and tear my mother's breast?" Think of this living flesh of the earth as you walk.

✦ As you walk along discuss the soil.

🔥 Where does the soil, which we are walking on, come from? Who gave it to us? (Point out lichens on rocks or old fences.) Lichens produce an acid which eats into the rock and makes tiny cracks and beginnings of soil. Mosses and ferns then begin to grow in this soil which the lichens gave-away to them. The moss forms more soil. The rock begins to crumble as more plants live and die giving their bodies to the soil. The bacteria works on the dead matter and the soil becomes better. Then larger plants can grow. It takes hundreds of years for this process of soil making to take place. That's why we walk carefully.

✦ If you see mushrooms or other fungus point out that this type of plant eats up dead plants and branches and cleans the woods as well as giving nitrogen back to the air. When you see signs of man's destruction of the soil or plants ask the group to tell you what they think the earth would say if it could only talk to us.

Everyone should be encouraged to notice all the patterns of energy which they come across — or vibrations which they can feel from any plant or animal.

Try to find a tree or other plant which is producing pollen. Gather some of it for next session and the spring equinox festival. Have everybody place it in plastic bags. If your climate is really cold and there is no pollen being produced yet, omit this step today. See directions for pollen gathering given in Session 2.

🔥 Indians believed that pollen was powerful "good medicine." Plants need pollen to produce their seed. We will gather some for our ceremonies just as the Indians did but remember to leave some pollen for the plant's own use. They can give-away some pollen to us but we must always be sure to take only a little from each plant.

✦ Remind everybody when they gather plant material or pollen to thank the plant for the give-away and to tell the plant we need its gift for our festival to help us live more harmoniously with the earth.

Chant

If the area in which you are walking is sufficiently private, do the Om chant as given below. However, if this proves difficult, the chant should be done as soon as they return from the walk so they will still feel close to plants, the rocks and the earth. The chant should be done in the ceremonial tepee area with vests on.

🔥 Sometimes, the Tibetans use the Om chant to help them feel the sufferings of all living things. By feeling their suffering this helps them to keep from unnecessarily hurting any living being. To do this they assign a special color for a living being to each syllable:

Om	— white	— This syllable stands for "the Powers"
ma	— green	— plants
ni	— yellow	— humans
pad	— blue	— animals
me	— red	— those who are unhappy or frustrated

hum — black — those who are angry or hate others. Those who we think are our enemies.

As we begin the chant, while we say Om, we make a wish that the energy from "the Powers" will flow abundantly through all living beings. Then, as we chant each of the other syllables think of the living being of that syllable and send the energy in you flowing out to help that being. When we do this we are doing what our "movement symbols" show — sending good energy out to all four directions from our centers. (Chant together.)

Wall hanging for the spring equinox festival

We will make a hanging by weaving together the colors of these syllables into a single unity. At times we are unhappy or frustrated or angry so that we are the red or black color. During those times we need good energy from other humans and from plants and animals. Other times, we are filled with energy and so we can give-away our good energy to other living beings. It is all a big give-away. See if you can show some of this interacting energy in your hanging.

Directions

Using one of the yarn strands, first give instructions in how to make a square knot. Have everyone make a *loose* square knot and check to see if anyone needs help. Have them make a second loose square knot and check again. When you are sure everyone knows how to make the square knot proceed below.

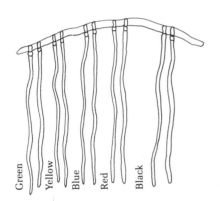

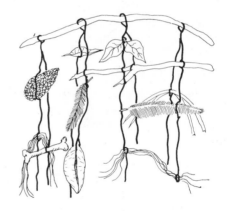

1. Pass out the necessary materials.
2. Have each person lay the strands on the floor or table in front of him so that they are straight and untangled. Beginning on the left, lay out the two green strands, then to the right of them, lay out the two yellow strands, to the right of that, lay out the two blue strands, to the right of that, lay out the two red strands, and last the two black strands.
3. Place the branch or dowel across the top of the strands.
4. Tie each piece of yarn onto the branch or dowel at the top. Be sure they are evenly spaced. Use a square knot and pull this one tight.
5. Beginning with the two green strands, tie them together using a loose square knot. Continue tying them together in a continuous chain until half the length of the yarn has been used. The last of this series of knots should be pulled tight.
6. Continue across the branch tying matching strands together in loose square knots until all strands have been tied.
7. Using the plant materials, weave them in and out of the holes which are formed by the centers of the knots. Weave a piece of plant material clear across all the colors of yarn or through just a few strands of yarn.
8. Depending on the amount of time available, plant material may be woven clear until the ends of the yarns or else the ends may be left free hanging as a fringe.

Not only is the chloroplast the overwhelmingly dominant mechanism whereby the light of the sun is transmuted into the substances supporting all life, the sugar and carbohydrates, but there are grounds for believing that it is from the exhalations of all plants in all time that an atmosphere with free oxygen has developed. Indeed, all food, all fossil fuels, fibres, all atmospheric oxygen, the stabilization of the earth's surface and its terrestrial water system, the melioration of climate and microclimate have been accomplished by the plant: all animals and thus all men were plant parasites . . . and this dependence persists unchanged.

IAN McHARG

Carefully tape or thumb tack the wall hangings to the wall in the ceremonial tepee area. Put on ceremonial vests and chant the Om chant. If time allows have everyone make a circle to chant. Then one at a time each person can stand in the center of this circle to feel the power of the sound around him as the others chant.

The objects which you found today that had special power for you should be taken home and saved until next session when we will use them to make a very special ritual object. Also, during the coming week, if you should find any other natural object which appeals to you such as a feather, an interesting tiny rock or even a small piece of broken glass which attracts you bring it along for the next session.

If you have a favorite dress or shirt which is especially important to you pull a thread from it and bring it along. Bring along a tiny piece of any object which is important to you.

The pollen, which was collected, should be put in jars with screw top lids to save for next session and the spring equinox festival. The "items of power" which everybody collected should be saved for next session. The wall hangings should be saved for the festival. If no pollen was found, you will have to go out and gather some during the week.

meeting area	
• double medicine wheel from Session 1 of the Energy cycle • materials needed on walk: small plastic bags to collect pollen, large sacks to collect plant material • materials for activity: for each person: one branch or dowel — 18 to 24 inches long yarn: 2 strands of black, 2 red, 2 blue, 2 yellow and 2 green. Each 24 inches long.	1 piece of twine, rope, or extra strong yarn to use as a hanger. • NOTE: The leader should gather ahead of time various plant items to be used in the wall hangings: twigs, leaves, pine cones, nuts, large seeds, cattails, dried weeds, ferns, etc. These will be available in case the group does not find enough material

ceremonial tepee area	
• ceremonial vests • chart of the Om chant. This chart, made before the session begins, should list each syllable of the Om chant, the color belonging	to that syllable and the living being which that syllable stands for. This information is given in the session itself

vegetation

The symbol for life and productivity, for peace and prosperity is pollen. Pollen symbolizes light.
STEPHEN C. JETT

2 pollen

During our walk, last session, I told you that the Indians considered pollen a very powerful "good medicine." Today, I will tell you more about this but, first, just what does *good medicine* mean? We've been talking about the Indian medicine wheel and "good medicine" for some time now. What do you think it means? (discuss) Medicine can mean "the Powers" as well as the helps which "the Powers" send to us to keep us in harmony with the earth. The medicine wheel is one of the greatest of these helps. Each Indian's own shield is "good medicine." Plants can be "good medicine." Certain places where we can feel the energy of "the Powers" are good medicine. Some of these places are mountains, deserts, near certain trees, and sometimes near waterfalls or springs of water.

Pollen was considered very powerful "good medicine." Do any of you know just exactly what pollen is? (discuss) Pollen grains are so tiny that you can hardly see the individual grains. (Show some which was gathered on the walk, or, if because of your cold climate it has been necessary to force willow branches indoors, gently shake off the pollen into a shallow container for this demonstration.) These grains carry the male cell of the higher types of plants — trees and flowers. These pollen grains are usually carried to the waiting female plant by bees or hummingbirds. But some types of plants, such as trees, release great clouds of gold pollen grains. The wind blows them about and rivers carry them along. The trees release so many millions of grains of pollen that some of them inevitably reach the female trees and then the seeds of the new tree are produced. Usually these seeds are contained in cones such as pine cones and fir cones. Fruit trees also need to be pollinated. Cottonwood and aspen trees and holly must also be pollinated.

The really amazing thing about pollen is that each tiny grain is protected by a very tough plastic covering. It's very thin and smooth like glass and it lasts, practically forever, when protected from air. Pollen is blown all over the country. Scientists find pollen layers in glaciers. There is a layer of permanent snow and then a thin layer of pollen blown up by the wind, then the next winter's snow. Pollen also settles down to the bottom of lakes. The protective cover of pollen preserves the grains so that scientists can use these pollen grains as a way to find out the history of prehistoric man. By boring into the peat bogs or the bottoms of lakes, the scientist brings up a column of old mud with all the layers of pollen still preserved by the protective covering of the grains. This pollen gives the scientist a record of what plant grew in a certain area clear back to the time when most of our country was covered with glaciers. By this method, scientists can find out exactly when primitive men first came to a particular area. Up to that time there are certain kinds of pollen from plants which always grew there. But as soon as man comes into an area — even primitive stone age hunting tribes, the pollen grains change and certain new pollens show up. One of these is rye. Rye was a sort of weed which came along with man in Europe. From the layers of pollen grains, scientists can tell when man first began farming.

Indians from many different tribes have always thought of pollen as being especially powerful "good medicine" of "the Powers", because they knew that plants needed pollen to produce food for them. For example, a corn plant will grow from a seed of corn which is planted in the ground but it will not have a real ear of corn on it unless pollen from another plant has fallen on it.

Corn must be planted in blocks, not in a single row, because it has to be cross-pollinated. The male cell is the tassel and the pollen from this has to be deposited on the sticky corn silk of another plant. Once the pollen has landed on the corn silk, the pollen grains begin to swell. Soon pollen tubes begin growing down the silk to where the ovules of the plant are. The ovules are where the seed develops. In most plants this is less than an inch away from where the male cells and female cells meet but in the corn plant the silks may grow 10 or more inches down the plant to reach the ovules — which are the actual kernels in the ear of corn. The individual corn silks grow until they extend into the ear where one is attached to each of the grains of corn. If any of these silks are broken, the kernel to which it is attached will fail to develop. That's why, sometimes, you get an ear of corn with no kernels in one part of it.

The Indians, of course, knew about all this long ago as they were the ones who developed corn for us. They realized that pollen was a very powerful substance because if a corn plant had pollen fall on it, corn was produced for them to eat. If pollen did not fall on the plant there was nothing for them to eat so they felt that pollen was a special gift from "the Powers." They used it in ceremonies and festivals because they felt it could help them to be more in harmony with "the Powers" who had sent them this great gift.

The transfer of pollen from male to female organs is most easily done by plants which have flowers. Flowers are quite new in the long evolutionary history of the earth. For thousands of years there were only green plants. Flowers came about rather suddenly and it is an interesting example of the giveaway. (Use a flower with pollen as an example while continuing the discussion below.) All along, insects had been eating off plants — boring holes in the outer stems and sucking up their juices. Some plants developed tougher skins to keep the insects out. Other plants developed a poison sap to kill the insects. But most of the plants remembered the giveaway and they put concentrations of their sap, called nectar, in a place where the insect could get at it without hurting the plants. Up to this time, the plants

If circadian rhythms bind us to the cycle of the earth on which we live, we have seen that light may slowly change our hormones and moods, in consonance with the longer annual revolution of earth about the sun. Light is only one of the many cosmic influences upon us. Earth turns in the winds of the sun, in the gravitational flux of the galaxy.

Since the dim beginning of man's history, human thought has been permeated with the belief that the movements of the planets and stars influence all earthly movements, from agriculture to health and social order. These astrological ideas were the basis for most of man's great religions, and throughout much of man's history his most important science . . . . From the Chaldeans to the Chinese, the Inca to the Iroquois, the great legacy of human learning and legend involved an appreciation of cyclic changes on earth, some of them well beyond the span of one or two generations. These cycles seemed influential for the future of life on earth. The object of the religions was to harmonize man with earth, and resolve how man belongs to the grander system of the universe. . . .

We have seen that sunlight may influence emotions by indirectly regulating the amount of calcium available for nervous activity. Gravitational changes, magnetic field changes from sun spots, or barometric pressure from lunar cycles may account for surges of excitement and agitation among vulnerable humans on earth. Our harmony with earth rhythms and the grander cosmos beyond is not a matter of philosophy, outside of our skins. Like the crab who feels the oncoming storm, and the other animals who share this planet with us, we respond to magnetic storms and changing forces. Our belief does dictate whether we will learn to identify these external rhythms and events, or continue to be influenced unawares. GAY GAER LUCE

had had to depend on the wind or on accidental brushing by animals to spread their pollen. But now the pollen bearing organs were near these pools of nectar. The insects which came to get the give-away nectar were getting pollen on their wings and legs and carrying it on to the next flower. The insects were much more efficient at spreading the flower's pollen than the wind so this meant more fruit could develop and therefore more seeds to start new baby plants. So, giving-away nectar by means of flowers, gave the flower-bearing plants a real advantage.

The plants began to try to attract the insects they used to fear. Some produced brighter flowers and some developed better smells; and, out of this effort a new kind of give-away developed on the earth. The plants got a very good way of pollination and the insects got a very good food supply among the flowers. What did we gain from this give-away? (Fruit, and the beauty and good smells of flowers.) And what do we get from the insects? (Bees give honey.) So, again, everyone gets something when all freely give-away to one another.

 NOTE: Background information concerning pollen in pahos.

In the cultures which use them, pahos are both intensely personal and symbolic. In those cultures which use the hollow reed types, the center is stuffed with symbols of personal meaning while the outside is decorated with cultural symbols which can be interpreted by everyone.

The "power" of the pahos stems from the part-of-the-self-powers inside the stick. These personal powers are intensified and sanctified by the power symbols of society on the outside. For these reasons, the pahos should contain something which is associated with strong feelings in the person.

 Today, we are going to use pollen in making prayer-sticks, or pahos, as the Hopi Indians call them. The Indians make these for special ceremonies. Ours will be quite different from the Hopi Indian prayer sticks. We will use them in our Spring Equinox celebration.

The most important thing about pahos happens while you are making them, because in a prayer-stick the Indians are trying to show their innermost, self, and feelings to "the Powers" so that "the Powers" will help them to understand these things. These important innermost feelings are a secret to each Indian. He only puts them in the paho for "the Powers" to see and not for anyone else.

In order to help you see inside yourself and find the most important things to share with "the Powers", I will give your four guidelines.

(Write these out for all to read.)

continued

continued

1. What is my most important goal that I am seeking?
2. What is the thing that I like the most about myself?
3. What is the thing that I most fear?
4. What do I cherish the most?

The answers you give to these questions will be written down and stuffed inside the pahos so that they are secret from everyone except yourself. You can either write them in words or use symbols. Since you know that they will be kept really secret you should try to go deep inside yourself, past all of the masks that you wear, and try to reveal to yourself the inner meanings of these questions. Remember, these secrets will be kept hidden and protected by the pollen which lasts almost forever — longer than most other things in the world.

Meditation

 To help you meditate on these questions we will play some meditation music. (Turn on the record which has been chosen for meditation.)

Directions for making pahos

PLAN I

1. When you feel you are ready, write down on the 4 pieces of paper what you have discovered from listening to the real, "self" deep inside you. Then put a pinch of pollen into each paper and carefully fold it and stuff the paper into one of the hollow reeds, or sticks.
2. If you wish, you can also put into the reed any other important items which you brought with you today.
3. Then close both ends of each stick with moss or cotton.
4. The outside may be decorated any way you wish, using felt pens, paints, old jewelry, etc. You may use the symbol books for ideas.

PLAN II — If you are unable to find cattails or reeds which are hollow, have already mixed up enough baker's dough so that each person will have 1 cup of dough.

Recipe for Baker's Dough
Stir together:

    2 cups flour   ¾ cup water
    1 cup salt

Form into desired shapes and bake for 20 to 30 minutes in a 350 degree oven. This makes two cups.

Do not double this recipe. If you need more dough mix up another batch using exactly the same measurements. Doubling the original recipe makes the dough the wrong consistency.

Other materials needed:
- pins with colored heads
- yarn (precut in 6 in. lengths) 4 per person
- cookie sheets
- old jewelry, sequins
- paints
- four sticks or dowels for each person
- pollen
- piece of aluminum foil

After each person in the group has written on the four pieces of paper, have them put a pinch of pollen in each one and fold them up very small. Divide their cup of dough into four equal parts. Each piece of paper will go inside a piece of the dough. The paper must be completely covered by the dough. One end of a piece of yarn should also be in the center of each piece of dough.

They may mold the clumps of dough into shapes and decorate them with the colored pins and old jewelry.

When the four clumps of dough are all decorated, they should be placed on a cookie sheet which is covered with foil. On the foil write the name of the person and draw a circle around the four pieces and the name. The graphite will not stick but the foil will indent and be readable after the dough is baked.

The clumps should be baked at 300 degrees for about 30 minutes, until nicely browned. While they are baking each person may decorate his or her sticks or dowels in the same fashion as the reeds were decorated in step no. 4 of Plan I above. Then, when the clumps are baked and cool, they are tied to the decorated sticks with the yarn.

While the pahos are being made, talk with the group about how the pollen stains their hands yellow. When the pahos are finished, point out that the pollen in them could last much longer than our lifetime and even longer than the biggest building in town or the oldest redwood tree.

At a National Institute of Mental Health Conference it was stated that very few useful drugs have been developed strictly on an empirical basis in the laboratory of the organic chemist. In most cases, they are improvements over what nature has already provided. Pharmacognosy Professor C. C. Albers of the University of Texas explained: "Plants provide blueprints for thousands of medical substances a chemist can synthesize. Plant explorers search for promising plants, then a valuable extract is produced and the chemists take over. They juggle and shuffle the molecules and come up with a variety of derivatives of natural product."

MARGARET KREIG

Now that we are beginning to understand the importance of pollen we can learn a special "power saying" of the Navajo Indians. They use this when they realize they are angry or unhappy and so they want to restore their harmony and balance with nature.

> Put your feet down with pollen.
> Put your hands down with pollen.
> Put your head down with pollen.
> Then your feet are pollen;
> Your hands are pollen;
> Your body is pollen;
> Your voice is pollen;

The trail is beautiful.
Be still.[24]

Follow this with the Om chant to concentrate the power which has come from making the pahos.

The pahos should be kept at the meeting area to dry thoroughly and to be used in the Festival next week.

Everyone should be reminded to bring flowers for the Spring Equinox Festival next week.

About pollen

Pollen comes in many shades — brown, black, orange, yellow, red, and green. Honey supplies the carbohydrates in the bees' diet while pollen supplies the protein, vitamins, fats and minerals. The workers feed pollen to the young nurse-bees. The nurse-bees make the royal jelly for the queen and the young larvae.

Some wind-pollinated plants have as many as 10,000 grains per stamen in flowers with many

Dr. Jonathan Lieff discovered the unique healing quality of mantras from using them with the inmates of the Boston State Hospital in psychotherapy programs for chronic psychiatric patients. He states: *The theory of the discovery of the healing properties of music rests on several assumptions. One is that meditation specifically aids psychoanalysis in that it increases free mental association. . . . The second hypothesis is that repetitive chanting of certain sounds operates as a meditation device, creating a mental set for the observer to witness himself. . . .*

Thirdly, specific sounds and specific phrases and specific rhythms have different physiological, emotional and mental effects that can be quantified. This effect depends upon interaction of a given sound with the body's nervous system centers, physiological centers, as well as with the symbolizations of the unconscious. In many systems of human endeavor, including ancient religious systems, a science of the effects of different sounds are described mostly in the form of monastic chanting.

DR. JONATHAN LIEFF

To practice Attunement, we begin with understanding the concept of oneness. This does not mean that everything is the same; it means that there is no real separation, that everything exists within a unified field of being. . . . To communicate with a level of life apparently outside us, we simply discover and attune to its corresponding reality within us . . .

We can draw an illustration of this from music. Middle C and its first harmonic, the next higher C note, are the same tonal quality but separated by an octave of energy. The two notes played in the same way possess equal amplitude but a different frequency of expression. The higher note is moving faster as a sound wave, hence we hear it as a higher pitched sound . . . they are still the same note and occupy the same tonal position in the scale. Because of this, whenever one C is struck, the other C's of higher octaves resonate in harmony and can be heard by one whose ear is sensitively trained.

So with the universe within us. In the microcosm of our individual being, we are harmonically related to all the macrocosm which represents higher octaves of what is within us. If we manifest a certain microcosmic quality, such as love, then there is a thrill of resonance throughout the universe of the love quality on all its levels of expression, on all of the octaves of its being . . .

I realize that this Awareness of limitless Love is not outside of me; it has a lower octave counterpart within me. I must find that counterpart and play it, like striking middle C in order to hear through resonance a higher C note. In other words, I must begin expressing on human levels a love released from limitations of prejudice, fear, hatred, separation. I must relate to the world around me as if all parts of it were my Beloved. I must see the reality of this love within me and in my life. I set the vibration of love resonating throughout my microcosmic life.

Then, in my moments of silence, I can rise on the currents of this resonance. I attract the higher octave counterparts of love to my awareness or, more accurately, by experiencing love in my microcosmic life I because sensitive to experiencing it in my macrocosmic life. The barriers of separation in my consciousness dissolve. There is no more within, no more without. There is only what I AM — the oneness of all.

DAVID SPANGLER

stamens each. Trees release pollen in the spring, grass and weeds release their pollen in middle and late summer.

About places where we can feel the energy of "the Powers"

This energy of "the Powers" may be somewhat the same as the prana energy of the Hindus and may be connected with the negative ions in the air. Positive ions produce depression and cause health disturbances. These positive ions are prevalent in city smog and certain bad winds such as föehn in Europe. Negative ions produce a feeling of well-being and promote healing. Negative ions are most prevalent in deserts or near mountains, the sea, lakes or waterfalls.

meeting area only today

flower for demonstration. If possible the flower should have pollen on it

materials for activity:
- pollen collected during the last session or forced willow branches and pruning shears and a shallow container for each person. If your pollen is to come from forced willow branches, use a pruning shears to cut off individual willow twigs and have everybody come to you for the twig. They shake the pollen off the twig immediately so none of the pollen is lost
- bits of old jewelry
- felt
- Elmer's glue

- felt pens
- paint in red, black, yellow and green colors
- string
- moss or cotton
- symbol books (See Session 3 of Autumn Equinox cycle)
- record for meditation and record player
- items which each person has brought with him or her to use in pahos
- each person will need:
  4 cattails or hollow reeds or bamboo sticks. If you cannot get any see Plan II listed in the Activity part of the session
  4 two-inch square pieces of paper
  pencil

Ritual has traditionally been the means of maintaining human activity in conscious accordance with the laws of nature. The purpose of ritual is to make a man a more conscious agent of cosmic forces. . . .

Ritual forms the basis of . . . "organic living." It is the binding agent of culture and articulates for man — through man — his place in nature and the nature of his place, so that there is a harmonious reciprocity between the culture and its environment, making of the two a seamless whole.   JOSE AND MIRIAM ARGUELLES

If you put God outside and set him vis-à-vis his creation and if you have the idea that you are created in his image, you will logically and naturally see yourself as outside and against the things around you. And as you arrogate all mind to yourself, you will see the world around you as mindless and therefore not entitled to moral or ethical consideration. The environment will seem to be yours to exploit. Your survival unit will be you and your folks or conspecifics against the environment of other social units, other races and the brutes and vegetables.

If this is your estimate of your relation to nature and you have an advanced technology, *your likelihood of survival will be that of a snowball in hell. You will die either of the toxic by-products of your own hate, or, simply, of over-population and overgrazing. The raw materials of the world are finite.*   GREGORY BATESON

3 spring equinox festival

Remember, we learned that each thing in the universe has its own rate of vibration. Our mind is like a radio or a television set. Our mind can transmit vibrations as well as receive them. A television set, which is out of adjustment, cannot receive clear pictures can it? If we do not work to keep our minds perfectly tuned with our bodies, our mind will not receive clear vibrations from the world. We become insensitive. We begin to live only in our own self-centered narrow world and soon the vibrations all around us fail to register. We miss out on all the hundreds of vibrations going on in the world around us.

During the great festivals at special times of the year, the Indians performed special rituals to get in harmony with the earth. One of the things these rituals did for them was to tune up their minds to enable them to feel more of the vibrations of other beings on the earth. The Spring Equinox Festival was a special time to get in tune with the plants.

At the time of the spring equinox we once again have equal light and dark during the day. Last September, we celebrated the only other time when light and dark are equal. This was our Autumn Equinox Festival. Ahead of us, now, is a time of more light from the sun — a time when the plants grow and the earth is warm. Our festival today will help us get in balance with this light-filled, warm earth.

The Indians had a special ceremonial eating of the first wild food which Mother Earth gave-away in the spring. So we will begin our festival, today, with that ceremony.

Celebration

Preparations

1. Everyone rubs all exposed parts of their body with a sweet smelling plant: sage, aromatic bark or leaves, thyme or other aromatic herb.
2. Everyone puts on their ceremonial vests.
3. All stand in a circle about the leader.

Wild food ceremony

- One person, chosen by the group, ceremoniously carries the food in on a wooden platter.
- The leader lights the smoke plant: eucalyptus, sage, pine needles, etc. He immediately blows it out and then blows the smoke from the plant to each of the four directions.

Spring Thanksgiving Chant

We give-away our thanks to Mother Earth for this (name of plant to be eaten).

We give-away our thanks to the flowers who give us such beauty and joy.

We give-away our thanks to the sun who comes closer to the earth, now, giving us more light and warmth after the long dark winter.

We give-away our thanks to "the Powers" by giving sacred pollen to the

east (face east and throw pollen over that part of the circle)

south (face south and throw pollen over that part of the circle)

west (face west and throw pollen over that part of the circle)

north (face north and throw pollen over that part of the circle)

We give-away our thanks to "the Powers" who give energy to all the beings of the earth so that they can give-away energy to one another in the eternal dance of balance and harmony.

- Then the leader and all others cross their arms over their chests — the right hand is on the left shoulder; the left hand, on the right shoulder. All stand silently for a moment.
- Then, holding hands in a circle do the Indian dance, chanting:

  "All things that must be — must be in balance and *that* takes practice."

- Sit down in a circle and eat the food.

All through the winter we've been learning about the energy systems of all the beings in the world. We've also learned about how we can give-away to other creatures. This is how we practice being in balance. When we do this, we are in harmony or balance with all the other living beings. Do you feel this energy flowing through you more these days? Do you feel closer to the birds and animals and plants you meet?

Today we will make our special spring equinox mandala shields. They will be on paper which looks just like old skins of animals which the Indians used. But now there are too many people in the world for each of us to kill an animal for its skin so we will make our own special paper to look like an animal skin.

Basic process for giving paper the look of old animal skin

- The grocery bag is opened flat by carefully pulling along the glued edges. If the glue is too tight, have them use scissors to cut along the seams in order to open the bag out into one large piece.
- Draw the design on the opened-out bag. See below on how this is to be done. Use heavy crayon with intense colors.
- Crumble the bag into a ball, open it and crumble it again. Do this 5 or 6 times.
- Lay the bag on several newspapers, design side down. With the iron set on high, iron the bag thoroughly.
- Repeat the process of crumbling and ironing at least 4 times. The more cycles this can be done the more like chamois the bag will become.

Design

- Review quickly the designs which have been used in the past so they will begin to think in terms of designs.
    Begin a _short_ discussion on what spring is:
      What it means to them.
      Goals for this particular spring.

Fears that occur only in the spring (flood, wind, etc.)
How spring relates to summer and winter.
How the weather of spring affects them.
How behavior differs in spring from behavior in winter and summer.

Keep the discussion short; merely beginning the thinking and feeling process. When you feel the group has been stimulated give them 10 minutes of quiet time in which each person makes one personal symbol design that expresses his or her individual feelings about spring. This is done in pencil on a scrap of paper. Pictures, words or symbols may be used.

- Divide the group into mini-groups of 4 each. The mini-group will make a mandala sketch which incorporates the symbols of each of the four members of the group. Provide at least 10 or 15 minutes for this. When the sketch is done, the design is then drawn onto the paper bag with crayon and put through the crumble-iron cycles. Each person gets at least one turn in this process.
- When each mandala is finished, the group can explain its meaning to everybody else.

NOTE: The group process of interrelating to make a group mandala which incorporates the symbols of the individuals is very important. Although the individual person could make his own mandala, the group process takes them a step beyond into the realm of explaining (thus clarifying and focusing) the meanings of their symbols.

This process sets up a situation in which each person is involved in a give-away of himself or herself through verbal communication. This moves them beyond the level of mere concept to the expression of that concept. They interrelate in order to symbolize the interrelationships involved in spring.

The Hopis believe that when they dance with full awareness of the energy from "the Powers" as their right foot stomps powerfully down on the ground they are awakening "the vibratory centers deep within the earth."[25] These vibratory centers resound all through the earth and call all living beings to live in harmony and balance. So the Hopis believe that dancing keeps us in harmony with the earth.

Dance

Directions

 Each person chants the pollen "power chant" which was learned last session as he dances:

> Put your feet down with pollen.
> Put your hands down with pollen.
> Put your head down with pollen.
> Then your feet are pollen;
> Your hands are pollen;
> Your body is pollen;
> Your voice is pollen;

The trail is beautiful.
Be still.

- As the music begins the leader throws a pinch of pollen in each of the four directions before the dancing starts.
- Do the basic Indian dance step pounding especially hard as the right foot comes down.
- Everyone dances in whichever direction they wish weaving through the four directions of the medicine wheel.

Everyone gathers in a circle, linking arms and recites the Om chant thinking of the colors and radiating compassion to all the beings.

Om	— white	— "the Powers"
ma	— green	— plants
ni	— yellow	— humans
pad	— blue	— animals
me	— red	— those who are unhappy or frustrated
hum	— black	— those who are angry or hate others. Those who we think are our enemies.

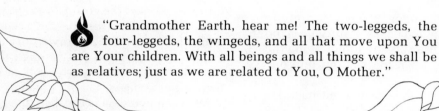

"Grandmother Earth, hear me! The two-leggeds, the four-leggeds, the wingeds, and all that move upon You are Your children. With all beings and all things we shall be as relatives; just as we are related to You, O Mother."

---

ceremonial tepee area only today

- Before the session begins, each person hangs up their wall hangings. Each person should be allowed to decide in which direction he or she wants to hang the wall hanging.
- The flowers, which have been brought, should be arranged by each person in vases or jars around the area. Each person also decides where he or she wants to place his or her paho for the ceremony. They could be put among the flowers or under the wall hangings but the choice is up to them.
- Chart of the colors assigned to each syllable of the Om chant.
- materials needed for ceremonies
  wooden platter
  sweet smelling plant: sage, aromatic leaves, thyme or other aromatic herb
  ceremonial vests

dried eucalyptus, sage, pine needles, etc.
matches
pollen
record player and Indian dance records
wild food — It is best to use wild food which can be eaten raw. If cooking must be done, it should be prepared before the session begins. See second session of the Energy cycle for list of books to help you find edible wild plants

- materials needed for activity
  scrap paper
  scissors
  large brown grocery bag for each group of four
  crayons or craypas
  newspapers
  at least 4 irons and extension cords, if needed

Thus art does not move exclusively in the opposite direction of meditation — as it might have appeared to a superficial observer, who values art only as a finished product — but it moves in the direction of meditation as well, namely in the state of conception. Thus art, and meditation compensate and penetrate each other. . . .

Thus art means the ever renewed concentric attack and the breaking through of selfhood toward infinity, the complete extinction of limitation by endless and as such uninterrupted turns of radiations and inhalations, it means the condensation of the universe to a microcosmic focus, and ever again the establishment of a magic balance between soul and universe. The object of art is the condensation of all the inconceivable streams, forces and effects of the universe upon the plane of human understanding and experience; it is the projection of psychic emotion into the infinite. The self dissolved and transformed into the whole . . . the integration of the one into the other, the passionless acceptance of the world into the liberated, i.e., unlimited soul.

Here art and religious life meet in a sphere of consciousness where all distinctions between self and non-self have disappeared. . . . Art in its highest attainments becomes religion, namely, when it succeeds to re-establish "the magic balance between soul and universe." The most perfect symbol for this ideal, however, is the Mandala, *in which the "concentric attack and the breaking through of selfhood towards infinity" finds its visible expression.*   LAMA GOVINDA

4 lotus flower mandala

We used pollen in our spring equinox festival and we used flowers, which produce the pollen. We used flowers not only because they are beautiful but because flowers can teach us many things.

Before flowers were developed each plant could only reproduce an exact copy of itself. For instance, the spores of mushrooms, the spores of mosses and the spores on the bottom of fern fronds could only grow to be exactly like the parent plant.

For plants to really begin to change, it was necessary to develop seeds and this took a long, long time in the earth's history. The first primitive plants began in the ocean about a billion years ago. Only in the last 200 million years have the first seeds been developed. Through all those 800 million years only very slow changes could happen in plants. Most of these changes happened by a change in climate or an accident to the plant. It took hundreds of millions of years of primitive plants before the next big change happened.

The ferns developed. Ferns produce male and female cells on the plant. During rain storms the male cells can swim to the female cells and form a new plant. But the male and female cells are on the same part of the same plant so there's still not much chance of variety. But, after a time, the reproducing part of the plant developed the ability to make what they call naked seeds. They had no protective coat. The plants which produced these naked seeds were spruces, firs and ginkgo trees. After that first step, gradually, true seeds developed.

All of the grasses, fruit trees and crops are seed plants. Seed plants have a terrific advantage. They can adapt faster to changing conditions. It no longer takes millions of years to change. They have this advantage because the male chromosomes of the pollen fuse with the female chromosomes in the plant and this combines their genetic inheritance. The chromosomes are what carries the details of the new plant: the form of the leaves, the shape of the blossoms. When the male chromosomes of one plant combine with the female chromosomes of another plant then there are possibilities of change and development. The evolutionary development of all the kinds of life we know, including ourselves, depends on this mixing of chromosomes. And flowers started it all.

You see flowers are more important than we thought. Many primitive people realized their importance, especially the Aztec Indians. They thought of flowers as special give-aways from the sun and they believed that within the flower petals there were messages from the sun. I'll read you an Aztec poem about flowers.

Aztec Flower Chant

The flowers are dancing:
the deep perfume
moves to the beat of a drum

The full flowers
tremble, the
flowers grow heavy
with Spring
bathed in sunlight

The sun's heart
throbs in the cup
His flesh
is the darkness of flowers

The god has opened his flowers:
flowers born in his house
are alive in this soil. [26]

Many people use flowers for meditation. We will move to the ceremonial tepee area to do our flower meditation.

Meditation directions

Begin with the relaxing exercises given in Session 5 of the Energy cycle. Then, give the directions below. Pass out a flower to each person.

1. Look in the cup of the flower. Look deep into the cup and see how the cup draws you into it.
2. Sit very quietly and look steadily into the cup of the flower. (allow a minute)
3. Now take a deep breath — all the while looking deep into the flower.
4. Now breathe out — still looking into the flower.
5. Breathe in and out; in and out (recite this very slowly several times).
6. Notice how the flower's center glows with light as you breathe in and darkens as you breathe out.
7. Continue to breathe deeply in and out and watch the light, deep within the flower, grow brighter and brighter. "The sun's heart throbs in the cup of the flower."
8. The light grows brighter. Our hearts beat to the rhythm of the drum beat in the flower. Our center and the center of the flower are pulsing together with the sun. You and the flower are both children of the sun. Breathe in the sun's energy and breathe it out. You are filled with the sun's light; filled with the sun's energy.

9. (Then, very gently) Take one last deep breath and gently put the flower back into the water.

Many people in India and Tibet meditate on flowers just as you did. In fact, they call the top of the head (point to the crown of your head), the thousand-petalled lotus and they say that the thousand petalled lotus flower opens through breath energy and then the real "self" glows like a shining jewel. Remember, our chant, om mani padme hum means, "Jewel in the heart of the lotus." The jewel of our real "self."

Move back to the meeting area.

The American Indian had some similar ideas about the importance of flowers. Remember, the Indian legend we told about the flowering forked tree and how the children turned into the tree. We also danced around the forked tree at the Winter Solstice. Here on page 180 in *Seven Arrows* (paperback, p. 182), we have a shield concerning this same idea. Notice that the flower has two stems. The flower to the left is a sunflower. The flower to the right is also a sunflower. This reminds us that we need both sides of emotions in us — happiness and sorrow, excitement and quiet. We need both the dark and the light side of the mind, the yin and the yang. The circle of this shield is the medicine wheel. The flower in the middle of the shield shows us that all these things are one.

In each of our sessions together we have been unfolding the petals, one by one, of this flower in the center of the medicine wheel so that we may see and understand the teachings of the medicine wheel. This is something that we can begin, now, together, but it will take most of our life to finish unfolding all the petals of this teaching.

Everything we have talked about in these sessions and the many stories we have heard — all are parts of the teaching of the medicine wheel. Remember we must move along the medicine wheel and look at each of these things from the four great directions — wisdom of the north, innocence of the south, sees-far of the east, and looks-within of the west. If we look at something from only one of these directions we do not really see it. We must try to see it from all the different ways.

Now, let us work together and we will unfold some of the petals of this medicine wheel flower. We will make a lotus flower mandala which unfolds so that we can show some of the teachings of the medicine wheel. Within this mandala book you can put anything which has come to you from moving around the medicine wheel these months we've been together.

✦ NOTE: Background information on the lotus flower mandala.

Designing the four layers of the lotus flower mandala will be the activity for this session and the next three sessions. One layer is designed each week and the book is assembled during the final session, session 7. These four layers draw together the symbolism concerning the four cardinal directions, the four elements and the four seasons which we have been developing all along.

The topside of each layer is a mandala; the bottom side or back side of each layer may contain random designs in a mandala pattern. The center of each layer of the mandala is the "self" because the "self" is the center of each individual's world.

As the "self" moves through the medicine wheel of the four directions, the four seasons, and the four elements of the earth it grows in understanding and the energy from all of these flows through the center, the "self", and out again. "It is from understanding that power comes," Black Elk said. As understanding grows, the flow of energy grows and real power comes to the "self."

Each lotus mandala will convey multiple meanings to its creator. This finished mandala will operate at many different levels simultaneously as it is unfolded, because the method used to construct it allows any random turning of the lotus mandala's pages to come up with a different combination. These combinations are random but meaningful as each combination will throw more light on the "self" which has created it. By understanding more, that "self" becomes more centered, permitting more energy to flow through. This, in turn, generates more powerful relationships to all the world around the "self", which, ultimately contributes to even greater understanding of the "self". This process can generate a never-ending, spiral of continuous growth and simultaneous centering.

"The essence of the mandala [is] a process of continual renewal."[27]

When finished, the lotus mandala book becomes an object of meditation. Turning through the pages so as to make different patterns is a meditation on the changeableness, yet unity, of all which happens to that particular "self."

Basic directions for the complete lotus mandala book

See note at the end of this session for overall plan outlining the steps to be accomplished each session. It will require four sessions for the group to complete this entire procedure. The directions for the first steps are given in this session; those for the remainder of the steps are given in session 7. You will need to refer to both sets of directions to make the sample mandala for today's demonstration.

Demonstration of a completed lotus mandala

Display the sample lotus mandala to the group. First show it to them closed up in book form. Partially open the lotus book and you will see the flower form with parts of all petals showing. Demonstrate this. Then you can open it in various ways demonstrating that each time a different combination of colors is seen. This will give a limited idea of the possibilities of the lotus mandala. The lotus mandala, which will be designed by each member of the group, will be much more complex as there will be four sessions to work on it. When this is completed, there will be an infinite variation in designs on each of the 8 sides unified by the colored outer rim and the centers of each layer.

Directions for beginning the mandala today

1. Distribute four 8 x 8 in. squares to each person.
2. Fold each paper into quarters and trim off the edges to make the petal form.

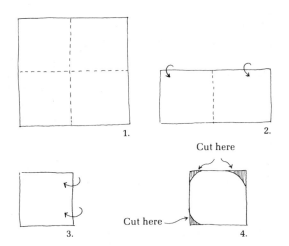

1.

2.

Cut here

Cut here

3.

4.

3. Unfold each of the four papers into a flat form. In all future directions this form is called the petal layer. Only one of these layers will be designed today.
4. Using a compass, make a 2 inch circle in the center of this petal layer on both the front and back of the paper. The center of the mandala will be designed next session.

5. Using a light pencil, make a half inch or one inch rim completely around the outer edge of the petal layer. This does not have to be exact. The size chosen, however, should be consistent on all future layers. Make this rim on both sides of the paper.

🔥 This layer will be north. What is the animal of the north (buffalo) and the color (white) and the season (winter)? So all these things will show on this north or winter layer.

- Because white is the color of north, the outer rim of this layer will be left white. You may make any kind of design to show winter on the rim but the background color must remain white. Blue is a good color for the designs as it is the color for ice.

- The symbols for winter are buffalo, snow, ice, snowflakes, snowballs, winter sports such as skiing, sledding, ice skating — whatever you like best.
- If you wish you may also include a drawing of any important thing which happened to you as you moved through the winter part of the earth's medicine wheel.
- If you want to include a buffalo drawing you may use *Seven Arrows* for ideas. The shield on page 181, (paperback, p. 182), has small buffalo pictures.

continued

continued

NOTE: After the rim has been finished, the group may make any kind of design they wish between the rim and the center: patterns of nature, Indian designs, yin/yang symbols, or even geometrical designs. Allow time to browse freely in all the available design books.

It is important to encourage the group to cover as much of their paper as they can with designs. As an example you may show everyone the mandalas between page 24 and 26 of *Mandala* by Argüelles. These are excellent examples of this process. Plate 9, the Tibetan Wheel of Life, presents a good example of how to use drawings of scenes from life. These three are the best examples to show at this time because many of the other mandalas in this book are too closely oriented to the four elements and someone may feel he or she should copy them.

If anyone has trouble designing the rim you may show them the shield on page 208, (paperback, p. 118), of *Seven Arrows*. For winter, though, they should use winter symbols and make up their own connecting design between the symbols.

When they have finished the front side of this layer, have them turn the paper over to design the back side.

Should anyone's inspiration fail for any particular layer during these four sessions, allow that person to freely and rhythmically draw a symbol of the element for that layer or the direction of that layer in time to music until a design forms itself. This should be done on a separate piece of paper — not on the mandala paper itself.

Introduction to the elements

Long ago people all over the world thought that everything in the world was made up of four main things which they called elements. These are the four things needed for us to live. What do you think they are? (discuss) Air to breathe, right. No, not food, because food is produced by other things. What do you need to grow food besides the sun, which is not part of the world? Earth or soil and water, right. So now we have three elements. What else is very important, especially in winter? Fire, right. So the four elements are earth, air, fire and water.

The back side of each of our petal layers will be one of the four elements and we will use the Tibetan colors for the elements.

In winter we can easily see our breath. Breathing is how we take in air so we will design the layer for air on the back side of winter because only in winter do we see our breath. The Tibetan color for air is green so the outer rim will either use green for the design or green as the background.

The Tibetans believe that deep breathing of air brings us movement, life and energy. The Toltec movement symbol, which we put on our vests, would be a good symbol for air because it shows movement and energy.

Symbols for air could be wind, clouds, and whirlwinds, a favorite Indian symbol. You could draw pictures of sports which use wind: kites, sailboats, balloons.

(Allow everybody to finish designing the air side of this layer according to the general directions given above for the winter or north side.)

Today we moved through the winter part of the earth's medicine wheel. We will have three more sessions to finish this lotus mandala. Put your completed layer carefully into your materials packet and I will collect them to keep until next session.

NOTE: Concerning the four elements.

The modern chemical elements associated with each of these ancient elements are as follows: earth (carbon), air (oxygen), fire (nitrogen), and water (hydrogen).

NOTE: Overall plan for lotus mandala book.

Session 4 · winter layer

topside

north, buffalo, white, winter (*Seven Arrows* symbols).

symbols for winter: buffalo, snow, ice, snowflakes, snowballs, winter sports.

underside

air — green.

symbols for air: Toltec movement symbol, wind, clouds, whirlwinds, sports which use wind: kites, sailboats, balloons.

(The centers of these two sides of the winter layer are not designed until session five.)

Session 5 · Spring layer

topside

east, eagle, yellow, spring (*Seven Arrows* symbols).
symbols for spring: eagle, flowers, pussy willows, birds, sports: marbles and baseball.

underside

fire — red.

symbols for fire: sun, energy, candles, campfires, lightning, jack o'lanterns, symbols for fires in Indian design.

(The centers of the two sides of the winter layer are done today as well as the centers for the spring layer. From now on the centers of the layers are done right along with the rest of the design.)

Session 6 · Summer layer

topside

south, mouse, green, summer (*Seven Arrows* symbols).
symbols for summer: mouse, foods from summer: strawberries, peaches, corn, watermelon etc., summer activities: camping, hiking.

underside

water — white.

symbols for water: designs of water drops, spirals or waves. Sports such as swimming, water skiing, fishing.

Session 7 · autumn layer

(The underside of this layer will be the title page.)

topside

west, bear, black, autumn (*Seven Arrows* symbols).
symbols for autumn: bear, colored leaves, nuts, apples, corn stalks, autumn moon, sports such as football.

underside

earth — brown.

symbols for earth: Indian symbols of snakes; rocks, mountains, places in nature; minerals extracted from the earth: gold, silver, jewels, coal or oil. Vegetables which grow in the earth: potatoes, carrots, peanuts.

ceremonial area	
one flower for each person — These flowers should be the type which has a deep cup such as a tulip. If possible, the flower should have a bright center at the bottom of the cup or lines radiating out from the center of the	cup. Daffodils are a possible second choice. These flowers should be kept in water until the meditation time and returned to the water afterwards
meeting area	
materials needed for activity: · each person needs: zip locking baggie. The name is written on a piece of masking tape attached to the baggie. All materials are kept in this baggie until the process is completed in Session 7 four 8 x 8 in. white paper squares. For best	results, use a good quality drawing paper. This will take the repeated foldings well. Drawing paper is also heavy enough so that felt pen markings do not show through to the other side. For a second choice, you could use a good quality bond typewriter paper *continued*

The key to this [Dakota Indian] metaphysic, as an organized system, is to be found in the number four, conceived as a principle of organization, and in some sense as a potency. The symbolism of this number is, or course, almost universal among the aborigines of America. . . .

There are four divisions of the terrestrial world. . . . Likewise there are four dividers of Time, the day and the night and the moon and the year. Of plants there are four parts, the root and stem and flower and fruit, and the kinds of animals are four, crawling and flying, and four-feet walking and two-feet walking. . . . Of celestial beings the four are sky and sun and moon and stars, and four are the winds "walking about the rim of the world." In the pattern of human life infancy, youth, maturity and old age form "the four hills" that mark its years. . . . Finally, all actions are to be performed in a fourfold manner, and in the ceremonies each subdivision of the sacred rites, from the pauses in a ceremonial march to the modes of suffering, is into the groups of four.   HARTLEY B. ALEXANDER

continued

- have available several books of designs:
  Mandala by Argüelles
  Seven Arrows by H. Storm
  see Session 3 of the Autumn Equinox cycle for other book titles. These books should be available for all the sessions through session 7
- sample lotus mandala. This is made by the leader before the session begins. Follow the "Directions for beginning the mandala" which are given in today's activity section. Complete all 5 steps. The 4 petal layers should be colored in a half inch wide rim all around the edge. One layer should be green, one white, one black and one yellow. After these rims are colored put the mandala together following the directions given in session 7. You do not have to worry about the order of the layers for this sample mandala

- watercolor felt pens. Do not use any other kind of felt pen or crayons as they show through
- pencils
- scissors
- Scotch magic transparent tape. The magic tape will take repeated foldings better

- optional: record player and record for use during these 4 sessions while the group is working on the lotus mandala. The record recommended is Sonic Seasonings by Walter Carlos (Columbia KG 31234). This is electronic music which recreates the sounds of each of the four seasons. An example of the technique used is that in the section on spring, bird sounds are suddenly stilled by rolling thunder followed by a spring rain. In a section on autumn, wind, sleet and very slow somber waves are heard

In India the lotus-flower (padme) is interpreted by the Tantrists as a womb. . . . It corresponds to the "Golden Flower" of Chinese alchemy, the rose of the Rosicrucians, and the mystic rose in Dante's Paradiso. *Rose and lotus are usually arranged in groups of four petals, indicating the squaring of the circle or the united opposites.*   C. G. JUNG

5 plant meditation walk

We've been talking about flowers and plants. As we know Indians talked to plants. If they were working in their corn field, they encouraged the corn to grow well and praised it for its strength. If they had to cut a wild plant for food or use it to make ropes or clothing, they first asked its permission before they cut it. Often they told it what they needed it for and thanked it.

For many years people thought that this was just superstition of the Indians. But recently scientists have discovered that the Indians were right after all. The scientists have found by means of research with special instruments that plants do have feelings. One of the men who learned this was Cleve Backster. He is a specialist on polygraphs, lie detector machines, which register the emotions of the person it is hooked up to by means of a pen which draws lines. When the line is fairly straight there is no emotion but when the line suddenly curves up then some kind of emotion is occuring.

One day, while Backster was working in his research lab he noticed that the house plant needed watering. So he watered it and while doing that he wondered if his polygraph would be able to register the water rising up from the roots to the leaves. He put an electrode on either side of a leaf and hooked it up to the polygraph. The water didn't register; but, after a minute, a sudden upswing contour appeared from the pen. He knew it was the same kind of mark which appears when a human being shows emotion. He thought that was interesting. So he decided to test for a pain reaction by putting a lighted match to a leaf. Just as he thought about that, the plant showed a prolonged upswing contour by the recording pen — a panic reaction. He hadn't even got the match out; he had just thought of it. He decided to do more research on this.

He found out that plants definitely do sense our emotions. They show fear when someone wants to harm them and they register emotions when some insect or animal near them is hurt.

It turns out that the Indians were right all along when they talked to their plants. Since plants can know our emotions, it is good that we show sympathy to them by doing the Om chant and extending our sympathy to the plant world.

Vibration and consciousness go together. Each kind of thing we feel in our head sends out certain vibrations. The plant can feel these vibrations and react. This is how our thought affects plants. But also this works the other way around. If we calm our minds of all violent thoughts we can learn to feel the vibrations which plants give off. Indians could do this. Plants help people to get calm and peaceful and tune out all the bad vibrations from bad emotions. That's why most Indians had sacred groves of trees where they went to meditate. The Plains Indians had cottonwood trees as their sacred trees; the mountain Utes had aspen trees; northwest Indians had cedar trees.

Today we will go for a meditation walk and see if we can tune ourselves into the vibrations from plants.

Meditation walk

We will do several things to help us turn our eyes off so that we can tune in with our other senses. Most people rely on their eyes to give them most of their information about the outer world and they neglect all the other senses. Indians learned to use all their senses.

FIRST, we will do a blind walk. Team up two by two. One of you close your eyes or tie a blindfold around them. The other person leads. All of us will be very silent so we can tune into the vibrations of the plants. The guide should try to take the other person near plants or trees which put off a strong smell. Also guide the person to damp places, very dry sunny places, and mossy places. If the guide notices a plant which he thinks is interesting, ask the plant if you may take one leaf and then hand it to the blindfolded person to crush in his fingers to smell.

Then reverse roles. The one who is blindfolded is now the guide and leads the other person in the same fashion.

The SECOND thing we will do is to listen to trees talk. Try to choose a place which has only one kind of tree or a single lone tree. Lie down under it with your eyes closed. Listen to the sound of the leaves talking to you. Then move to another type of tree to listen. If possible, try to hear both deciduous trees and evergreen trees. Some trees such as aspen, poplar, cottonwood, and birch trees talk a lot. Pine trees sigh and moan. Some trees clatter.

Now, we are ready to meditate.

Choose a sunny open place which is quiet and have everyone lie down. Try to choose a spot where everybody may look up at leaves which are backlit by the sun.

We have opened all our senses to the world around us. Now we will tune our minds to the vibrations around us coming from plants or the earth and find out what these vibrations can tell us. The Pueblo Indians have a little "power saying" which helps to tune them into nature.

"Up here is quiet. My feet are quiet. My hands are quiet. My eyes are also quiet. They see a bird flying quiet, a tree blowing quiet."[28]

Allow up to 10 minutes for this meditation. It is easy for everybody to enter into this as the leaves and light make fascinating patterns.

Walk quietly back to the meeting area. Pass out sunflower seeds on the way.

These sunflower seeds come from the sunflower. Why does it have that name? Do you know? (Beacuse it follows the sun.) All plants tend to move toward the sun but sunflowers do this even more. The sun is the source of the food energy for the plant and the source of our energy too.

Today we will design another layer of our lotus mandala book. (Pass out the materials packet and art supplies.)

This layer will be the fire layer. Last week we did the air layer. Using your compass, make a 2 inch circle in the center of the petal layer.

Now, we will design this center. This is your true "self" — which is so often hidden deep inside that no one can see it. It's like the center of a flower where the golden pollen is, and this center is often hidden deep inside the petals. But we saw it glow with light in our flower medita-

tion last session, didn't we? You really know what your true "self" is like but you don't often let others know. But, today, you can feel free to draw this true "self" on your lotus mandala because it will be protected by all the layers of the mandala book.

Meditation

We will meditate a moment before we design this important center.

Put the record which you have chosen on the record player. If you are using the

continued

continued

Sonic Seasonings record, play any part which would recall to the group the outside meditation they just did. Bird calls or calm, peaceful music. You may use any other record for this purpose if you prefer. Have everyone sit with eyes closed. Be sure the extra yellow and orange colored felt pens are handy.

- Close your eyes and think of how you felt when we were outside meditating under the tree. Remember the sound of the leaves and listen to them and let them speak to your mind now and calm it. (wait a moment)
- Feel the vibrations from the trees flowing through you.
- Remember how the sun shone on the leaves. "The sun's heart throbs in the cup of the flowers," the Aztec Indians say. The sun gives-away its golden, glowing light to the leaves, to the flowers, and to us. It's the same golden energy in each of us. Think of that golden glowing energy deep inside you — the real you.
- Breathe slowly in and out (wait a moment).
- Watch the golden light get brighter as you breathe in and darken as you breathe out, slowly. (Allow a long moment of quiet.)
- Now, open your eyes, and draw in the center circle of your petal layer just what you saw deep inside yourself just now. Just take up a color and draw with it and you will see a symbol of your real "self" in the center of the mandala layer.

When they have finished this, then they draw the half inch, or one inch, rim around the outside of the petal layer.

Fire layer

Today we will do the fire layer. Think about fire for a moment. Why do we need fire? Where does fire ultimately come from? (the sun) The symbols for fire are: light of the sun, energy, fire, candles, campfires, lightning, jack o'lanterns, symbols for fire in Indian design books. Design the outside rim using any fire symbols you wish. The Tibetan color for fire is red so the outside rim should either have red as a background or the design should be red.

For those having trouble getting started on their fire design, show them the Star Water shield on page 210 of *Seven Arrows* (paperback, p. 342) Or show them the following pages in *Mandala*: page 106 and plate 12 near page 120.

When they have finished the rim, then they may go ahead and fill in the rest of this layer.

Spring Layer

Turn your paper over. Last week we did the north or winter layer of our mandala book; today we move along the earth's medicine wheel to east or spring.

What is the animal of the east (eagle) and the color (yellow)? The outer rim of this layer will be yellow — either the background or the design.

The symbols for spring are: eagle, flowers, pussy willows, birds, sports such as marbles, baseball or whatever you like best. The east is where the Morning Star lives part of the year. The Indians believe that the Morning Star gives man understanding.

Center of the mandala

The center of each mandala shows your real "self". So for this center on the spring side of the layer, you may copy the center from the other side if you still feel just that way or you may do a variation of that design if you've changed just a bit. I have a poem which might give you some more ideas for how you want to design the center:

> I am
> the center
> I am
> the point
> from which each direction goes
> . . . a thousand suns surround me
> And I am the sun
> burning in the center
> I am
> my rays go out
> and penetrate the night
> I am
> a million jewels blazing
> in my solar sight
> . . . I am
> a silent witness
> to what in me
>> forever learns
>> forever burns
>> forever turns.[29]

Allow everyone to finish designing this center. When they have finished it have them take out the winter layer, which they did last week, and do the centers on both sides of this layer. They may copy the centers they already did or they may do variations on them.

We have just finished two layers of our lotus mandala book. I'd like to tell you some of the amazing things about the lotus plant.

A thousand years ago, long, long before there were any white men in this country so there were no cities, no roads and no big buildings, in a lake in Manchuria in northern China, there were sacred pink lotus flowers growing. Their seeds dropped into the water and sank to the bottom and were buried in the mud there. After many years the lake dried up but still the lotus seeds lay buried there. Through the years more dirt and dust blew in on top of them. During all these years the seeds lay there. As these years went by, in our country white men arrived, they began building cities and roads and moving west. Hundreds more years went by. Still the lotus seeds lay there under the mud.

Then hundreds of years later, some people were in that part of Manchuria studying the ancient civilization by digging into the soil for ruins of cities. They found the lotus seeds. They were stored in a museum for some years. Finally, someone noticed that the seeds had never rotted, and, since they knew that lotus seeds have a very hard protective cover, they thought that possibly the seeds were still alive. So they softened the hard coating by using sulphuric acid and planted the seeds. Then, in the spring of 1952 pink blossoms of the sacred lotus bloomed again in a pond in Washington, D.C. in our own country. Imagine, the seeds had lived for a thousand years! This amazing long life of the lotus seed is one of the things that makes them a special flower.

Lotus flowers were considered very important in ancient Egypt, and now in China, Tibet and India. In all these countries, the lotus is the symbol of spiritual growth. You see, the lotus grows up from the darkness of the mud in the pond bottom up to the surface of the water. The blossom opens only after it has raised itself above the water's surface. So the blossom opens in the pure air and sunlight, untouched by either water or mud. Yet it is rooted and nourished in the mud of the pond bottom. Because of this way of growing, people use it as a symbol for the unfolding of our true "self."

Our body and emotions are needed for our true "self" to become whole just as the lotus needs the mud of the pond bottom. But the "self" cannot be seen by others until it understands the body and emotions. Then, the true "self", which was formerly hidden, like the center of the lotus flower by layers of petals, can shine forth in its full beauty. This is what the Om chant refers to when it says: "the jewel in the heart of the lotus."

All of you remember when Black Elk was nine years old and first saw the four-rayed daybreak star herb. This herb had a four-rayed flower of understanding. And, later, when he was older, Black Elk said, "It is from understanding that power comes . . . for nothing can live well except in a manner that is suited to the way the sacred Power of the world lives and moves."[30]

The center of the mandala, which we have designed today, shows this "understanding self", which Black Elk tells us gives us power.

 We will move to the ceremonial area and do the Om chant.

 Do the chant several times.

Now, we will think of all the living beings which belong to each syllable. On the *ma* syllable, the plant syllable, remember to direct your thanks to the plants for giving-away their teachings to us today.

meeting area	
sunflower seeds strips of cloth for blindfolds materials needed for activity: • materials packets for lotus mandala book • compasses • books for designs: *Seven Arrows*, *Mandala*, etc.	• watercolor felt pens — be sure you have extra yellow and orange colored ones today • pencils • record player and *Sonic Seasonings* record
ceremonial tepee area	
chart of the colors assigned to each syllable of the Om chant	

So . . . we see in water a mediator and balancer between contrasts; it takes what is superfluous at one place and bears it over great distances to where it is needed. Water as the bearer of warmth acts as a great regulator of the gain and loss of heat of the planet. The visible expressions of this are the clouds and the weather with all its different elements of pressure, temperature, humidity, wind and so on.   THEODOR SCHWENK

6  water

Remember the Indian legend about Star Water? In this legend, water from the Universe — Star Water, which fell on the earth, was used as a symbol of the good energies which "the Powers" give-away to us. Some of the signs of this good energy were understanding, love, truth and joy. Why do you suppose the Indians used something so commonplace as water as a symbol for such important things? (discuss)

Yes, water is necessary for life. So, although it is common it is about the most valuable thing in the universe — far more valuable than jewels or gold because water is the element in the world which understands best the give-away.

We know that water is necessary for life but most of us never really give this much thought. Today we'll go into this a bit more. We know that plants need water to grow but have you ever thought about how much they need? To produce only 20 tons of fresh food crops, 2000 tons of water will have to go through the plants during the time of their growing.[31] This 2000 tons of water is equal to a bathtub filled 25,000 times and that's a lot of water. The water comes into the plant through its root system and is given off into the atmosphre by its leaves. It enters the atmosphere as water vapor. It stays in the atmosphere for a period of from a few hours to about 10 days and then it returns to the earth either as rain or snow to give us water again. It may come back down to earth close by where it left the plant or a thousand miles away depending on the weather system. So you can see that water does a lot of travelling. It makes this cycle from ground to atmosphere and back down as rain or snow about 34 times a year. To do all this it has to be always on the move — either hurrying down to the sea in rivers or falling on the earth as rain or moving through us or the plants, or filtering down through the ground.

The different surfaces of moving water are very sensitive to the forms around them. Maybe you have put a small bit of wood in a current in a large stream and watched how it moves. It dips down some places and swirls around in another place. All these movements are the current of water reacting to the slightest differences in the creek bottom or to any object in the stream. The different surfaces of moving water are extremely sensitive.

Remember, in our milk light show, we saw that when two different layers of liquid met the most activity occurred. As they met, they began to turn and form spirals. The edges of these different layers are where water is most sensitive — so sensitive that it's been proved to be susceptible to influences from the moon and other planets.

Primitive people knew that water was influenced by the moon and planets but modern scientists are just recently finding this out. American meteorologists found that there is more rain in our continent on the third to the fifth day after both the new and full moon. Australian researchers have duplicated these findings.

Of course, we all know that the moon affects the tides. For many years people have thought that the full moon affects people's behavior and now this has been proved. But it is now thought that one of the main ways in which the moon and planets and sunspots affect people is through their effect on the water in us. Most of our bodies is water because water makes up most of each individual cell.

One of the most interesting proofs of this effect on the liquid in our bodies came from the work of a man in Japan. He was a special researcher on albumin in blood. Sometimes this curdles into small fluffy lumps and sometimes not. He found, after studying this for many years, that the changes in this curdling of the albumin happened when sunspots pass across the central meridian of the sun. At this particular time the sun directs the most concentrated beam of particles toward the earth. So it is proved that sunspots on the far distant sun directly affects our blood. This is quite amazing isn't it?

From all this you can see that water is more sensitive to changes than we thought. This sensitivity to change helps to make water the great balancer on the earth.

Water helps make soil. It can seep into the tiniest crack in a rock. When it freezes the water expands and cracks the hardest rocks. Repeated freezing of cracks over long periods of time helps make soil. Water carries fine soil down to river bottoms and spreads this out in fertile bottom land. Most of the world's crops are grown on this give-away from rivers. This is how water brings about a state of balance everywhere. It erodes high cliffs, brings them down to fill up bottom lands for farms. It carries fish down to the sea to help populate the ocean and then carries the fish back up to lay their eggs in fresh water rivers.

Water brings nutrients to the plant's roots. It gives these nutrients to the plant and then goes on out the leaves of the plant hurrying back up to the sky where it soon returns to the earth to give-away more water as rain to whoever needs it — plants or animals or man.

Water is the element which knows most about the give-away. It gives of itself freely, always willing to change its form when needed by any plant or animal. Water comes to us from the sky or from plants such as the juice of fruits; it stays with us for a brief time, picks up the waste products from our food; and then moves on its journey.

Water tries to balance everything out. Water balances the needs of plants and animals and remakes the world to keep this balance.

The Toltec Indians had a legend about this relationship of water and the earth which I'll read to you now.

In the beginning

The Earth was a virgin,
    nothing grew from her.
    No trees
    Nor flowers,
    No mountains
    And no streams

She was only
    Endless matter,
    turning through
    endless space.

She was lonely
    and tired
    of waiting
    for something to create.

Then the Clouds
    found the Earth
    and the Earth
    felt the
    Clouds surround her
    and she felt the
    thrill of
    Life in her spirit.
    She was no longer
    alone.
    Now,
    She could create.

And the Clouds
> Found the Earth to be
> what the Clouds
> Had always wanted,
> A place to stop
> And
> A place to create.

Then the Clouds
> gathered together in
> Great excitement
> The Clouds
> grew dark
> With the weight of Creativeness
> With the weight of love.

And the Clouds
> rained down
> upon the Earth.

And she,
> The Earth,
> Reached up
> To touch the Clouds
> With mountains of stone
> From her breast.

And the
> Creative forces of the Clouds
> Washed the mountains
> And
> Formed the rivers.

Then, she,
> The Earth
> Released the seeds
> Of her flesh
> And
> Trees sprang forth
> with leaves.

And grass
> Leaped from her flesh
> To meet
> The fresh rain
> Bushes

And reeds,
> And flowers,
> Sprang into being,
> As a result of
> Her love for the rain,

The Clouds
> Feeling the force
> Of her love,
> Rolling thunder
> And
> Flashing with lightning
> Sacrified
> Part of his own spirit.
> And the spirit
> Of the rain-drops
> Entered into every bush,
> And reed,
> And flower,
> Into every tree
> And every living thing. . . .

And the Earth,
> now radiant
> with their creation
> Brought forth her own water.
> It came in the form of tears,
> Tears of love
> And
> Tears of joy.
> And
> Those tears
> Are called springs."[32]

It is this water, created by the Clouds and the Earth together, which is the element which helps to keep all on earth in balance. The Toltecs are the people who use that balance chant which we often say:

> "All things that must be
> must be in balance
> And — *that* takes practice.

Designing the water layer of the lotus mandala book

Use water colors so as to experience the flow of water.

Remove another petal layer from the packet. Last week, we did the element, fire; this week we will do the element, water. The Tibetan color for water is white so the background of the outer rim will be left white and the design can be any color you wish.

The symbols for water are: design of water drops, spirals or waves, sports such as swimming, water skiing, fishing etc.

An excellent idea for the water layer is to design the entire mandala as the ripples formed by a rock dropped into a pond. The center is the rock, "the self", which creates the ripples in the world around it. One ripple band

continued

continued

around the center could be water drops; another band, waves; another band, spirals; another band, the things which water gives-away to us.

For the center design

I have printed the Center poem, which I read to you last session, on a card so you can see all of it. Let's read it again. (discuss) What do you think those last three lines mean? Your understanding "self", here in the center learns forever because it keeps understanding more and more about all that is around it. Forever burns — the energy, which the sun gives-away to us, burns in us now and the more understanding the "self" gets, the more the sun's energy burns in us and the "self" can become so powerful that it goes on forever. The Tibetans believe that truly great selves leave the world for a time when the body wears out but they always come back again with a new body, as a baby, so that they continue to help the rest of the people in the world to understand more.

Forever turns — we move through all the dozens of things we do each day, we are forever turning as the earth turns through the day and as it turns round the sun through the year.

You may now design the center — your understanding "self." You may copy the design from our previous session or you may vary the design if something from the Center poem inspires you.

Designing the summer layer

Turn your paper over. Last week we designed the spring layer. Now we will move along the earth's medicine wheel to summer or south. What is the animal of south (mouse) and the color (green)?

The outer rim of this summer layer will be green — either the background or the design.

The symbols for summer are: mouse, foods which summer gives-away to us such as strawberries, peaches, corn, watermelon. Also you may draw any of the activities which you do in summer such as camping, hiking, lying in the sun.

If you wish, you may include a drawing of any important event which happened to you last summer or an event which you are looking forward to doing this coming summer.

The directions for designing this center should be similar to the directions given for designing the center on the water side of the layer.

Water helps to keep the earth in balance; but we, humans, take even more of a part in balancing the earth. We must keep in balance the energy from the four directions and the four elements. We are in the center, keeping the balance of all things on earth. That's what the Toltec movement symbol, on our ceremonial vest, means. Let's chant the balance song.

> "All things that must be
> must be in balance
> And — *that* takes practice."

meeting area only this session

materials needed for activity:
materials packet for lotus mandala book
compasses
books for designs
watercolor felt pens

pencils
several Milton Bradley water color boxes and fine brushes
record player and *Sonic Seasonings* record

That terrible arrogance of the white man, making himself something more than God, more than nature saying, "I will let this animal live, because it makes money"; saying, "This animal must go, it brings no income, the space it occupies can be used in a better way."

LAME DEER

7  animals

In our Om chant we sometimes think of colors for each of the syllables. Each of these colors stands for a living being in the world. We've been doing several sessions on our relationship to plants — the green color in the chant. Today we will think about our relationship to animals — the blue color in the Om chant.

What animals do you like? Why don't you like others?

Discuss: Ask the group if anyone fears a particular animal. Ask if he or she has ever been bitten by that animal? Discuss this aspect, too.

Do you think animals can know when we are afraid of them? Dogs will growl and bark furiously at one person and not even bark at all at another person. Why? Remember, we talked about how everything gives off certain vibrations which other creatures can pick up. Fear certainly affects the vibrations of our mind and body. A dog can feel that. Some people think fear makes a change in our odor, too. Generally, a dog will growl at someone who is afraid of him.

Some people seem to attract animals by their good vibrations. Dogs follow them and cats like them.

Many of you mention fear of snakes. Snakes also can detect man's emotions. Snakes never bite someone who is not afraid of them or not hurting them. The Indians say, "Snake does not bite man, snake bites what man is thinking."

One of the Hopi Indian ceremonies has a Snake dance ceremony in it. The purpose of this ceremony is to bring rain for the final growth of the crops in August. Before the ceremony, the Snake Society people hunt out on the desert for the rattlesnakes. When they find one, they bless it with cornmeal, wave the feathers of a buzzard over the snake to calm it and pick the snake up and put it in a sack. The snakes never bite these Snake Society people because they are not afraid of them; also, they talk to the snakes before they pick them up.

They bring all the snakes back to the kiva. Here the men sit in a circle and let all the rattlesnakes loose to wander freely, to get used to the people. The men sing continuously during this time to calm the fears of the snakes. Often, most of the snakes will curl up and go to sleep on those men who are the most calm and gentle.

On the day of the ceremony, the snakes are all put into a shade house made of green cottonwood boughs. The dancers enter the plaza. As they go by the kiva, each one stomps powerfully on the sounding board which is placed over the top of the entrance to the underground kiva. This makes a deep powerful rumble. It awakens the vibration centers deep within the earth to resound all through the earth to call up "the Powers" from the earth. The power enters the men. First, the Snake chief stops in front of the snake house and gently picks a snake up in his teeth, just behind the head. He holds the snake's body close to his chest with his left hand. They dance together around the plaza. Each of the other men dances with a snake. Then these snakes are let loose upon the ground and each man picks up another snake until all the snakes have been danced with.

In this ceremony, the snake is both a symbol of mother earth and of rain. In many Indian tribes the snake means rain. When a snake wriggles along the ground, it has a rhythm like lightning. It also moves like the wind and the rivers flowing to the sea. This is why it is a symbol for rain. So snakes are very sacred creatures to the Indians.

In the Hopi snake dance the snakes are used not only to unite mother earth and the rain so that rain comes for the crops but also to release the power that recharges all the psychic centers of the Indians' own body. In this way the snake is a symbol which renews the life of both man and the earth.

Indians refer to snakes as the snake people just as they sometimes call deer, the deer people and rabbits, the rabbit people. All the living creatures are considered as just different kinds of people and just as worthy of respect as human people.

There's a Yaqui Indian legend from Mexico about the snake people.

THE SNAKE PEOPLE

"Long ago there lived a Yaqui by the name of Habiel Mo'el. He was an orphan, but he had many relatives all over the Yaqui country. This man did not enjoy hunting as most young Yaqui men did. Instead, he liked to travel from house to house and from pueblo to pueblo, attending fiestas and eating and chatting with his friends and relatives.

The only weapon he ever carried was a big, thick club. He lived at the foot of the hill, Mete'etomakame. One day he started out for Hekatakari where there was to be a little fiesta. When he came to Maata'ale, the monte became too thick for passage, and he turned around and went to Jori. From Jori he cut across toward Betaconsica, where an arroyo empties into the Rio Yaqui. Travel

there was very difficult, for the undergrowth was extremely dense. He crawled on his belly under branches, crawled over them, or pushed past them.

When he came upon a sort of clearing, a big snake appeared, crawling across his path. Habiel Mo'el hit the snake right in its middle, but it vanished into the underbrush before he could strike it again. So he continued on his path toward the rancheria at Hekatakari.

Suddenly, what had been nothing but thick monte stretching before him became a large Yaqui pueblo with many people in it, moving about their business. Habiel Mo'el felt very strange. As he walked between the houses, a cabo from the guardia came up to him, and greeted him.

He told Habiel that his chief would like to see him at

the guardia. So the two went over there . . . the officials were sitting about. To one side a young girl was sitting. About her waist was a bandage of leaves.

The head Kobanao spoke to Habiel, 'We have brought you here to ask you why you beat a girl this afternoon as you were traveling along between Jori and Bataconsica.'

Habiel was very surprised. He replied that from Jori to this place he had met no one on his journey. 'I did not beat any girl,' he said.

'You struck a girl this afternoon, and you are liable to punishment. Why did you do this?' insisted the kobanaom.

Habiel could not remember having done so; and he repeated this. Then he explained where he had come from and his route, saying that he had seen no girl on the path. He respectfully asked their pardon, but insisted that he had done nothing at all.

The head kobanao turned to the girl, who was seated to one side, and asked her if this were the man who had beaten her.

'Yes', she answered. 'And he is still carrying the stick with which he beat me and almost killed me. That is the man.'

Habiel said that he had never seen the girl before and that he remembered nothing of it. He again asked their pardon, but disclaimed guilt. The kobanaom considered the matter among themselves.

Then the head kobanaom said, 'We will pardon you this once, since it is your first offense. But after this, when you are traveling, never harm anyone at all who may cross your path offering you no danger. You may go this time.'

Habiel thanked them and left. As he went out, he found himself in the middle of the monte with no sign of a village.

He traveled on toward his destination. It was dark when he arrived at Hekatakari and the house of his relative. He greeted the little old man whose name was Wete'opoi.

They sat down to a meal and Habiel told Wete'opoi about his strange experience concerning the appearance and disappearance of the large Yaqui pueblo, and of his accusation.

The old man listened and then said, 'You have done a great wrong. All animals, as well as people, have their authorities and their laws. You hurt a snake which crossed your path, doing you no harm. The authorities of that group took action against you. You must never again do that thing. The chiefs of the snakes met when the girl complained. They turned into people to punish you. I will give you some advice. Never hurt any snake, coyote, or any kind of animal, which is just crossing your path and offering no harm. If a snake lies coiled in the path, kill it. You are defending yourself then. But always kill it completely, never let it get away or it will complain and its chiefs will punish you.'[33]

 Discuss the ideas in the legend and sum them up.

If one really tries to understand animals, snakes, and birds as the Indians do, we see that they have just as much right to live as we do. They have their place in the world and we have ours. We should treat them with respect because they are brothers and sisters.

*Awareness of the earth, consciousness of its proximity, of its inescapable influence —
even when not obvious — presents aesthetic and psychological possibilities largely
overlooked or forgotten. Each individual, in canyons and beyond, is deeply affected by his
physical surroundings. If it can reach him, knowledge of the earth as reality, rock as
material of the universe, landscape as momentary expression of natural process, is a rich
and vital source of sanity and calm for modern man.*   DAVID LEVESON

Pass out the materials.

 Today we design the last layer of our lotus mandala books. On the back of petal 4 of this layer we will make our title page. Put a check mark with your pencil on this petal so you will be reminded to put your title in this space. The title may be *Lotus Mandala* or you may make up your own title if you feel like it.

Today we design the last of the four elements: earth. The Tibetan color for earth is yellow but we will use brown, instead, because most of our earth in this country is brown.

Either the border design itself or the background should be brown. The symbols for earth are the Indian symbol for the earth, the snake, rocks, mountains. In fact, any drawing of any place on earth which appeals to you could be used. Things which we get from the earth directly are: gold, silver, jewels, coal or oil for heat.

The center design may be copied from the previous layers or you may do a variation today.

If you have the record, *Sonic Seasonings*, play the autumn side today as background.

Designing the autumn layer

Turn your layer over. Today, we move along the earth's medicine wheel to autumn. The direction is west. The color of west is black and the animal is the bear.

You may use black felt pen on the white background for the rim.

The symbols for autumn are bear, colored leaves, nuts, apples, seeds of all kinds, corn stalks, autumn moon, sports of fall such as football.

If someone needs inspiration, the shield opposite page 208, (paperback, p. 118), in *Seven Arrows* has a good idea for a border design for autumn.

The center design is now put in the white empty circle.

Assembling the lotus mandala book

1. Number the petals of all the layers with a very light pencil. Follow the diagram given below.

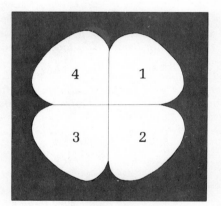

continued

The word, *vehicle* is a technical yogic term for body.
*The essential idea is that by producing a particular kind of vibration through a vehicle
it is possible to draw down a particular kind of force through the vehicle or to produce a
particular state of consciousness in the vehicle. Such vibrations can be produced by
means of Mantras each of which represents a particular combination of sounds for
bringing about certain specific results.*   I. K. TAIMNI

2. Using a very light mark, put a dot in the center of each layer where the two folds cross.

3. Then, draw a line from this center dot to the outer edge between petal 4 and petal 1. You don't have to draw this line through the center design as you can't erase it, here.

4. Cut along the line drawn in step 3 above. Cut only to the center dot. Cut all 4 petal layers in this same manner.

5. Place the autumn layer, which will be the outside layer or cover of the finished mandala book, flat on the table. Make sure that the earth side is down on the table; the autumn side up.

6. Place the winter layer directly on top of this layer, lining it up so that it is even with the petals of the first layer. The winter side faces up; the air side down.

7. Place the cut edge of petal 4 of the winter layer and the cut edge of petal 1 of the autumn layer evenly alongside one another. Using mending tape, tape the cut edge of petal 4 of the winter layer to the cut edge of petal 1 of the autumn layer.

8. Next place the summer layer on top of the pile, lining up all evenly so that the petals are in the same position. Tape petal 4 of the summer layer to petal 1 of the winter layer.

9. Next place the spring layer on top of the pile. Tape petal 4 of the spring layer to petal 1 of the summer layer.

10. Then, beginning with petal 1 of the spring layer, fold it down over petal 2 of the spring layer. Then, continuing to fold, fold on over to the right onto petal 3 of the spring layer and on up to petal 4 of the spring layer. Then continue to fold all these petals over to the left onto petal 1 of summer and down to petal 2 of summer, then over to petal 3 of summer etc. Continue around until all are folded into the single petal form. This constitutes the completed form of the lotus mandala book.

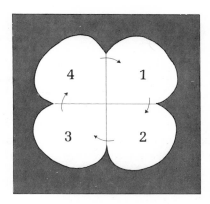

11. Erase all pencil lines.

🔥 The lotus mandala book is you and the earth and the medicine wheel turning through the year. We will now put our names on the book. Here are three ideas of how to do this. You can use any of these ideas or follow your own idea.

1. Write along the edge of the center, your true "self", on the petal which forms the cover.

2. It's fun to write your name in a spiral form intermixed with the patterns on the petal which forms the cover.

3. You may write your name on the layer of the direction in which you are now.

To live in harmony with Nature is the necessary condition for survival. This is surely the teaching of Shinto. . . . Nature is not an inanimate force which mankind is entitled to exploit to the utmost of human power. Nature is a goddess whose laws we must obey if we are to win this goddess' benevolence. If we break her laws, we shall arouse her anger and shall incur the punishment that is the inescapable penalty for committing this grievous offense against her. Awe, not greed, is the emotion that ought to govern our attitude toward Nature.
ARNOLD TOYNBEE

As they turn through the assembled mandala book point out that the earth supports all life on it just as the earth layer of our mandala supports and encloses our lotus mandala.

Move to the ceremonial tepee area.

An interesting thing about animals is that they can pick up vibrations from the earth before an earthquake happens. The burrowing animals move out of their holes days before an earthquake. The scientific instruments can register the earth tremors when they happen during the earthquake but they don't pick up the vibrations days before as animals do. This tells us more about the vibrations which are present but which we do not feel.

Today, let's do the Om chant with special concentration on the syllable, *pad* which is the blue syllable for animals. We will concentrate on sending out strong sympathy vibrations to animals because now we know a little more about how they can pick up our vibrations.

(Do the Om chant together.)

We will keep your finished lotus mandalas here to use in a special ceremony next session. Also when you come to the next session bring with you any leftover yarn, string, small bits of rope, or cord which you have at home.

About snake symbolism

The frequently irrational fear of snakes is sometimes explained as a real fear of the unconscious element in the human psyche. The snake, according to Jung, symbolizes the unconscious. The snake is also an earth symbol and, at the same time, a spiritual symbol. The presence of a snake in the older myths is an indication of a "hero myth" as the snake is a frequent counterpart of the hero.

The function of the snake symbol, combining the earthly and spiritual, is best expressed in the Quetzalcoatl myth. Quetzalcoatl, the deity of the Toltecs and Aztecs, combines the quetzal bird, symbol of heaven and spirit, and the serpent, coatl, symbol of earth and matter. Quetzalcoatl reconciled the opposites: conscious and unconscious, matter and spirit and established a religion that lasted for centuries.

meeting area	
materials needed for activity: materials packet for lotus mandala book compasses books for design watercolor felt pens	pencils Scotch magic transparent tape record player and *Sonic Seasonings* record Center poem
ceremonial tepee area	
chart of the colors assigned to each syllable of the Om chant	

8  entanglements

Explanation of the entanglement

The entanglement is created by the movements of everybody in the group throughout the meeting area as they move about to take part in the various activities. Each person carries a ball of yarn and unwinds it to leave a trail of yarn behind. Initially, the end of the yarn is tied to the frame and each time the ball is carried back to the frame the yarn is tied to it again. Each time one piece of yarn crosses another a knot is tied to join them. If a person steps outside the frame, the yarn is tied to the frame and the ball is left behind. It is picked up again on re-entering the frame and the unwinding and knotting process continues.

The main idea of the entanglement is that each person leaves a visible line of yarn behind as he or she moves about to various places within the frame.

Laying out the work areas

Measure the largest available free space which you have on the walls of your meeting area. Mark off on the floor an area no bigger than this space. Enclose this space with a rough frame made of 1x2s. Reinforce the corners with extra wood, if necessary, so that the entire frame can be lifted onto the wall later. This area will be labelled *area C*. For this area you will also need a box of balls of different colored yarn.

Area A will contain the mandala books from last session and should be located immediately to one side of *area C*.

Area B will contain paper and felt pens for making drawings of movement symbols. Scissors will be needed to cut them out. This area should be located on the other side of *area C*.

Procedure after the group arrives

Divide the group into two sections: A and B. After all the directions for the entanglement have been given, group A will go to *area A* to look at the mandala books. Group B will go to *area B* to make movement symbols which will be attached to the entanglement. The Toltec movement symbols, see session 8, show how each person's energy interacts with all the directions of the world. These symbols will be attached to the completed entanglement wall hanging.

As the individuals in the two groups move through the intervening *area C* they create the entanglement by unwinding the yarn behind them while they are within *area C*.

Beginning the session

◆ Today, our entire group will make an entanglement which will show the pattern of our interaction with others. Everybody should be consciously aware as they move about the room that the work they do on the entanglement is affected by what has been done by others working before they got there, and that, after they leave, their entanglements will influence what the next people do.

◆ Explain the directions given above and give each person a different colored ball of yarn so they can begin. After each of the 2 groups has had time to work in each of the 3 areas, gather everyone together in another part of the room so that the entanglement is not disturbed.

◆ In the last few sessions we've been talking about our relationship to the earth, to the plants and animals on it, and to the air and all the vibrations coming to us through the air. This science of relationships is called ecology.

Today, I'm going to tell you a story about the wanderings and relationships of a single atom which we will call X.

"X had marked time in the limestone ledge since the Paleozoic seas covered the land. Time, to an atom locked in a rock, does not pass.

The break came when a bur-oak root nosed down a crack and began prying and sucking. In the flash of a century the rock decayed, and X was pulled out and up into the world of living things. He helped build a flower, which became an acorn, which fattened a deer, which fed an Indian, all in a single year.

From his berth in the Indian's bones, X joined again in chase and flight, feast and famine, hope and fear. He felt these things as changes in the little chemical pushes and pulls that tug timelessly at every atom. When the Indian took his leave of the prairie, X moldered briefly underground, only to embark on a second trip through the bloodstream of the land.

This time it was a rootlet of bluestem that sucked him up and lodged him in a leaf that rode the green billows of the prairie June, sharing the common task of hoarding sunlight. To this leaf also fell an uncommon task: flicking shadows across a plover's eggs. The ecstatic plover, hovering overhead, poured praises on something perfect: perhaps the eggs, perhaps the shadows, or perhaps the haze of pink phlox that lay on the prairie.

When the departing plovers set wing for the Argentine, all the bluestems waved farewell with tall new tassels. When the first geese came out of the north and all the bluestems glowed wine-red, a forehanded deermouse cut the leaf in which X lay, and buried it in an underground nest, as if to hide a bit of Indian summer from the thieving frosts. But a fox detained the mouse, molds and fungi took the nest apart, and X lay in the soil again, foot-loose and fancy-free.

Next he entered a tuft of side-oats grama, a buffalo, a buffalo chip, and again the soil. Next a spiderwort, a rabbit, and an owl. Thence a tuft of sporobolus. ·

All routines come to an end. This one ended with a prairie fire, which reduced the prairie plants to smoke, gas, and ashes. Phosphorus and potash atoms stayed in the ash, but the nitrogen atoms were gone with the wind. A spectator might, at this point, have predicted an early end of the biotic drama, for with fires exhausting the nitrogen, the soil might well have lost its plants and blown away.

But the prairie had two strings to its bow. Fires thinned its grasses, but they thickened its stand of leguminous herbs: prairie clover, bush clover, wild bean, *vetch, lead-plant, trefoil and Baptisia, each carrying its own bacteria housed in nodules on its rootlets. Each nodule pumped nitrogen out of the air into the plant, and then ultimately into the soil. Thus the prairie savings bank took in more nitrogen from its legumes than it paid out to its fires. That the prairie is rich is known to the humblest deermouse; why the prairie is rich is a question seldom asked in all the still lapse of ages.*

Between each of his excursions through the biota, X lay in the soil and was carried by the rains, inch by inch, downhill. Living plants retarded the wash by impounding atoms; dead plants by locking them to their decayed tissues. Animals ate the plants and carried them briefly uphill or downhill, depending on whether they died or defecated higher or lower than they fed. . . ."[34]

Then, one year, while X was part of a tree by the river, a beaver ate the tree and he became part of the beaver. When the beaver died, a spring flood carried his body down to the sea. So X lay imprisoned in the sea and couldn't make any more trips through the creatures of the prairie.

This was the story of long ago, during the Indian's time, before the white men came. But, later, when the white man came things were different, unfortunately. Here is an example of what happened then. A farmer arrived in the New World from Sweden and cut up the rich prairie sod with his plow. Up until then the prairie had many different kinds of plants and animals as we noticed in the story. All of these were important to the land because they gave-away freely to one another and kept the prairie land fertile and healthy. But now the farmer wasn't interested in keeping all of these different plants and animals alive; he only wanted to grow wheat to sell at the market.

When he saw all the hundreds of passenger pigeons around he just shot them because they weren't of any use to him. So soon after they were all killed off, insects and bugs started coming on his land, eating his crop of wheat. And soon after that his land started washing away down the creeks. This was due to the fact that the land was always bare when the spring rains came because he had killed off all the plants, which he called weeds, and the wheat wasn't up, yet, in early spring.

Soon this once rich land couldn't grow enough wheat to make money easily. The farmer moved on and was followed by a man who brought cows for a dairy. He tried to stop erosion by planting alfalfa but he kept plowing up the prairie to plant corn and oats to feed his cattle and the corn used up the fertility of the really deep layers because it has long roots. The good top soil continued to wash away.

Erosion experts built dams to try to check the erosion but the dams just made the rivers raise their beds as they were filled with eroded soil.

Because of all this white man's farming and other activities, an atom, which was released from a different rock by a root, made his whole journey from rock to river in one single century while it had taken atom X hundreds and hundreds of years. While this new atom was in the lake behind the dam he did get to make a couple of quick journeys by giving himself away to water plants, fish and ducks. But pretty soon the engineers built a sewer too, and the poor atom was washed away into the sewer and there he lay imprisoned in the gooey mud and could no longer give-away to anything.

The interrelationships of land are so many and so complex that we cannot begin to understand all of it. If we can't understand something it would be stupid to kill it. Some people say about a weed: "What good is it? Let's get rid of it." Does that make sense? We know the land is a give-away to us and every part of it plays a role in this give-away. The rich, black soil of this country was built up by fungi, insects and animals. All gave-away to one another. All of these creatures were giving-away to one another for ten thousand years to build up the soil of the prairies and we have destroyed it in less than a hundred years because we do not understand the give-away.

Each kind of living thing which interacts gives-away to others. Take a look at the floor — at the yarn, which we have laid down as we moved about the room since we first came into it. The pattern on the floor shows our interaction. Complicated isn't it? We

[The methods of modern theoretical physics classify the world] *not into different groups of objects but into different groups of connections. . . . The world thus appears as a complicated tissue of events, in which connections of different kinds alternate or overlap or combine and thereby determine the texture of the whole.* WERNER HEISENBERG

could call it an entanglement. Did you ever think of the fact that in some ways we draw lines in space whenever we move? We really do because, as we've learned, our vibrations affect things around us and we, in turn, are affected by other's vibrations. By looking at the maze of lines we've drawn just since we came into this room, we get an idea of how complicated an entanglement our relationship is.

Someone pull a bit on one of the lines of yarn. See how it affects all of them. Even lines of yarn on the far side of the room moved a bit. This is really true of how things interact all the time even though we can't always see it this clearly. Remember, that although reality is a complicated interwoven system of various vibrations, man's five senses are tuned into only very small bits of it at one time. We learned that when we talked about energy and vibrations. There's a lot more entanglements going on than we know about. So that's why we have to be careful when we think about changing nature.

Let's think about various ways in which nature's harmony might be changed and the result of that change. Supposing we think of a forest with trees and a stream and animals and birds. What would happen if someone thought the forest needed more water and diverted a bigger stream through it? (discuss) What if someone thought the floor of the forest should be covered with more plants and went in and planted a close growing ground cover? What would happen if someone thought it needed more rabbits and turned loose a truckload of rabbits.

✦ Discuss as many aspects of this as the group can think of. Let them stretch their imaginations and use fantasy if they wish. The main point is that everyone sees that too much of anything — even if good in itself — can be destructive of the whole environment.

🔥 If man were not on earth, nature would harmonize all creatures for the good of the whole. All the creatures on earth know the give-away except man. But man does live on the earth and so the Indians believed it was man's duty to put himself in harmony with the earth.

✦ With help from the group, lift the entanglement from the floor and hang it on the wall by the outside supports. Let everybody look it over and talk about how everything is connected with everything else in it.

🔥 We will make a wall hanging of this entanglement by doing the following things:
· weaving new pieces into it from the material you brought.
· making loops of different colored yarn and putting them together in long chains such as colored paper Christmas chains.
· unravelling rope ends.
· attaching movement symbols.

✦ When finished with the above steps, the lotus mandala books are attached to the wall hanging by paper clips. Everybody attaches the books in the direction on the medicine wheel where they feel they are now. When all of these have been hung on the entanglement, proceed below.

🔥 I want to read you something from Black Elk's book. Remember, when Black Elk had his vision and was up in the tepee in the sky, two men came from the east and between them was the day-break star (the morning star).

"They gave him the herb and said, 'With this on earth you shall undertake anything and do it.' It was the day-break star herb, the herb of understanding, and they told me to drop it on the earth. I saw it falling far, and when it struck the earth it rooted and grew and flowered, four blossoms on one stem ... and the rays from these streamed upward to the heavens."[35]

Your lotus mandala books have four blossoms like Black Elk's day-break star plant, the herb of understanding. Because of your lotus mandala, you understand more and this spreads light through your world.

Dance of the Four Directions

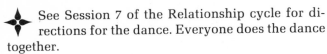 We will do our dance of the four directions to put all in balance so that we can be in harmony with nature.

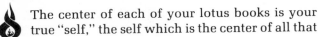 See Session 7 of the Relationship cycle for directions for the dance. Everyone does the dance together.

The center of each of your lotus books is your true "self," the self which is the center of all that moves around it. The entanglement gives you an idea of all the different things which move around your "self". But your "self" cannot be hurt by anything outside it. It is really in harmony with everything unless we muddy this "self" up by any of the things which we just mentioned in our dance. But now we have stamped on all those things and our true "self" is glowing pure and bright within. The movement symbols on the entanglement remind us that this true "self" is the center which takes in energy from "the Powers" and moves it out to all the four directions.

The Om of our chant stands for this pure bright "self" glowing within each of us, which can send out vibrations of light and joy and sympathy to all the earth. All these things of the earth are represented to us here today by the entanglement.

Om chant

While doing the Om chant face the entanglement. Link arms or hold hands while chanting.

If possible, leave the entanglement up on the wall for the next few days so that the group has more time to work on it. It becomes more impressive, the more work done on it. Everybody should take their lotus mandala books home with them today.

NOTE: Ask the group to bring vegetables to put in a soup which we will have next session. Each person should also bring a bowl and a spoon.

We need to become vividly aware of our ecology, of our interdependence and virtual identity with all other forms of life which the divisive and emboxing methods of our current way of thought prevent us from experiencing. The so-called physical world and the so-called human body are a single process, differentiated only as the heart from the lungs or the head from the feet. In stodgy academic circles I refer to this kind of understanding as "ecological awareness." Elsewhere it would be called "cosmic consciousness" or "mystical experience."

ALAN WATTS

meeting area only

- yarn — if possible provide a different color for each person so that his or her movements through the entanglement may be seen in the finished work
- old rope
- any kind of fibers, synthetic or natural, which can be worked into the entanglement
- yarn, string, cord etc. which the group brings from home

- paper and felt pens
- scissors
- pieces of 1 x 2 wood to make a rough frame for supporting the entanglement
- hammer, nails and other tools necessary to make the frame
- the lotus mandala books from last session

You know, we open ourselves like the air, and the world flows through us like the wind. . . . We have no boundaries — we are all we experience, know, feel — all of which interacts with everything, making us of the entire earth. . . .

As our bodies do not grow and unfold from choice and decision, neither do our minds. Disharmonious and destructive acts arise automatically from disharmonious conditions. Through the old ways, we are in harmony with all circumstances — the correct and harmonious course of action is always to be found in us if we are in touch with ourselves.

GAYLE HIGH PINE

1 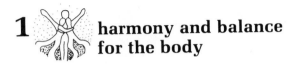 harmony and balance for the body

◆ NOTE: Cook the bones, which you have secured from the butcher, for 2 hours or more before the session begins so that all the meat and marrow are loosened. The entire pot, including the bones, meat and liquid, is brought to the session.

The pot is simmering when everyone arrives and each person puts his vegetables into it. The soup continues to simmer during the first part of the session.

In our last session we talked about how nature keeps everything in balance in a forest. We went on to talk about how too much of anything just might be destructive of the whole forest. For this reason we should be careful about changing any one thing when we don't really know what it does to the forest or the whole system. That seems to make sense when we think of nature but how about our body which is another kind of whole system? Do we really know what is going on inside of us? What do you think? (discuss) What are some of the most important processes going on inside of us, which are necessary for our life? (heart circulating the blood, lungs circulating oxygen, food digesting, brain processes). Supposing you had to consciously think each time you wanted your heart to beat. What would happen? (discuss)

Supposing you had to tell your brain to move all the muscles necessary for each step you took. Let's try it. Now, instead of just walking across the room try to listen to my directions and then make your brain give all that information step by step to your body. It's a very interesting experiment.

You are going to begin walking. You have to tell your brain that you are going to lean forward slightly and shift your balance forward. The brain has to send this message down to the muscles involved. But if you don't do the next thing quickly enough you will fall forward on your face so you send a panic message to the brain: "I've got to lift one foot slightly off the floor." The brain sends this message back down to the muscles which lift the foot. Then you've got to tell the brain that your leg has to relax and swing forward. The brain, in turn, sends this message down to the muscles. But when this foot reaches the floor you can't keep that leg relaxed or it will crumple under you. You've got to send another panic message to the brain to be sure that it stiffens up the leg again so that it will take your weight. The brain does this.

You've taken one step now. But, now, you've got to bring your rear foot up — not even with the front foot but on past it. To do this you've got to swing your weight forward on the front foot. Send the message to your brain and it will relay it down to the muscles. Then, the rear leg has got to be relaxed so that you can lift it slightly and swing it on past the other foot. You tell the brain that. There are more orders involved in this than before but you're tired of doing all that thinking by now and you hope the brain can figure it out for you. In the middle of all this you remember you've got to tell the brain to stop the muscles from swinging the foot at some definite point or it will go clear on up and you might topple over backward. So you send another emergency message to the brain to tell the muscles to set the foot down. And then you send another message: "Don't forget to tell the muscles to stiffen the leg as it comes down or we will all fall over."

Pretty exhausting isn't it? Have you had time to think of anything else these few minutes? No. Supposing you had to be telling the brain how to keep you breathing during this time and also how to keep the blood moving. You'd be in trouble, wouldn't you, because you can't consciously think of all that at once? The walking process is only one of the processes going on inside us all the time. The walking process is a brain/muscle interaction. In addition to that, we have the blood circulation system, the lung system and the digestion system to name a few systems. Then we have pains to deal with and our emotions. We also have outside energies hitting us all the time which our body automatically adjusts to — visible light, x-rays, radio waves, infrared radiation, air pressure, gravity's pull, etc. It's all very complicated. If you had to consciously tell your body what to do about all that you'd fly apart in a minute, wouldn't you? The point is that all the time our brain coordinates more things going on inside and outside the body than you could possibly even understand if you studied for years and years. So we have to learn to trust our bodies — to pay attention to the whole body and not just try to impose our will on it by telling it what to do. After all our thinking, rational mind is only a tiny part of the whole brain. Forcing the body to produce only one thing for our limited purposes can ruin it just as people have ruined the prairie soil by producing too much wheat.

We don't often think of how complicated our body is until we've imposed our will on it in some way and it breaks down. Maybe you've strained a muscle while playing ball? What really happened? You've played ball hundreds of times without this happening. If you will really look closely at what was going on in your head, you'll find that you strained a muscle because you tried to use your body in a way that was not in harmony with the whole body. Perhaps, you were tired before you began but friends wanted you to play. You tried to please them rather than listen to your tired body. Or, maybe you were trying to impress a friend with how well you could do and you forced your body to do something it wasn't ready to do.

Let's take skiing. Any of you who ski know about someone who broke a leg because they insisted on taking one more run when they were really too cold or too tired. Can any of you think of any times when someone was hurt because they didn't listen to their body? (discuss)

For a long time people thought that they could just push their bodies around exactly as they pushed nature around and get away with it; but lately, with new scientific studies it is becoming obvious that many illnesses are the result of such behavior.

One of the most obvious examples of illness caused by getting our bodies out of balance with nature is the jet plane syndrome. It seemed like a good thing to be able to fly to Europe so quickly but then more and more people began realizing it was impossible to do anything for at least 24 hours after they arrived. They became sick easier. Airline stewardesses suffered definite physical breakdowns from the constant time changes. The rhythm of night and day is one of the most basic rhythms in all plants and animals. This rhythm is upset by the rapid time change of jet travel to Europe. Recently, many business firms have taken this into account and they do not allow their executives who will be making crucial decisions to attend any meetings within 24 hours, or sometimes 2 days, after they arrive.

The body has a natural rhythm. Some of you can get up early in the morning, easily. How many of you can do that? And some of you have a terrible time getting out of bed, not only on school days, but even when something good is happening. There's a basic reason for this difference in people. Body temperature reaches a high point in the evening and a low point in the morning in some people. But, in others their body temperature reaches a high point in the morning and so they are full of energy then. The people whose temperature doesn't reach the high point until the afternoon find it difficult to get up and don't work well until the afternoon.

This daily temperature change in the body has been known about for a long time but, recently, it's been discovered that practically everything in the body has a natural rhythm of more activity at a certain time of the day and less at another. Even our emotions and moods have a natural up and down rhythm. All of this is terribly complicated isn't it? If we try to control it we are in trouble. The only thing we can do is to learn to help all parts of the body stay in balance.

What causes you to get sick? (germs) Is this really true? Why aren't you sick all the time? The germs of most common illnesses are present in the air and on our skin all the time. What do you think happens to cause us to be sick only some of the time?

Something in you causes a difference in your relationship with the germs which are around you all the time. Most of the time we live in balance with the germs but then something happens. We get very tired or our emotions cause us to be depressed. The balance is changed and the germs affect us; we are sick.

Some people get panicky and want to kill all the germs so no one can get sick. This same type of people wants to spray insecticides on plants to get rid of all the bugs which eat our crops. That was done for a time and what happened? (discuss) One thing, we killed the bees which pollinate plants. Now, fruit orchard owners have to import bees each spring to pollinate the fruit. We even killed off butterflies and many birds which formerly ate the bad insects. People didn't know all that would happen just from spraying bugs which ate the plants. But remember, we can never change just one thing can we?

What would happen if we really did try to kill off all the germs in the air? We would not be able to bake bread because yeast floats in the air. We couldn't make cheese because a kind of germ makes cheese. We couldn't even digest our food because bacteria living in our intestines does that for us and they would be killed. We have to learn to live in harmony with germs, too. They are living beings just like us who give-away some good things to us but can cause us trouble if we get out of harmony with them.

The Indians had people they called "medicine men" who cured the sick people by helping them get back into harmony with nature. The medicine man heals because he knows that all things on earth have their own vibration rate. If some physical injury or emotional trouble has disturbed this natural rhythm of the person then the medicine man helps the person get back into harmony with nature and himself.

The mandala is used in Tibet to heal people. The word *heal* and the word, *whole* are related. The mandala helps to make you whole by putting all the parts of you together so it helps to heal, too.

One of the most famous healing ceremonies of the Navajo Indians is called the Beautyway. It's quite a long ceremony lasting several days in which people fast, and chant and at the end the medicine man does a sandpainting, sort of like a mandala. The sick person sits in the middle of this painting while the chant is sung. When the person is healed the sandpainting is destroyed because it's power has been used up. The chant is very long but I will read just a small part to you:

"Happily I recover . . .
Happily may I walk.
Happily, with abundant dark clouds, may I walk.
Happily, with abundant showers, may I walk.
Happily, with abundant plants, may I walk.
Happily may I walk.
Being as it used to be long ago, may I walk.
May it be beautiful before me,
May it be beautiful behind me,
May it be beautiful above men
May it be beautiful around me.
In beauty it is finished."

Discuss the nature things in this chant in relation to their lotus mandala books and healing

 The person is again walking with nature so everything is beautiful and that person is healed and whole.

Many Indians believed that dancing helps your trouble — whatever it is. This is a chant from the Pueblo Indians:

"When trouble comes to me
I have to go and dance.
I dance until the dust receives my trouble.
The dust takes my trouble to the mountain.
The mountain grows with the dust of trouble.
The place for my trouble to be."[36]

Dance

 Today we will do our Dance of the Four Directions. See session 7 of cycle II. Who wants to tell me what words to write on the papers which go in the middle for the dance, so we can stamp on them?

 Discuss the emotions or troubles each person wants written down for the dance.

Go to the ceremonial area for the dance. After the dance, return to the meeting area.

 An important item in healing ceremonies of Indians were bone rattles.

Among many primitive people who hunted animals for their food, bones were considered the eternal part of both animals and people. They never broke the bones of an animal they were eating but carefully gathered them up and either buried them or put them out on a platform for the vultures to pick clean. They thought that if the bones were whole then the animal could come back to life again. Medicine men used bone rattles for special ceremonies. We will make some today to use for our Summer Solstice Festival.

Directions for bone rattles

1. Remove the bones from the soup and place in several bowls. Rinse the bones in cold water and dry them.
2. Each person uses 3 bones.
3. Thread the twine or yarn through the bones and tie them to the stick.
4. Decorate the bones with felt pens.

Serve and eat the soup.

 Return to the ceremonial area to do the Dance of the Directions again with the bone rattles.

The bone rattles should be kept at the meeting area for use in the Summer Solstice celebration. They may, of course, be used any time during the intervening sessions.

meeting area

- bones — At a butcher shop ask for the type of bones which will be hollow after they are boiled. They should be small bones such as lamb bones. There should be at least 3 for each person. See note in the actual session for preparing them
- paper towels
- one stick for each person
- masking tape to secure the string to the stick
- scissors
- colored twine or yarn
- felt pens

ceremonial tepee area

- paper and pencil

The "waterfall effect" was known to Aristotle. It is a dramatic example of illusionary movement caused by adaptation of the image / retina system. *It remains a problem as to whether the adaptation takes place in the retina or in the brain . . . We do not know precisely why the image-retina system is upset by continued stimulation by movement, because we do not know exactly how it works. We have already seen . . . that movement is represented in separate neural channels, and that different channels indicate different directions of movement. It is reasonable to assume that these channels can become adapted, or fatigued, with prolonged stimulation (as happens with almost all other neural channels) and that this unbalances the system, giving illusory movement in the opposite direction. . . .*

A curious fact about the waterfall effect is that it occurs hardly at all if the moving field covers the entire retina and moves as a whole. It is relative *movement in different parts of the retina which produces the effect. . . . This fact — that stimulation of the whole retina gives very small or no after-effect — is fortunate, for it is largely because of this that car drivers seldom experience the effect, even when stopping suddenly after a lengthy run.*

R. L. GREGORY

2 the waterfall effect on vision

This session is held at a waterfall. No other experience produces such a powerful visual illusion as the "waterfall effect." Because of this it is very important that the group visit a waterfall even if this necessitates an overnight trip due to distance. It is possible to experience this visual illusion from certain water fountain sculptures but much more difficult. If it is impossible to visit a waterfall, rent the film, "Introduction to Visual Illusions." This color film rents for $15 from Pyramid Films, Box 1048, Santa Monica, Ca. 90406. In no way does it produce the powerful effects which the waterfall illusion does but it does give a clear idea of how the eye can be fooled. If you cannot afford the film get the book, "Eye and Brain" by R. L. Gregory (McGraw-Hill Book Co.) There are some interesting visual illusions in it.

Last session, we discovered a bit more about what happens if we try to impose our will on our body instead of keeping both in balance. Today we are going to try an experiment which shows us more about balancing all the information from all the parts of our bodies including our eyes. To do this, we are going to carefully watch a waterfall. Waterfalls were considered "good medicine" by many Indian tribes. Sometimes Indians would meet at a waterfall to make peace after a period of warfare. They felt that the "good medicine" of the waterfall would help them. Today, we will experience some of this power of the waterfall.

I would like you to join me in a little experiment. . . . How many of you will agree that you see me? I see a number of hands — so I guess insanity loves company. Of course, you don't "really" see me. What you "see" is a bunch of pieces of information about me, which you synthesize into a picture image of me. You make that image. It's that simple. . . . In my everyday thinking, I see you, even though I know intellectually that I don't. Since about 1943 when I saw the [Adelbert Ames] experiment, I have worked to practice living in the world of truth instead of the world of epistemological fantasy; but I don't think I've succeeded. Insanity, after all, takes psycho-therapy to change it, or some very great new experience. Just one experience which ends in the laboratory is insufficient.

GREGORY BATESON

At the waterfall

◆ Allow time for everyone to have a good look at the water, then announce that you are going to try the experiment. If there is any steep drop or cliff be sure everyone is holding on to something before proceeding as this experiment produces dizziness in some people.

🔥 You must carefully follow my directions to make it work. We'll begin now. First, find one of the surges of water at the top of the waterfall. With your eyes follow it down to the bottom, without looking away. When you get to the bottom, immediately, move your eyes back up to the top and follow another water surge to the bottom. Continue doing this until I give the next order. (Allow about 2 or 3 minutes to go by.) Now, look to the left at the rock (or trees or grass — whatever is there).

◆ Let them discuss what happened to them. Most will experience it immediately. The land area adjoining the waterfall will flow uphill. If any person failed to experience it ask another person to help him with it.

If there is a rainbow in the water call attention to it as it will be discussed later in the vision cycle. Have the group move around to find out that seeing the rainbow depends on where they are in relation to it.

🔥 What part of our body do we use to learn most of what we know? (the eye) What kinds of things do we learn about through our eyes? (discuss) Do you really think that we can see exactly what is going on around us? What did we learn from the waterfall? Were the rocks moving or not? But they were moving to us. What does that tell us about our ability to really see the world as it is out there?

The whole thing of seeing is fascinating. Since the Indians were hunters they were especially aware of the problem of seeing. We take it for granted but the Indians knew it wasn't that easy. They knew that the five senses — eye, ear, smell, touch, taste can mislead if they weren't careful, just as we noticed that our eyes told us the rocks were moving but they weren't. "The Powers" give-away to us a sixth sense — intuition or wisdom to help us keep the five senses in order so that no single one of these senses can get complete control of us and cause us to leave the balance and harmony of "The Beauty Way." The Indians used meditation and prayer to develop this sixth sense so they could gain control of their five senses. We all have this sixth sense but we don't learn about it without meditation. When a young Indian boy wanted to study under a medicine man or shaman he went to the older man and said, "I come to you because I want to see." This is where we get the word, *Seer* for a wise man. It, literally, means "one who sees." The young Indian boy would spend many years learning the knowledge of the medicine man before he felt he was really beginning to see.

As we know, seeing involves much more than the eye. Vibrations of different kinds striking the eye begin the process. Signals carried from the eye to the brain are changed by various things which happen in our nervous system. These changed signals are then combined with information from the other sense organs and with the information already stored in our memory. All of this, together, makes up what we see. As each person has different things stored in his memory each person can see the same thing differently. This doesn't mean that one person is correct and the others are all wrong. It just means each person sees the same things differently, sometimes. Indians say that each of us sees from his own position on the medicine wheel. Unless we realize that, and use our special sixth sense of wisdom or intuition, the gift from "the Powers", we find ourselves arguing or fighting with other people. Sometimes, we become disgusted with others because they can't see things our way. We have to move on the medicine wheel to see. If we stay the same place, we see only from that one direction and we can never really see the whole thing.

We will be learning more about seeing in the sessions coming up.

We have begun to understand that our consciousness is not single but dual, that we exist both in linear time and outside of this particular construction. . . . Man is, or rather can be trained to be, sensitive to quite subtle sources of information, sources often overlooked in our personal world. These sources exist within ourselves (the part of the nervous system which we have considered "involuntary"). They exist on earth as subtle geophysical forces, such as negative ionization of the air, the rhythmic shifts in the earth, and the constant, invisible force of gravity. These energies can be sensed in other people in a form of communication termed "paranormal."

Yet all these phenomena have often been relegated to the realm of "paranormal" simply because our conception of what is normal and possible with man has been radically too low.

ROBERT ORNSTEIN

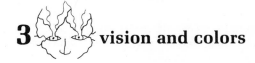

3 vision and colors

Film

 Show *American Time Capsule*. This film consists of a series of scenes, each of which lasts only a second. The entire film is only 3 minutes long.

What did you see in the film?

Let everybody talk about it at length. If a particular scene is mentioned which only one person saw, show the film again. Tell everyone to watch for that scene. More will see it the second time but not everyone. Let them discuss how much more they saw this time. Again, it might be true that one person sees a scene no one else saw. Prove that it was there by showing the film a third time. Then discuss what is going on.

Remember, we said last session that our eyes aren't the only thing involved in seeing. Our eyes receive the vibrations from "out there" but this is combined with information stored in our memory to form the picture we see. Now, this film shows us more about how this happens. Some of you didn't see particular scenes because you didn't happen to be that interested in that particular thing. For instance, the horse wasn't seen by some of you because, since you weren't so interested in horses, you weren't able to see it as it went by so fast. But others of you, who really love horses, saw that scene because horses are important in your memory and this information allows your eyes to register and transmit that thought to your brain so that you can hold onto it long enough to recognize it.

NOTE: In one particular group where the film was shown, only one girl saw the horse on the platform the first time. The film was reshown often. It wasn't until the sixth showing that all saw this particular scene. Other scenes varied in how many saw them but none so much as this one.

The fact that some of you saw one scene and not others shows us, again, that what we see depends on our position on the medicine wheel. If we had not shown the film over and over there would be a fierce argument by now with one group claiming the rest were crazy because they didn't see the same thing. But, because we showed it often enough, most of you eventually saw most of the scenes. But, often in our life we don't get a second chance to repeat an experience so each of us comes away from the experience convinced we really saw the whole thing whereas we really saw just the part we were conditioned to see by our interests or dislikes or by our

position on the medicine wheel. Now you may begin to understand why the Indians put so much emphasis on seeing in all its forms.

There's another thing which might help us to understand that we can't trust our eyes alone. Which direction does the sun rise every morning? (east) And which direction does it go down? (west) O.K. we all agreed. But stop and think a minute. Does the sun rise up over the edge of a world which stands still or does the world turn so that we can begin to see the edge of the sun as our world turns, and as it continues to turn, we see the entire sun? It's an illusion, isn't it, that the sun appears to rise and move across the sky and then sink in the west? We *know* that better, now, than at any other time in human history because the astronauts have been away from the earth. They saw the earth turning and then, the sun's light shining on different parts of the earth.

Another illusion concerning our seeing isn't quite so easy to prove but it's just as definite a fact. We all think that the colors we see out there are real colors. The tree is green; the car is blue. But really this isn't exactly so "out there"; it really happens "in here" in one's head. The colors we see are the result of certain kinds of energies striking our eyes and being interpreted by the brain.

The sun puts out energy. We experience this energy as many different wave lengths. Some of these are as long as 100 meters (as long as the tallest tree) and some as small as 1 trillionth of a meter. We can only see a very tiny section of all these wave lengths — the part called "visible light." In this small area, between 4 and 7 — ten millionths of a meter in wave length, we

can see the colors — red, orange, yellow, green, blue and violet and all the combinations of these.

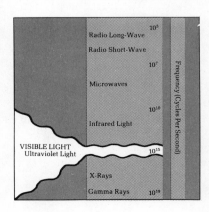

These colors are not necessarily "out there." It's just that the light waves which appear red to us have a lower frequency rate than the light waves which appear blue to us.

To give you some idea of how many other wave lengths of light there are which we don't see at all, let's talk about infrared rays. These have a lower energy than the red color waves. If we could see these infrared waves we would be able to see 10,000 more colors than the six main ones we see now. We are really blind to most of the colors. The only way our bodies show us that the infrared waves are there, is that we can feel them as heat from the sun or from a fire of some sort.

Another type of light wave which we can't see is called radio and TV waves. These have an even lower frequency. We can't sense them at all with our bodies but we make use of them.

Higher frequency waves than the visible light are called ultraviolet. These are the ones we know about because they give us sunburn. X-rays are of a still higher frequency but we can't see them or even feel them. We do use them to take pictures of bones. These ultraviolet waves might seem to us an amazing color if we could see them.

It's still difficult to believe that the colors we see out there are really in our heads, but we can do an experiment to help us understand that.

Each of you take two white cards and one black and one green crayon. Now, on one card draw a traditional picture of a Christmas tree — no decorations, just the tree. Color it green. Fill it all in solid. Now, put that card under a book or on the floor and take the second white card. Put a small black dot in the middle of the card. Tell me, do you see any other color on this card besides black? Now, we are ready for the experiment.

Hold both cards in front of you side by side. Look at the Christmas tree for 30 seconds as I count. *Now*, look at the black dot. What do you see? (a pink after image of the tree) Look again, there's no color on the card now is there? So, was the color "out there" or "in here" in your head?

If we were totally aware, we could see and feel many things which are invisible to most people. Some great Indian medicine men and some white people like Edgar Cayce *can* see more than most people. I'm going to tell you a story to help you understand how this can be possible. You have to use your imagination as I tell the story.

Imagine you are a tiny creature only one cell big and you have only two dimensions: you are only ¼ in. long and ¼ in. wide but you have no height or depth. You live on the surface of a pond. Because you are only long and wide you can only see just at the surface of the pond. You can't see above it or below it. There are other creatures like you and you play with some of them. You see them as they approach you or move away. It's a very simple, clear world.

But one day a dog comes along and walks into the pond to get a drink. He walks in just a short way. The water comes up to his ankles. All of a sudden you see four little circles which are far apart in your world. That's all you see, because you can't see up to where the dog's legs go on up. Then the dog's master throws a stick for him and the dog goes in deeper, and suddenly, like magic you see a great big long oval. The four little circles just disappear. Then, the dog sticks his head down to get the stick and you see another slightly smaller circle suddenly appear. Then the dog walks out and the big circles vanish and, suddenly, here are the same four small circles. The whole thing is a complete mystery to you. You don't see any connection between these different sets of circles. They just come and go according to magic. But the man on

But I can't go out and try to see this way. I'll fail, I'll go mad. All I can do is try to gag the commentator, to hush the noise of useless interior babble that keeps me from seeing just as surely as a newspaper dangled before my eyes. The effort is really a discipline requiring a lifetime of dedicated struggle; it marks the literature of saints and monks of every order east and west. . . . The world's spiritual geniuses seem to discover universally that the mind's muddy river, this ceaseless flow of trivia and trash, cannot be dammed, and that trying to dam it is a waste of effort that might lead to madness. Instead you must allow the muddy river to flow unheeded in the dim channels of consciousness; you raise your sights; you look along it mildly, acknowledging its presence without interest and gazing beyond it into the realm of the real where subjects and objects act and rest purely, without utterance.

ANNIE DILLARD

the bank sees the whole thing. He sees the dog enter the water, drink, go after a stick and come out. It's all the same dog. He sees this because he can see more than you. The man has another dimension.

What do you think about this story? (discuss)
If we can learn to see or feel in more ways, many things could make sense to us such as telepathy, clairvoyance, healing at a distance. All of these might not be mysterious at all if we could really see how they are interconnected.

The medicine men of the Indians knew a great deal about this because they had learned to see more by meditation and other techniques and especially by their vision quest. The medicine wheel teaching is part of this search to see more.

Next session we will tell an Indian legend about learning to see more.

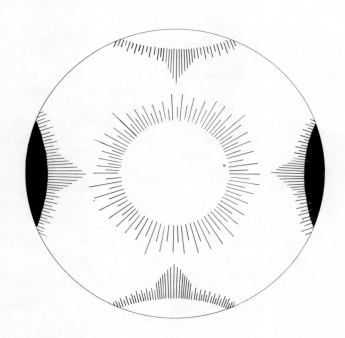

meeting area

film: *American Time Capsule*. This film may be rented from Mass Media Associates Inc., 2116 North Charles St., Baltimore, Md. 21218. The rental cost is around $10.00	projector 2 white cards for each person green crayon for each person black crayon or felt pen for each person

vision

According to his vision, he made up his medicine bag, which he opened only when he was alone. His medicine bundle and pipe were his own portable church, very like the ark. The objects in a man's medicine bundle — stones and pebbles, an oddly shaped root, the claws or bones of an animal — as well as his peace pipe, were not mere inanimate things. They had a life of their own and they had great power.   RICHARD ERDOES

4 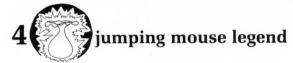 jumping mouse legend

◆ Begin the session by showing the shield on the cover of *Seven Arrows*.

◖ You've all seen this shield before as you've looked through the book. Today, we will hear the Indian legend for this shield as told by the Indian Peace Chief.

◆ Read "Jumping Mouse." It begins on page 68 and ends on page 85. The legend is printed in italic type. Decide ahead of time how much of the additional material interspersed between the sections of the legend would interest your group. Include those parts as you read the legend.

When the legend is finished, allow discussion to continue as long as they wish. Bring out how limited it is to see only one reality — our own. Show the cover shield again.

◖ Remember when Jumping Mouse looked in the river and saw his reflection. This cover shield shows all the signs of the mirroring. All of us mirror the world in different ways. We have already learned how we mirror one another and how nature can mirror our emotions. All of these ways are the many reflections of the world and are symbolized in this shield.

We are coming nearer to the time when we will go on our Vision Quest just as the young Indian does. Before we do that we must make our *medicine bags* to put a special plant, which we might find, that is *good medicine* for us. If you find any rock or curious piece of wood or other object which feels like an object of power, save it to put into the *medicine bag*.

Today we will design the bag and begin making it. We will finish the work next session. In designing your bag, think about all the things which you have learned about which have special power for you and work these into your design. This could be symbols for yin/yang or spirals. It could be clouds or lightning or trees or other things from nature. Your own animal for the direction of the medicine wheel is another symbol to use. I will pass out paper for you to work with during your preliminary designing.

Directions for medicine bag

1. Use the 8 in. cardboard circle for a pattern to mark around so as to make a suede circle. Then cut it out.
2. Using the leather punch, punch holes around the circumference of the circle about 1 inch from the outer edge. The holes should be about an inch apart.
3. At this point, have each person stop to design the medicine bag. Call attention to the fact that the holes may be worked into the design for greater effect. Encourage them to try several different designs on their paper before working out the finished design.
4. When the finished design has been chosen by each person, this is transferred to the suede. Felt pens may be used or the special coloring dye pens. Test the effects of the pens on both sides of a scrap of suede. Some suede has a nap which makes it difficult to draw on.

Jumping Mouse gave-away both his eyes but in the end he got much more back, didn't he? The Tibetans have a "power saying" about this type of give-away: "Giver, gift and receiver — all these are one." This means that we are all one in the universe. As we know, energy goes from one kind of being to another. It flows on. Atoms move from one thing to another — from rock, to plant, to us. So by now everything on earth has atoms which were once in every other type of being. We really can't say who is the "giver" or which thing is the "gift" or which one gets the gift, because in a few seconds the one who gets the gift of an atom of oxygen from the *giver*, the plant, will in turn give this *gift* to another being. So the first one who was the receiver may now be the *giver*. The gift, the oxygen atom, by now, may have combined with a hydrogen atom and become a water molecule. He, in turn, becomes the giver because water gives-away its life to everything else to keep it alive. Now, you can begin to *see* how dumb it is for people to fight with one another or for countries to fight wars when we are all each of us both the giver, the gift and the one who receives the gift, all the time in the "give-away." Sometimes we give and sometimes we get energy but the energy is there all the time if we just learn to really see that it is. During these sessions of the Vision Cycle we are beginning our vision quest by learning more about what seeing really is.

 Move to the ceremonial tepee area.

Remember, when we made the lotus mandala books, the center of the book was a design showing our true "self." This true "self," deep within us, knows all about the give-away just like Jumping Mouse did.

The *Om* in our chant stands for this true "self" which can give-away to all the beings in the world and send out vibrations of light and joy to all the earth.

Let's do the Om chant and think of the animals, plants and other beings which each syllable stands for. As you think of the being which belongs to that syllable give-away your loving energy toward that kind of being.

meeting area	
Seven Arrows book materials for activity: • one precut cardboard circle 8 inches in diameter • suede leather — enough to provide 8 inch circles for each person. The medicine bag is a very important ritual item so we use leather for once	• leather punch • leather thong for each person about 12 inches long • felt pens • coloring dye pens for use on leather. See session I of the Energy Cycle
ceremonial tepee area	
chart of the colors assigned to each syllable of the Om chant	

Among all the conditions which an animal must survive — temperature, food, humidity — light seems to be the most important synchronizer of animal activity. GAY GAER LUCE

5  light

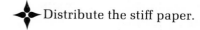Distribute the stiff paper.

Everyone make a tube out of this paper. Tape it together to hold it. Now, close one eye and put the tube to the other eye. Look very closely at something. You can look at the lines on your hand or the grain of the wood in a chair or table, or a plant leaf.

Allow 5 minutes or more for this activity and then let everyone discuss their discoveries.

By using the tube, you find out that you see from a different perspective don't you? You found out new things about objects which you see — everyday objects which you thought you knew all about. You can begin to understand still more about the Jumping Mouse legend. You begin to understand still more about *seeing*.

We've been talking about seeing but we haven't mentioned much about light. Without light we wouldn't see. Where does light come from? (the sun) We've been noticing all along how important the sun is to the Indians. When an Indian child was very young, his grandfather would take him out just before sunrise when the glow of the rising sun could be seen behind the mountains. The old man would tell the child that the mountain was the house of the sun so he must learn the shape of the mountain just as well as he knew his mother's face. The sun rises from a different place behind the mountain each day. The old man would point out where the sun rose at the winter solstice and how it would move day by day along the edge of the mountain toward its summer house. When the sun reached a certain spot on the mountain, maybe behind a large standing rock, was the time to plant squash. When it reached another prominent point, a break in a line of cliffs, it was time to plant corn, and when it reached the summer house it was time for the big festival. In this way the child learned the rhythm of the sun coming and going through the year and how he, himself, must learn to live in harmony with the sun by regulating his actions with it.

Recently, it has been proved that Stonehenge, the great ring of huge stones in England, was a giant computer for telling where the sun appeared at solstices and when there were eclipses of the moon. Chaco Canyon in New Mexico has just been proved to be another giant computer for the same purposes. It was designed by our own southwest Indians hundreds of years ago.

These facts have amazed many scientists who find it difficult to believe that these so-called primitive people could do such complicated mathematics, astronomy and engineering to produce such places. But these great monuments do show how important the sun and moon were to these people.

Often, in the cities now, we can't even see where the sun rises because the way is blocked by buildings so we might not think that the sun is as important to us as it is to Indians. But the sun influences us just as much as it ever did, the difference is we don't know it while the Indians did. But, recently, scientific studies have shown us just how important the sun is to the daily rhythms of our body. Sunlight times us to the rhythm of our planet. You know sunflowers are named that because they turn their flowers toward the sun as it travels across the sky. We are just as much influenced by the sun as these sunflowers but in different ways. The sunlight times our sleeping and waking. Light affects our pituitary gland, the master gland in our body which controls many basic systems of our body. The different amounts of light and darkness throughout the year influence our hormonal systems and keep them in tune with the seasons of the earth. Light affects our moods.

One scientist, who has studied the pineal gland which is affected directly by light, believes that light is as potent as any drug and that, eventually, we will use different wavelengths of light and different timing of light to help people in certain diseases.

One of the most interesting things produced by sunlight is the rainbow. (If your group saw a rainbow at the waterfall refer to that.) Just what is a rainbow? Is it a thing, an object? Can you ever get to the pot of gold at the end of the rainbow? (discuss)

First, let's think about the colors themselves. The sun's light is spread out by the water drops in the air. The colors are the white light of the sun spread out according to the energies of the photons of light. The ones with less energy we see as red; the ones with more energy we see as blue. As we learned the other day the colors are not "out there" but they are in our head. But is the rainbow "out there" at all, then?

The best way to think of it is that the rainbow is a relationship, not a thing at all. It's a relationship between three things — what do you think they are? (The human eye, the raindrops and the sunlight at a certain angle.) If these three things are not in the correct relationship, there is no rainbow. Lots of times all three of these things are there — our eye, the rain and the sun but there's no rainbow. The rainbow only happens when these three things are in the right relationship.

This is interesting because we've been learning a lot about relationship — our relationship with plants, with the earth, with "the Powers." In the rainbow you can get a glimpse of some other things. Love doesn't exist except in a relationship between two or more people. Hate doesn't exist except in a relationship of two or more people. There has to be two or more people in a certain relationship for that to happen. We make love happen or hate happen by our relationship just as we make a rainbow happen by our relationship to the raindrops and sunlight.

Rainbows are symbols for various relationships which are very important to Indians. For one thing Indians felt the rainbow combines the power of the sun, the air and the water to make things grow for our life. Many Indians see rainbows in their visions. It is a sign for "the Powers." It is also a sign of the union of all people which will some day happen. The different colors stand for the different races of people.

One white man, Vinson Brown, had such a unity dream when he was a child. At the end of his dream: "Slowly a bow formed in the sky, a rainbow of people marching to glory, a rainbow of unity and a vision so marvelous in its sense of beauty and joy that I can never forget it nor hope to see anything its equal." [37]

He had this dream, often, through four years and then when he was nine it stopped. That summer he spent some time on a ranch in Nevada and saw an Indian reservation where the Indians were very poor and had lost hope. The white man had killed their spirit. They did not fit the Indians of his dream and he didn't understand so the dreams stopped.

But, later, when he was a grown man he learned that the Toltec Indians long ago had had just such an idea which their leader, Quetzacoatl, had told them. He had told them that in the future the white man would come bringing the Indians great trouble and sorrow. But that a few hundred years later there would be a new kind of whiteman and the whites and Indians would join together as brothers and build a world of peace and love among all kinds of men and between men and the earth. Perhaps you will grow up to be that new kind of white man.

The Toltec Indians are the same ones who have the "movement symbol" which we made a few sessions back for our vests. Remember, the movement symbol shows the movement of eternal energy through man and out to all beings in all the directions so that we all live in harmony with one another.

Remember, Black Elk who had his vision when he was nine years old. When he was carried into the air he saw the tepee with the rainbow door. The six old men who were "the Powers" were inside. In our session last fall we learned only about a part of his vision concerning the give-away to Black Elk of the sacred day-break-star plant. But in his vision many more things happened. He was given a bay horse and rode with many horses through all the world and he was shown the "sacred hoop of the world." This means that all the people of the world are really one circle — together, just as a hoop is round and has no end. After many adventures he rode back to the tepee.

He said, "As I rode in through the rainbow door, there were cheering voices from all over the universe, and I saw the Six Grandfathers sitting in a row, with their arms held toward me and their hands, palm out; and behind them in the cloud were faces thronging, without number, of the people yet to be.

'He has triumphed!' cried the six together, making thunder.'"[38]

But most of his life, Black Elk thought he had failed. He was supposed to make the sacred tree bloom at the center of the hoop of the people. But he didn't fail because he told about his vision to a white man who wrote it down in the book, *Black Elk Speaks*. He wrote the book long ago in 1932 but it wasn't the right time and hardly anyone read it. The book was reprinted in 1961 and since that time the words of Black Elk have changed the hearts of thousands and thousands of white men and the sacred hoop of the people is beginning to grow together again because of that. The white men are learning of the Indian's reverence for the earth and because of that, the sacred hoop of all the people is coming together as the Six Powers told Black Elk it would.

A really interesting thing is that the white man, a poet, who wrote down the vision of Black Elk is now called Flaming Rainbow.

Shortly before Black Elk died, when he was very old, he took Flaming Rainbow up to the top of Harney Peak in the Black Hills where he had been taken on his vision when he was nine years old. He wanted to say something to the Six Powers before he died. It had been very dry for a long time — a real drought. The sky was clear and it remained clear for most of the ceremony. Just before the end of the ceremony the white man noticed that thin clouds were forming around them and, as Black Elk said his last prayer, a

thin rain fell and low thunder was heard. Black Elk's last prayer was: "In sorrow I am sending a feeble voice, O Six Powers of the World. Hear me in my sorrow, for I may never call again. O make my people live!"[39]

Black Elk stood weeping on the top of the mountain as the rain fell on him. Soon after that the sky cleared again and the drought continued.

Black Elk's prayer is beginning to come true, now, as we begin to learn more from the Indians about how to live in a good relationship with the earth and all the creatures on it. The rainbow is a sign to us of the coming of this new relationship.

Completion, greater fullness, a wider grasp of the multitudinous aspects of life — these are what man and the gods must strive for. Not perfection and 'goodness'; never these.

SHEILA MOON

Finishing the medicine bags

◆ The designs on the medicine bags are completed today. Some people may want to add rainbows to their design.

When all the design work on the leather circles is finished, form the decorated leather circle into a bag by threading the leather thong drawstring through the holes which were punched during session 4. Pull this drawstring tight. This draws the leather circle up into a bag shape.

Tie the colored felt strips to the drawstring. The strips may be braided together before they are attached. Each person may choose his own combination of the four medicine wheel colors. All one color may be used if someone wants to use only the color of the direction he is, now, on the medicine wheel. All four colors may be used to show movement through the medicine wheel.

At the beginning of our session, today, we heard one way in which Indian children are taught to live according to the sun. The second day of the Pawnee Indian Hako ceremony is devoted to the sun. Its course is followed throughout the day and a special song is sung at each stage of the sun's journey. I'll read you a small bit of this ceremony as described by a medicine man:

"Whoever is touched by the first rays of the sun in the morning receives new life and strength which have been brought straight from the power above. . . . We think of the sun, which comes direct from the father of life, and his ray as the bearer of this life. While we sing, this ray enters the door of the lodge to bring strength and power to all within. . . .

As the sun rises higher the ray, which is its messenger, alights upon the edge of the central opening in the roof of the lodge, right over the fireplace. We see the spot, the sign of its touch, and we know that the ray is there. The fire holds an important place in the lodge. . . . Father Sun is sending life by his messenger to this central place in the lodge.

As the sun rises higher . . . the ray is now climbing down into the lodge. We watch the spot where it has alighted. It moves over the edge of the opening above the fireplace and descends into the lodge, and we sing that life from our father the Sun will come to us by his messenger, the ray. . . .

Now the spot is walking here and there within the lodge, touching different places. We know that the ray will bring strength and power from our father the Sun as it walks within the lodge. Our hearts are glad and thankful as we sing. . . ."[40]

When you get home, today, make a mark on the wall where the sun shines one of its rays into your house. If possible make the mark at sunset. Then a few weeks from now, when the summer solstice happens, make another mark on the wall. You can see how far the sun has travelled to get to his summer house in just these few weeks. Then you can watch the sun reverse his direction and begin the journey back to his winter house. In some Indian homes these marks are made regularly. Stonehenge and Chaco Canyon are really just a gigantic way to do this marking of the sun's journey.

meeting area

one piece of stiff paper for each person. Use architecture or biology bond paper or thin cardboard
masking tape
optional: pictures of Stonehenge or Chaco Canyon in New Mexico
materials for activity:
suede leather circles from session 4

12 in. length of leather thong for drawstrings — one for each person
felt pens
coloring dye pens for use on leather
black, white yellow and green felt. This should be cut into narrow strips to be used in decorating the bags

I was there to move softly . . . over the ground. Discover fire and become inside the balance. Survive and be strong within the earth. Discover new gods, mysteries, devils, and rituals. Pray for help and warmth and rain, and somehow live to be given new eyes.

GINO AUGUST SKY

6  vision quest

General idea of the Vision Quest

A vision quest could be an overnight trip to a country or mountain setting or it could be a day trip where everyone can spend the day alone or an hour alone. A park in the city is also possible if the time of day is chosen when there are not many people. For a city park, the best time of day would be just before the sun rose so each person could be there alone as the sun rose.

If the vision quest must be done within walking distance of the usual meeting area, again, the time of day is most important. The single most important requirement for the vision quest is that the person be completely alone, out of sight from other people. The other requirement is quiet. Be sure the site is not near a freeway, highway or busy street.

Sunrise is one good time of day. Sunset is the other but there is often more noise this time of day. If the quest is done at the time of the setting sun be sure that everyone is allowed a good hour alone after the sun goes down because twilight is a powerful part of the day. If the quest is done at sunset and twilight tell the group of Don Juan's saying "Twilight is the crack between the worlds." At twilight we can see more.

Have you ever been riding in a car with the radio on and you get near power lines so that you can't hear the music because of all the static? That's how it is in our lives, sometimes. Usually our minds are so noisy because the rational part of our mind is continually making plans for the future and remembering the past. Also we are often carrying on conversations inside our head. It is never quiet enough inside us to be able to hear the other part of our mind. This part of our mind is where our creativity comes from and our appreciation of beauty. This part of our mind can hear "the Powers" when they speak to us. But if our rational mind is always going strong, we can never hear the other part of our mind and then we get frustrated and caught up in our own little problems and we can't really see the beauty all around us.

When we go on a vision quest, we turn off the noisy talking, rational side of us so that the other side of our mind has a chance to be more aware of all the things within and outside of us which we normally don't see or hear. We have a chance to really be aware of the earth, the plants, the clouds and of everything around us. Then we learn more about ourselves because all of these things tell us new things about ourselves.

We call this a vision quest because a vision is what happens to you when you allow your mind to wander freely without worrying about anything or planning anything or remembering anything of the past. You just *be.* You let all the things around you come into you freely.

When the Indians went on a vision quest they often discovered their true names. Our beginning names were given to us when we were born but those names don't really tell who we are deep down inside, do they? To find that out we must begin our vision quest and then we will learn. Sometimes an Indian would take the name of an animal because "the Powers" spoke to him through that animal or the animal, itself, taught him something about the world. Some of the Indian names like this are Night Bear, Dancing Elk

Woman and Little Black Crow. Sometimes the Indian took names like Green Willow Woman, Singing Rock or Woman of the Sun because a plant or rock or some other natural object was important in their quest. Sometimes the Indian took a name like "Not Afraid of Knowing" or "Sees the Sun" or "Sees the Rock" because these were emotions or states of mind which helped him to *see.*

While you are on your vision quest if a name comes to you, write it down. It will be your true name.

You will carry your medicine bag with you. Put into it such things as a bit of soil from a special place you find or a feather. Feathers are important to Indians because the birds can fly high in the air, close to Father Sun and so when they drop a feather for us to find it is considered a gift from "the Powers." Other things you might want to put in your medicine bag are unusual rocks, the leaf of a plant, or a pressed flower. All these things are kept in your medicine bag to take out and look at when you are unhappy or troubled in any way.

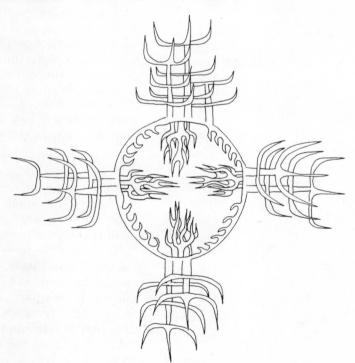

✦ Drive or walk to the area of the vision quest.

🔥 Walk around wherever you wish. Don't think about anything — just walk. Let "the Powers" guide you whether to turn right or left. Just turn in the direction which makes you feel good. If you find a

place which you like stop there awhile. Explore this small area completely so that you know exactly what is there in each direction.

You can make a mandala of this place. Put yourself in the center and lie down on the ground. Line your body up with your head pointing to the east where the sun rises. See what natural object is at your feet then. Stretch your arms out on the ground and see which natural objects stand in each of those directions. In this way you and the objects around you make a natural mandala. You are in a special relationship with all around you. Sometimes you can feel the power of the earth this way or the energy from the plants.

You can look at the sky and see as a bird would. Remember the eagles in "Jumping Mouse."

You can roll over on your stomach and look through the grass as a mouse would and see what you learn. Talk to the clouds, the animals, the grass and plants. Remember they are your brothers and *do* have something to say to you if you really listen.

Hold your palm of your hand near the leaves of various plants and make a stroking motion with your palm just as close to the leaf as you can without touching it. Think of the plant as a special friend as you do this. Sometimes you feel the energy of the plant responding to you.

Most important of all be aware of the Seventh Arrow, the Power which holds all things together.

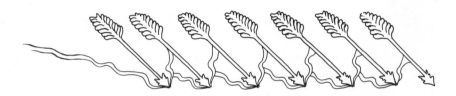

Vision walk

Be sure that everyone knows the boundaries of the area they are to walk in and the signal for returning. This could be a whistle or a shout.

After the walk

Gather everyone together and give the following short explanation. Don't ask any questions. In fact, talk of what occurred on their vision quest should be discouraged. It is better to let it sink into their minds without dissipating the experience by talking.

In our *Seven Arrows* book, the Indian, Hawk said to the young man on his vision quest: The things that happened to you on your vision quest were "the things that you are. When a man seeks to discover who he is, he ultimately discovers also who his brothers are. And he learns about the Universe around him."[41]

We began our vision quest, today, but the rest of the week will be a continuation of it as you meditate on it in your mind. Your dreams will also be a part of it.

After Black Elk got back from his vision, he was thinking about all the wonderful things which he had seen. He was sad because he thought everybody should know about it but he was afraid to tell because he thought no one would believe him because he was only nine years old. He could see it all so clearly and vividly but he couldn't talk about it. When he was older he explained that "when the part of me that talks would try to make words for the meaning, it would be like fog and get away from me.'" As he grew older the meanings became clearer.

What we experienced on our vision quest might be very clear to us in our head, but it might be just as difficult as it was for Black Elk, for us to talk about it. That is why it is good to make a drawing or some art object or a dance from something you saw on your vision quest. Then, the thing you make speaks to others about what you experienced and they feel some of it much better than if you tried to say it in words.

If, in your dream you get an idea for a poem or a work of art or a ceremony write it down. This is a gift

Don Juan squatted in front of us. He caressed the ground gently. "This is the predilection of two warriors," he said. "This earth, this world. For a warrior there can be no greater love. . . . This lovely being, which is alive to its last recesses and understands every feeling, soothed me, it cured me of my pains, and finally when I had fully understood my love for it, it taught me freedom."
CARLOS CASTANEDA

A diablero is a diablero, and a warrior is a warrior. Or a man can be both. There are enough people who are both. But a man who only traverses the paths of life is everything. Today I am neither a warrior nor a diablero. For me there is only the travelling on the paths that have a heart, on any path that may have a heart. There I travel, and the only worthwhile challenge for me is to traverse its full length. And there I travel — looking, looking, breathlessly.

DON JUAN

from "the Powers" for your vision quest. Next week, we will work on it together and this will be a part of our Summer Solstice Festival.

During the week, while you are meditating on the events of your vision walk, if any special idea for art or a ceremony comes to you be sure you write it down. Carry paper and pencil with you and be sure you keep them by the side of your bed, too.

Return to the meeting area

If you have driven to the vision quest area, let the group do the next step at the parking area.

Allow a few minutes for everybody to draw the beginning ideas for their vision shield. Tell them to just draw a quick circle and put themselves in the center. Then around that, put a quick drawing of whatever was most important to them in their vision quest. This is so they don't forget it.

Before everyone leaves, give out the materials for making the vision shield if someone wishes to do it at home. Make sure that they bring the shield with them next week or return with the materials to make it during the session if they decide to do it that way.

The vision quest was begun today but it will take all the rest of your life to complete it as each year of your life you will learn to *see* more.

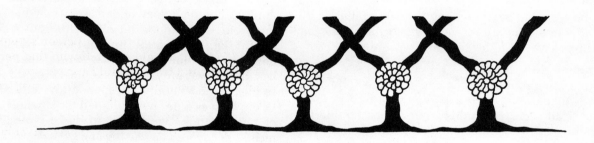

meeting area	
squares of scraps of cloth to wrap soil in small plastic bags rubber bands for closing bags	medicine bags one piece of paper and a pencil for each person

Presumably there are many subtle changes in our metabolism that are consonant with seasonal changes. As automatic data analysis reveals unsuspected rhythms in man, we may begin to see cycles with very long periods that are not now documented. There are annual symptoms, and even psychoses that seem to be related to our glandular adaptation to the seasons. For instance, we secrete something known as ''summer hormone'', a thyroid product that helps to reduce body heat. But little is known about it or about how the secretion is triggered to anticipate the hot summer months. GAY GAER LUCE

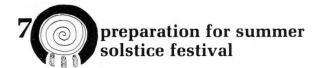

7 preparation for summer solstice festival

The group, as a whole, plans this festival as they have now learned many techniques for celebration. See sessions 2 and 3 of the Autumn Equinox cycle, 9 and 10 of the Relationship cycle and 2 and 3 of the Vegetation cycle.

The planning and the beginning of the preparations are done today. The preparations are completed and the festival is held at the next session, the Summer Solstice Festival.

The vision shield should not only have symbols related to each person's own vision quest but should also tell who that person is. Dreams and fears should be shown on it, too. The new vision quest name may be written on the shield for all to see.

Use *Seven Arrows* and all other design books as references for finding symbols to fit what each person is trying to say on his shield. Allow plenty of time for making the shield but be sure to save enough time so that the group as a whole may go on to plan and work for the festival. Anyone who wishes to do intricate borders or designs may want to take their shield home to finish it. The vision shields should be used in the Summer Solstice Festival at the next session.

Planning the festival

Black Elk had his vision when he was nine years old. By the time he was sixteen he began to be very troubled in his mind. In the intervening years "the Powers" had often warned him of danger and helped him find buffalo to eat but he had not figured out how he was supposed to bring the message of "the Powers" to his people. During his sixteenth year, whenever he heard thunder he thought it was saying to him, "It is time." The Morning Star, or as Black Elk called it, the "day-break star" seemed to be saying the same thing to him.

By the following spring, when Black Elk was seventeen, he had become so troubled that his parents asked an old medicine man to try to see what the trouble was. After working with Black Elk and hearing of his vision, which Black Elk had never told anyone before, the old medicine man said that Black Elk would have to perform the vision for his people in a special ceremony.

So Black Elk, with the help of his parents and the medicine man, performed the Horse Dance. They set up a sacred tepee and painted the symbols of his vision on it and over the door they painted a rainbow. Black Elk purified himself with sweat baths and fasting and he taught the songs which he had learned long ago in his vision. The medicine men and the young men who learned the songs were training to perform the horse dance. They had four horses for each of the four directions. The horses were of the same color as the color for each of these directions. The riders were painted with lightning running down their legs and across their chests.

On the day when they performed the Horse Dance, the thunder clouds came up out of the sky and stood around the horizon and rumbled. The people all joined the dance. At the very end of the dance all the riders on their horses had a race for the sacred tepee to see who would touch it first and get the power from the dance of the vision.

For the first time in years, Black Elk was very happy. Many people had been cured during the dance. The entire world seemed very beautiful and harmonious. As Black Elk said: "From that time on, I always got up very early to see the rising of the day-break star. People knew that I did this, and many would get up to see it with me, and when it came we said: 'Behold the star of understanding.' "[42]

Because Black Elk had been granted a vision by "the Powers", it was his responsibility to share it with his tribe through a ceremony. On our vision quest, each of us was granted understanding in some way by a new or clearer vision of something in nature, therefore, we must share it with one another just as Black Elk shared his vision. Today, we will plan, together, how to share our vision at the Summer Solstice Festival. We can use the energy given to us by "the Powers" in our vision to help others to see.

Each of you has already written down a poem or song or bit of words or an idea for a work of art. These came to you during your vision quest or afterwards in a dream. Let's see how we want to use all these "give-aways" from "the Powers."

✦ Explain as much as you wish from the Sun Dance of the Plains Indians and the Niman Kachina of the Hopis. These two important ceremonials are held at the time of the Summer Solstice.

Background on the Sun Dance

Sun Dances of the Plains Indians are spiritual gatherings. The sun, the symbol of "The Great Power", shines strongest and the growing power of the world is strongest in June. The Sun Dance revitalizes the world and its inhabitants. The Cheyenne Indians felt that the power or energy of the earth can run down as it is used by plants, animals and people. It must be renewed by ceremonies. This can be lik-

Man is like a bird with two wings that potentially can lift him to the pathway-of-the stars (spiritual life). Too often, however, he is like a bird with a broken wing. One wing is the physical conscious thinking process, and the other is the spiritual, including the subconscious dream pattern. When both wings are functioning with the rhythm of the Beauty Path (Spirit Path), they have mighty power, and can carry the soul to joyful heights.

DAVID VILLASENOR

ened to the entropy concept of modern science. The Sun Dance ceremony, not only was to get a share of the sun's new energy due to the fact that the sun's rays shine most directly on the earth at the Summer Solstice, but the people offer their energies for the use of the sun. This latter concept has its origin hundreds of years ago in the Toltec beliefs. The sacred ceremonies restore the harmony necessary to keep the creation going.

The Sun Dance was held during this time because plants are at the height of their growing season in late June. Some tribes now hold their Sun Dance on the 4th of July. Fires were built to represent the sun's heat — the force which makes living things grow. A remnant of this custom still exists in modern Europe. Pagan northern Europeans also made fires on the eve of the Summer Solstice. To this day, in the alpine region fires are lit on the summits of mountains or at high alpine huts on the eve of St John's Eve which is the Summer Solstice.

Many Indians vow to fast and dance for several days and nights in a Sun Dance because they had been helped in some special way by "the Powers" during the previous year. On the last day of the Sun Dance a race is held. Endurance is emphasized all through the Sun Dance.

Background of Niman Kachina

Niman Kachina of the Hopi Indians occurs just after the Summer Solstice. It is a ceremony for the four energies — germination of plants, heat of the sun, life-giving water, and the magnetic forces around us. Spruce branches are very important in this ceremony because they have a magnetic force which draws rain. This is also the home-going of the Kachinas who have been with the Hopis since winter began. See pages 242 to 256 of the *Book of the Hopi* by Frank Waters for more information. Some in the group may want to read about the ceremony of the Horse Dance as Black Elk performed it. See chapter XV in *Black Elk Speaks*.

When you have finished the explanation of these ceremonies, ask the group what part of their vision quest each wants to share with the group as part of the Summer Solstice Festival. As one person begins to talk about his or her experiences on the vision quest and what can be done with them, all of the others will immediately want to begin telling their ideas. Try to keep some sort of notes on this first burst of creativity so that it is not lost. As the things are told they may be sorted out under headings such as:

dances	group actions
songs	food
meditation	ceremonies
mandalas	music

body painting. The recipe for body paint is given in session 10 of the Relationship cycle. See pages 224-225 of *Seven Arrows* for ideas for painting the dancers to conform with where they see themselves on the medicine wheel. For example, if someone is mainly of the south and is a mouse who sees close he is painted green. He will have a yellow stripe across his eyes to show that he cannot see far yet. He needs to move in the eastern direction on the medicine wheel.

After completing the sorting under the above headings and others, the tasks can be assigned on a group or individual basis and the planning can proceed from there. There may not be enough time to get all accomplished during the time span of one session. Whatever remains to be done can be finished during the following session, the Summer Solstice Festival.

About clan groups for ritual preparations

In many Indian tribes one clan is in charge of a particular ceremony; another clan has charge of a different ceremony. During a particular ceremony the clan in charge, takes precedence in all affairs.

In some other tribes, for instance, the Zuni, a particular clan is assigned to each season and it has charge of any ceremony during that season. This allows leadership for many different sections of the group.

According to the Zuni system, there are the four direction clans and the sky and the earth clans but in the center is the midmost point. They are called the People of the Center. The Center or the midmost point is made up of all the divisions and goes beyond all. It takes precedence above all else. See the pillow

game in session 6 of the Relationship cycle for a further understanding of this concept.

If you decide to follow this system, divide the group into four clans according to their place on the medicine wheel. You could also have a sky and earth clan. Each clan could be assigned a color using the *Seven Arrows* color system or any other color system. The rainbow, containing all the colors, could be the symbol for the Center. It is probably advisable to keep this Center as a symbol and not assign any group of people to it.

This concept of clan groupings is of utmost importance for permitting change yet insuring overall stability in a group. It is the structure used by most long-lived steady-state cultures in the world.

---

meeting area

materials for activity:
one precut circle of drawing paper 18 in. in diameter for each person
compasses
watercolor felt pens
crayons
colored pencils

Seven Arrows book
other symbol and design books. See session 3 of the Autumn Equinox cycle for a list
further materials for this session will depend on the group decisions so they cannot be listed here

---

Summer Solstice Festival

This festival is completely planned by your own group. Our give-away to your celebration is this translation of an Indian chant which harmonizes each individual's medicine wheel with the turning of the earth's medicine wheel:

Now we all move, we're moving with this earth.
The earth is moving along, the water is moving along.
The grass is moving, the trees are moving, the whole earth is moving.
So we all move along with the earth, keeping time with the earth.[43]

Future Cycles

For your next festival as the earth turns through the summer, we suggest

Interdependence Day — July 4*

Now we *know* we are not independent but *interdependent.*

And, as the earth's medicine wheel continues turning, it is time for the Autumn Equinox cycle once again, but, because of our experiences together we will be one level higher up on the spiral of awareness as we go forward to a new vision of the earth.

*For *The Unanimous Declaration of Interdependence,* see the following page.

The Unanimous Declaration of Interdependence

When in the course of Evolution it becomes necessary for one species to denounce the notion of independence from all the rest, and to assume among the powers of the earth, the interdependent station to which the natural laws of the cosmos have placed them, a decent respect for the opinions of all mankind requires that they should declare the conditions which impel them to assert their interdependence.

We hold these truths to be self-evident, that all species have evolved with equal and unalienable rights, that among these are Life, Liberty, and the Pursuit of Happiness. — That to insure these rights, nature has instituted certain principles for the sustenence of all species, deriving these principles from the capabilities of the planet's life-support system. — That whenever any behavior by members of one species becomes destructive of these principles, it is the function of other members of that species to alter or abolish such behavior and to reestablish the theme of interdependence with all life, in such a form and in accordance with those natural principles, that will effect their safety and happiness. Prudence, indeed, will dictate that cultural values long established should not be altered for light and transient causes, Mankind is more disposed to suffer from asserting a vain notion of independence than to right themselves by abolishing that culture to which they are now accustomed. — But when a long train of abuses and insurpations of these principles of interdependence, envinces a subtle design to reduce them, through absolute despoilation of the planet's fertility to a state of ill will, bad health, and great anxiety, it is their right, it is their duty, to throw off such notions of independence from other species and from the life support system, and to provide new guards for the re-establishment of the security and maintenance of these principles. Such has been the quiet and patient sufferage of all the species, and such is now the necessity which constrains the species Homo Sapiens to reassert the principles of interdependence. — The history of the present notion of independence is a history of repeated injuries and usurpations all having in direct effect the establishment of an absolute tyranny over life.

To prove this let facts be submitted to a candid world.

1. People have refused to recognize the roles of other species and the importance of natural principals for growth of the food they require. 2. People have refused to recognize that they are interacting with other species in an evolutionary process. 3. People have fouled the waters that all life partakes of. 4. People have the face of the earth to enhance their notion of independence from it and in so doing have interrupted many natural processes that they are dependant upon. 5. People have contaminated the common household with substances that are foreign to the life process which are causing many organisms great difficulties. 6. People have massacred and extincted fellow species for their feathers and furs, for their skins and tusks. 7. People have persecuted most persistantly those known as coyote, lion, wolf, and fox because of their dramatic role in the expression of interdependence. 8. People are proliferating in such an irresponsible manner as to threaten the survival of all species. 9. People have warred upon one another which has brought great sorrow to themselves and vast destruction to the homes and the food supplies of many living things. People have denied others the right to live to completion their interdependencies to the full extent of their capabilities.

We therefore, among the mortal representatives of the eternal process of life and evolutionary principles, in mutual humbleness explicitly stated, appealing to the ecological consciousness of the world for the rectitude of our intentions, do solemnly publish and declare that all species are interdependent; that they are all free to realize these relationships to the full extent of their capabilities; that each species is subservient to the requirement of the natural processes that sustain all life. And for the support of this declaration with a firm reliance on all other members of our species who understand their consciousness as a capability, to assist all of us and our brothers to interact in order to realize a life process that manifests its maximum potential of diversity, vitality and planetary fertility to ensure the continuity of life on earth.

ECOLOGY ACTION EDUCATION INSTITUTE[44]

a note on the way of the mountain

The earth speaks to us if we know how to listen. I have always felt that it speaks most powerfully in the presence of a great mountain. In all parts of the world such great mountains have been considered sacred. In Tibet there is Mt. Kailas, sacred to both Hindus and Buddhists, in Japan, Mt. Fujiyama, a sacred Shinto mountain, and in the Near East, Mt. Sinai, sacred to primitive people and Judeo-Christian peoples. In our own southwest, the Hopis and Navajos have just fought a legal battle to save their sacred San Francisco Peaks. Here, in Silverton, where 13,000 foot peaks stand in each of the four cardinal directions, I have found others for whom mountains are sacred and powerful teachers. Our *Way of the Mountain* center, provides a focus for sharing such teachings from the earth.

Our first publication is *Earth Festivals*. We plan a quarterly journal published at the time of the equinoxes and solstices. This journal will exchange information and help for people who are trying to find their *place in nature* and understand the nature of their *place* so that there is harmony and balance between the two. Based on the idea that "the primitive world-view, far-out scientific knowledge and the poetic imagination are related forces"[46] in this search for balance, the journal will provide a focus for gathering and disseminating ideas on how to combine these forces in the personal life of your own household with its children.

Because the importance of the presence of children for *real* learning by adults is not generally acknowledged, in our first publication, *Earth Festivals,* the discussion in each session was geared to the children who are present to show how to set up such situations where true learning occurs for all ages. Future issues of the journal will be for adults but each issue will contain articles translating the material covered in that issue into ritualistic, "doing", terms for use by everyone: adults and children.

In our culture knowledge has been split up and compartmentalized so that anyone who crosses the boundaries is suspect but, as it becomes more obvious that "reality" is a dynamic web of interrelated events, the whole idea of learning must change. The ecological point of view provides the basis for this change. Each issue will celebrate one season on our changing earth at many levels: scientific, practical and psychological. Each article will concentrate on the many learnings which come from the deep relationship of one individual to a particular plant, or a certain climate or to the feel of the land in one particular part of the country. The importance of this emphasis on the relationship between a person and a *particular* environment was explained by Gary Snyder at a recent reading of poetry based on the feel of the Pacific Northwest country. He pointed out that, "Local ecosystems speak to you if you know how to listen but you've got to listen well in one place, first."[46] Then you can go to other places and the earth will continue to speak to you but the earth will never really speak to you if you haven't learned to listen well in one particular place.

We hope you will send us any comments or ideas you have concerning your own relationship to the earth. We welcome any articles, poems or artwork which is connected with the earth and its rituals and its living beings. Unsolicited manuscripts are welcome but should be accompanied by return postage. Write us and we will put your name of the list for free sample pages from our first issue of the Way of the Mountain Journal.

Dolores LaChapelle
Way of the Mountain
P.O. Box 542
Silverton, Colo. 81433
Interdependence Day, July 4, 1976

dyeing recipes

Basic recipe for using tree barks for dyes

½ cup bark
1 oz. wool

Soak the bark overnight in 2 cups water. The next morning bring this to a boil and simmer 2 hours. Add hot water as necessary to maintain the original level. Then take it off the stove. Pour it through cheesecloth to remove solids. Then add 2 more cups of water to make 1 qt. altogether. Boil the yarn for 30 minutes in this solution. Rinse and dry.

Fresh bark is more potent but dried bark may also be used. Because of the tannin in them, bark dyes usually become darker with time.

birch bark makes a pale rose color
alder bark makes a light brown
dogwood bark makes a richer light brown

Basic recipe for using lichens from trees for dyes

½ cup lichens
1 oz. wool   1 oz. wool

Cover the lichens with water and soak them overnight. Next day bring the water to the boiling point and boil for one hour. Strain the lichens out with cheesecloth and add enough water to make 1 pt. Put the yarn in this, bring to a boil and boil for 30 minutes. Rinse and dry.

Birch leaves

½ cup fresh leaves
1 oz. wool

Cover the leaves with water and soak overnight. Next morning boil for 1 hour, strain and add water to make 1 qt. Boil the yarn for 30 minutes, rinse and dry. This makes an interesting yellowish-brown color.

Oregon grape root

½ cup root
1 oz. wool

Cover the chopped up bark with water and soak overnight. Next morning boil it in 2 cups water for 2 hours. Strain out the particles and add water to make 1 qt. Boil the wool in this solution for 30 minutes, rinse and dry. This makes a dark yellow.

morning star

Symbolism

Due to recent discoveries in the field of particle physics the scientific view of "reality" is changing from the 19th century idea of matter as bits of solid material objects to the idea of a web of relationships which moves and changes constantly. This dynamic web resembles the "reality" of Eastern mystics.

In the East the yin and yang symbol stands for this continual change yet unity of all things; however, as Jung pointed out we, in the western world, have so overlooked the necessity for this union of opposites that we have neither a word nor a symbol for it. Most of our symbols still deal with reality in the dualistic terms of our European heritage; however, our new world heritage, the culture of the American Indian, provides a powerful symbol for this union of opposites. It is the Morning Star which stands between the darkness of night and the light of day and only appears when night and day are balanced. It appears suddenly as a brilliant being in "tranquil suspense" between the day and the night, earth and sky, reconciling these opposites and symbolically reconciling all human opposites, showing the unity and mutual relationship of all things and events.

This powerful symbol was developed by the Toltecs who lived long ago in the high clear air of Mexico. To this day in the mountains or the deserts of the west, the Morning Star needs no explanation. It still speaks as it did to the Indians but in many parts of the country we have dimmed and silenced it and thus there is need of an interpreter. D. H. Lawrence, who lived in Mexico for a time, seems to have grasped some of its meanings as a symbol for the continually changing relationships of the universe when he wrote: ". . . I am the Morning and the Evening Star, and lord of the day and the night. By the power that is put in my left hand, and the power that I grasp in my right, I am the lord of the two ways . . . When the fingers that give touch the fingers that receive, the Morning Star shines at once, from the contact . . . and thus there is neither giving nor taking, nor hand that proffers nor hand that receives, but the star between them is all . . . ."[*]

Astronomical information

Venus, the Morning Star of the Indians, has been important to many other cultures in all parts of the earth. Apart from the sun and moon Venus is the most brilliant object in the sky. It is a mysterious planet because it appears and disappears and is sometimes very bright and other times only as bright as an ordinary star.

The brilliance of Venus is not due to its size but to the high degree of reflectivity from its cloud cover and the fact that it is nearer to us than any other planet. It reflects 59 per cent of the light falling on it compared with 29 per cent for the earth and only 7 per cent for the moon. Venus reflects about as much light as freshly fallen snow.

Venus goes through phases just as the moon does. These phases cause it to become brighter or darker. When Venus is closest to the earth it's dark side is toward us. As it moves away from the earth it's bright side begins turning toward the earth. At this time, the planet appears as a slender crescent in the morning sky. It becomes brighter and brighter as its phase and its apparent distance from the sun increases, until it becomes a brilliant, glowing being appearing in the east before dawn.

As it moves onward, Venus changes to a three quarter phase and draws back toward the sun's line of sight, so it becomes steadily less obvious. Then it ceases to be visible at all except during the hours of daylight thus, ordinarily, we do not see it. When Venus is full it is so close to the sun that it is difficult to see.

Elongation is a term referring to the angular distance between a planet and the sun as observed from the earth. Venus appears low down in the evening sky gradually shrinking as its angular distance from the sun increases. The time between Venus' evening elongation (Evening Star) and the morning elongation (Morning Star) is about 144 days.

The following table will help in following Venus throughout the year:

1976 morning star January to April
      evening star August to December
1977 morning star April to November
      evening star January to March
1978 evening star March to October
      morning star November and December
1979 morning star January to June
      July to September is not visible
      evening star October to December
1980 evening star January to May
      morning star June to December
1981 morning star January and February
      evening star June to December
1982 morning star February to September
      evening star late December
1983 evening star January to August
      morning star September to December
1984 morning star January to April
      evening star July to December

music

This is some of the music we've found which works in many of the rituals in *Earth Festivals* but we can't guarantee it will work for all groups. Giving advice on music to use is difficult for two reasons: first, because of all the aspects of rituals for a "natural way" of life there is probably more confusion about music than any other aspect and, second, because pre-teen and teenagers are so deeply involved with the "top 40".

For generations people of the Western world looked for inspiration in music which was classed as uplifting or spiritual and which got its effect from a series of rising chords which culminated in a musical climax. This no longer fits the new culture. Much of the so-called "new spiritual music" from spiritual groups or communities is not musically sophisticated enough for teenagers. Some people turn to music from India and Bali as this music does not build toward climax but it is not suitable for kids as it takes time to get used to it. The raga form from India has influenced some contemporary Western music and in some settings can appeal to kids.

The group called *Oregon* is just about the best for this east-west synthesis. They are excellent musicians using oboe, English horn, guitar, sita, and tabla. Try their album, *Distant Hills*. John Fahey does not appeal to everyone but kids move freely to it. *Yellow Princess* and one side of the album, *Of Rivers and Religion*, are especially hypnotic. *Inside Taj Mahal* by Paul Horn, consisting of single flute and chanting inside the Taj Mahal is good.

Robbie Basho is more controversial. He does do some interesting things with some excellent guitar solos on each of his albums. *The Voice of the Eagle,* dedicated "in the spirit of love and respect to the American Indian," has the only song which I can unhesitatingly recommend to all groups, *Moving Up A Ways,* which Basho says "depicts the spiritual and physical evolution." The song fits the theme of moving along the medicine wheel used in *Earth Festivals.* It could be introduced at the Winter Solstice Festival as it has the line, "We are all ONE in the Sun." It could be used often thereafter and is especially effective with the poem in the Summer Solstice Festival. Kids really like it. Some of the songs on this album do not come off as well because Basho tries the same type of singing as used by Indians.

Some of the older albums of the Moody Blues, who were influenced by Eastern music, have some worthwhile songs for *Earth Festivals* on them. On the album, *A Question of Balance,* the last cut, *The Balance,* is good for putting people into meditative states. It is about "seeing" and "understanding". The entire song is about "being in balance" and so fits one of the continuing themes of *Earth Festivals.* Two other songs on this album fit the rituals: *Minstrel's Song* provides a good concluding song for celebrations. It's about unity and love and has a strong rhythmic beat almost like a chant. *Dawning is the Day* is really about finding your true "self". An even older album, *Threshold of a Dream,* has three pertinent songs: the *Om Song,* a good introduction to the Om chant used in the Energy cycle; *Thinking is the Best Way to Travel,* about "seeing" and other themes in the Energy cycle; and *Voices in the Sky,* about listening to nature, the birds and the sea. Although this album is old to adults it is new to most kids as they've never heard it.

Moving to music that is more for adults. There is a little known album, *Red Buddha* by Stomu Yamash'ta on Island label, which has one cut, titled *Mandala,* which provides a very intense sound participation in being a mandala. The chaos and confusion often surrounding one is built up, becoming very intense and then resolved very suddenly.

Meditative is one word for this type of music. Another term is *trance* music. *Trance* can be defined as a temporary trip away for our usual reality consciousness giving one a feeling of oneness with all life and encouraging an opening to the whole of reality without imposing one's own narrow ego-awareness on it. Below are a few possibilities to investigate. These albums may or may not appeal to kids.

The group, *Fleetwood Mac,* has one cut on the album, *Vintage Years,* titled *Albatross,* and one cut on the album *Bare Trees,* titled *Sunny Side of Heaven,* which give excellent results. They are short and should be recorded on a tape loop.

A record, which can almost be guaranteed to induce a mood of timelessness for anyone who likes music, is Keith Jarrett's *Köln Concert.* He improvises before a live audience in Köln, Germany. People who refuse to listen to anything but classical music have heard Side 1 and been entranced.

We've been jumping all around the world but coming back to American Indian music. Because the Indian has a special way of producing tones and of passing from one tone to another that is so different from our music many people find it strange. Once understood it is very powerful. If you want to investigate Indian music write Akwesasne Notes, Mohawk Nation, via Rooseveltown, N.Y. 13683 and send 50¢ for a single issue of their national Indian newspaper. It has excellent listings for authentic Indian music.

Do consult the kids in your own group as to the music to use. If you cannot find any of the lesser known records listed above write Finn Hill Arts.

natural incense

To burn natural incense you need a charcoal block. Another name for this is self-lighting charcoal. Charcoal blocks may be bought at religious supply stores for about 10¢ apiece.

Fill a bowl or ashtray or small tin can with an inch or two of sand. Put the charcoal block on the sand and light it with a match. It catches fire immediately and burns across the top of the block with a quick flare. It then settles down to a slow smolder. Sprinkle the natural ingredient you wish to use over the top of the block. You may use natural plant material such as sage, pine needles, cedar bits or eucalyptus. These will smolder and let off a natural odor. Sprinkle more needles or bits of the plant over the block from time to time. One block burns for approximately 40 minutes.

Don't restrict yourself to the common plant materials used for incense. Try anything you come across in nature and see if it works. The petals of some species of flowers have an agreeable odor when burned but the petals of other species have an unpleasant odor. Always be sure the material you use is cut up into tiny bits or use a small part of the plant such as needles.

To burn sweet grass without a charcoal block, braid three strands together when still green. After it dries out one end is lit and the plant material is whirled around in a circle so that the smoke and sweet smell gets into every part of the room.

solstices and equinoxes

The passing of the sun through the equinoxes and solstices marks the beginning of our four seasons and thus marks our changing relationship to the changing earth.

All the peoples on earth do not have this particular relationship to the earth as their *place* on the earth may not have four seasons.

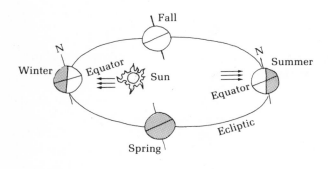

The word, solstice, comes from two Latin words: *sol* meaning sun and *sistit* meaning stands. Summer solstice occurs about June 21 and winter solstice about December 22. Near these dates the sun reaches its extreme northern and southern points in the ecliptic and appears to stand still before it turns back on its apparent course. Actually, of course, the earth moves around the sun and hence the sun appears to move against the background of stars.

The axis of the earth's rotation is tilted in respect to the plane of the earth's orbit around the sun so that the north pole tilts away from the sun in the northern hemisphere's winter and toward the sun in the summer.

The word equinox means equal night: *equi*, equal and *nox*, night. At the equinoxes day and night are of equal length. Solstices and equinoxes do not necessarily fall on the dates which are given on your calendars as will be seen from the tables in this appendix. The information used in compiling these tables comes from the Nautical Almanac Office of the U.S. Naval Observatory in Washington, D.C.

Dates of solstices and equinoxes

The time used in this table is Universal Time, which differs from the time in ordinary use by an exact number of hours. These corresponding times are shown in the second table; an asterisk denotes that the time is on the preceding day.

The beginnings of the seasons in Universal Time in the northern hemisphere are:

	spring equinox			summer solstice			fall equinox			winter solstice		
	date	hour	min.	date	hour	min.	date	hour	min.	date	hour	min.
1976	March 20	11	50	June 21	6	24	Sept. 22	21	48	Dec. 21	17	36
1977	March 20	17	43	June 21	12	14	Sept. 23	3	30	Dec. 21	23	24
1978	March 20	23	34	June 21	18	10	Sept. 23	9	26	Dec. 22	5	21
1979	March 21	5	22	June 21	23	56	Sept. 23	15	17	Dec. 22	11	10
1980	March 20	11	10	June 21	5	47	Sept. 22	21	9	Dec. 21	16	56

Universal Time	Eastern Daylight Time	Eastern Standard Time and Central Daylight Time	Central Standard Time and Mountain Daylight Time	Mountain Standard Time and Pacific Daylight Time	Pacific Standard Time
0h	*8 P.M.	*7 P.M.	*6 P.M.	*5 P.M.	*4 P.M.
1	*9	*8	*7	*6	*5
2	*10	*9	*8	*7	*6
3	*11 P.M.	*10	*9	*8	*7
4	0 Midnight	*11 P.M.	*10	*9	*8
5	1 A.M.	0 Midnight	*11 P.M.	*10	*9
6	2	1 A.M.	0 Midnight	*11 P.M.	*10
7	3	2	1 A.M.	0 Midnight	*11 P.M.
8	4	3	2	1 A.M.	0 Midnight
9	5	4	3	2	1 A.M.
10	6	5	4	3	2
11	7	6	5	4	3
12	8	7	6	5	4
13	9	8	7	6	5
14	10	9	8	7	6
15	11 A.M.	10	9	8	7
16	12 Noon	11 A.M.	10	9	8
17	1 P.M.	12 Noon	11 A.M.	10	9
18	2	1 P.M.	12 Noon	11 A.M.	10
19	3	2	1 P.M.	12 Noon	11 A.M.
10	4	3	2	1 P.M.	12 Noon
21	5	4	3	2	1 P.M.
22	6	5	4	3	2
23	7 P.M.	6 P.M.	5 P.M.	4 P.M.	3 P.M.

useful books

This is *not* a bibliography, it is merely a list of books which we think will be useful to those who use *Earth Festivals*. During the course of the sessions in *Earth Festivals* knowledge is drawn from many different fields. For example, in one session there may be specialized knowledge which only a housewife could have acquired and, a few paragraphs further on, there are references to theories from subatomic physics. We cannot assume that everyone using the book will have a background in all the fields covered. Fortunately, books are beginning to be published which attempt to bridge some of the gaps existing between various disciplines. Most of these books are not too difficult. Occasionally, we list a particular book for an in-depth study but this fact is always noted along with the title.

The list contains books under two categories: general books and books which provide background material for a specific cycle. All books listed are also published in paper unless specifically noted otherwise.

General Books

These books provide a general background upon which the more specific sessions of *Earth Festivals* were based.

American Indian Thought

John Neihardt's *Black Elk Speaks* (Lincoln: University of Nebraska Press, 1961) provides the single most important source in beginning to understand the spiritual values of the American Indian. A detailed presentation of the rituals of the Oglala Sioux is given in Joseph Epes Brown (editor), *The Sacred Pipe: Black Elk's Account of the Seven Rites of the Oglala Sioux* (Norman: University of Oklahoma Press, 1953). The best book on the Toltec and other origins of American Indian thought is Laurette Sejourne, *Burning Water: Thought and Religion in Ancient Mexico* (N.Y.: Grove Press, 1960). Other books which are valuable in this field are: Frank Waters, *Book of the Hopi* (N.Y.: Viking Press, 1963); John Lame Deer and Richard Erdoes, *Lame Deer Seeker of Visions* (N.Y.: Simon and Schuster, 1972); Hartley Burr Alexander, *The World's Rim Great Mysteries of the North American Indians* (Lincoln: University of Nebraska Press, 1953); and Tony Shearer, *Lord of* the *Dawn* (Healdsburg: Naturegraph Publishers, 1971). These books are just about the only books available which are both for the non-specialist and worthwhile for understanding the traditional inner vision of the Indian. There are dozens of books about and by Indians in this field at the present time but they don't give you much real help to increase your own understanding. Hyemeyohsts Storm's *Seven Arrows* (N.Y. Harper & Row, 1972) is in a special class and, furthermore, is required in many sessions in *Earth Festivals.*

It is difficult for some people to understand how primitive cultures could have a view of reality in some ways similar to modern science. We are listing two books to help in this understanding. The quickest way to get information is to read one chapter in Laura Thompson, *Culture in Crisis a Study of the Hopi Indians* (N.Y.: Harper and Row, 1950), since reprinted. Not in paper. This book contains one chapter, "Time, Space and Language" written by Benjamin Lee Whorf which pulls together all his ideas from a linguistic analysis of the Hopi language. It is a mind-opening introduction to how we structure reality by our use of language. For a more detailed study see J. B. Carroll, (editor), Language, Thought and Reality: Selected Writings of Benjamin Lee Whorf (Cambridge: M.I.T. Press, 1956).

Mandalas

José and Miriam Argüelles' *Mandala* (Berkeley: Shambhala Publications Inc., 1972) is the best all around introduction. C. G. Jung's Mandala Symbolism (Princeton: Princeton University Press, 1972) extracted from Jung's *Collected Works* contains a fascinating collection of mandalas done by Jung's patients as they progressed in their efforts toward individuation. It also contains good background material on mandalas in general. The commentaries which Jung provided for Richard Wilhelm's *Secret of the Golden Flower* (N.Y.: Harcourt Brace Jovanovich Inc., 1931) provide more interesting background material on mandalas.

Art

The only general book on art which we recommend as a background for *Earth Festivals* is José Argüelles, *Transformative Vision* (Berkeley: Shambhala Publications Inc., 1975). This is not an easy book but it is worth reading to gain an understanding of what went wrong with art in the western world and why and how

we are returning to the real sources of art. M. C. Richards' *Centering in Pottery, Poetry, and the Person* (Middletown: Wesleyan University Press, 1964) is one woman's very beautiful account of what she learned from her total engagement with art. Edith Kramer's *Art and Therapy with Children* (N.Y.: Schocken Books, 1971) gives useful insights into what art can do for children. Not in paper.

The Psychology of Jung
(Analytical Psychology)

The best general introduction to this field is by a Jungian analyst: June Singer, *The Boundaries of the Soul* (Garden City: Doubleday and Co., 1972). The best book for parents and others closely involved with children is Frances G. Wickes, *The Inner World of Childhood* (N.Y.: Appleton-Century, first published in 1927, republished in 1966). No one has done anything nearly as good because this book shows the affects of the adult's unconscious on children and vividly proves that the child's dreams and fantasies reflect the adult's unconscious. This book also shows the importance of fairy stories and fantasy for children. Not in paper.

The best way to begin to understand Jung is to read C. G. Jung, *Memories, Dreams, Reflections* (N.Y.: Vintage Books, 1963). This book is an autobiography.

Ritually Relating to the Earth

The only background book we can list here is an old one written by a Thomist philosopher but he does understand what true festivity is and can write very clearly and simply: Josef Pieper, *In Tune with the World, A Theory of Festivity* (N.Y.: Harcourt, Brace Jovanovich Inc., 1965). It contains only 65 pages and is not in paper.

Ecology

For a clue into the full implications of ecology try reading Gregory Bateson's *Steps to an Ecology of Mind* (N.Y.: Ballantine Books, 1972). It's the best but we've not succeeded in getting a great number of people to read it as it is difficult. Stewart Brand of *Whole Earth Catalog* fame has been trying to get people to read it for years too. He even wrote a book about the importance of reading Bateson's book. We suggest you begin by reading Part VI, for an overall view. No other book ever attempted to do what this book does. Because reading requires use of the left brain it is really cognitive learning but, somehow, the book succeeds in giving one the type of almost mystical knowledge of unity which only comes from right brain learning.

Aldo Leopold's *A Sand County Almanac with other essays on conservation from Round River* (N.Y.: Oxford University Press, 1966) provides interrelationship writing at its best.

Peter S. Stevens' *Patterns in Nature* (Boston: Little Brown and Co., 1974) is a "stunning synthesis of art and science." The book contains beautiful photographs along with explanatory text on why the small resembles the large in nature. "When we see how the branching of trees resembles the branching of rivers, how crystal grains look like soap bubbles and the plates of a tortoise's shell, how the fiddle-heads of ferns, stellar galaxies, and water emptying from the bathtub spiral in a similar manner, then we cannot help but wonder. . ."

William L. Thomas, Jr. (editor), *Man's Role in Changing the Face of the Earth* (Chicago: University of Chicago Press, 1956) is a basic book in this field. A massive book, 1193 pages, it brings together the best of the papers from the seventy participants at the International Symposium of the same name. Get it from the library and browse. You will learn amazing things. It is in paper, also.

Topophilia is the term for "love of place". Yi-Fu Tuan's *Topophilia A Study of Environmental Perception, Attitudes and Values* (Englewood Cliffs: Prentice-Hall Inc., 1974) is a rather limited book for the inherent greatness of the subject but it is the only one we've got. Chapters 8, 9 and 10 and 14 are well worth reading.

Steady-state culture is the only name we have so far for the kind of culture which does not exploit the environment. The best book so far is Herman E. Daly (editor), *Toward a Steady-State Economy* (San Francisco: W. H. Freeman and Company, 1973). It is a collection of essays on the subject. The essays by Georgescu-Roegen, Boulding, Daly, and Schumacher are the best for background for *Earth Festivals*.

Psychology

Charles T. Tart's *Altered States of Consciousness* (N.Y.: John Wiley & Sons, Inc., 1969) is the basic book in this field. Papers in it cover altered states, the hypnagogic state, dreams, hypnosis, meditation and drugs. Andrew Weill's *The Natural Mind* (Boston: Houghton Mifflin Co., 1972) is another good background book because it has good information on children and altered states. Weill shows that altered states are natural for the human being and that children alter their states of consciousness often.

We will list only a few of the most useful books in the field of meditation. Chogyam Trungpa, *Meditation in Action* (Berkeley: Shambhala Publications, 1970) provides a good introduction. The next two books provide an easy introduction to what is termed *insight meditation* or *jnana yoga,* or *Learning III,* the term used by Gregory Bateson. A. Sujata, *Beginning to See* (Santa Cruz: Unity Press, 1975) is a little book of almost cartoon like pictures perfectly matched with the few words of text. Joel Kramer, *The Passionate Mind* (Millbrae: Celestial Arts, 1974) is from his taped lectures. It does begin to open your mind. Any book by Krishnamurti is excellent.

Tibet

The spiritual thought of Tibet is referred to often in Earth Festivals. The best introductory. book is John Blofield, *Tantric Mysticism of Tibet* (N.Y.: E. P. Dutton, 1970).

Transpersonal Psychology

The best source for information on transpersonal psychology is *The Journal of Transpersonal Psychology,* P.O. Box 4437, Stanford, Ca. 94305. The best book for information on the right and left brain studies is Robert E. Ornstein, *The Psychology of Consciousness* (San Francisco: W. H. Freeman, 1972). Joseph Chilton Pearce's *Exploring the Crack in the Cosmic Egg* (N.Y.: The Julian Press, 1974) gives information on some of the exciting possibilities which may come from right brain learning. Pearce points out that one of the functions of the right brain, which he terms *Reversibility Thinking,* "forms as a possible function (developed or not) somewhere around the sixth year, and generally atrophies as an open-ended possibility, through neglect and inhibition, somewhere around adolescence." Of even greater interest is the possibilities he outlines if this *Reversibility Thinking* were encouraged instead of inhibited. He provides more information on younger children in this context than any other book.

Although A. H. Maslow's, *The Farther Reaches of Human Nature* (N.Y.: The Viking Press, 1971) was written before the term, *transpersonal,* acquired wide usage, he outlines just such a psychology and furthermore, points out the importance of helping children to look within themselves.

Transpersonal Education

There are three books available so far with specific information on transpersonal education: Gay Hendricks and Russel Wills, *The Centering Book, Awareness Activities for Children, Parents and Teachers* (N.Y.: Prentice Hall, 1975) provides brief exercises for relaxing the body and mind, for seeing and some dream work for children. It contains a very useful section listing answers to questions asked by teachers and parents on transpersonal education. Gay Hendricks and Thomas B. Roberts, *The Second Centering Book* and Gay Hendricks and Jim Fadiman, *Transpersonal Education* are both due from Prentice Hall in 1976.

Background Books for the Cycles

In addition to the above books there are specific books used as source material for each cycle. For further background reading consult the Notes for each cycle in the back of *Earth Festivals*.

Autumn Equinox and Relationship cycle

David Leveson's *A Sense of the Earth* (N.Y.: Natural History Press, 1972) is the best kind of writing, scientific and poetic, about the relationship of man to the rocks and form of the earth. Richard Grossinger's *Solar Journal* (Los Angeles: Sparrow Press, 1970) is still more poetic yet factual about the sun and the earth and man. In *Pilgrim at Tinker Creek* (N.Y.: Harper Mag. Press, 1974) Annie Dillard writes of her deep relationship to her *place*.

Energy cycle

There seems to be some new concepts of energy but ideas have not crystallized enough to provide a book; however, some clues about these forms of energy are given in the following books. Fritjof Capra's *The Tao of Physics: An Exploration of the Parallels Between Modern Physics and Eastern Mysticism* (Berkeley: Shambhala, 1975) is not an easy book to read for those with no background in physics because some parts are difficult but the author does not take the easy way out and resort to formulas as most physicists do. He writes, as clearly as possible for non-physicist readers, concerning the theories of atomic and subatomic physics, of relativity theory and of astrophysics and relates the world view emerging from these theories to the mystical traditions of Eastern religions. More important, he explains the importance for each of us in our daily personal lives of the findings of modern physics.

Lawrence Le Shan's, *The Medium, the Mystic and the Physicist* (N.Y.: The Viking Press, 1974) is a much less technical book which shows the similarity of "reality" as viewed by these three categories of people. He also writes of a very interesting healing experiment which demonstrated this "reality".

Alan Watt's *Does It Matter?* (N.Y.: Pantheon Books, 1970) is excellent on matter, interrelationships, flow and energy.

Vegetation cycle

Edgar Anderson's *Plants, Man and Life* (Berkeley: University of California Press, 1967) gives a real in-depth study of the relationship of man and plants and therefor is not an easy book but is excellent. Peter Tomkins and Christopher Bryd's *The Secret Life of Plants* (N.Y.: Harper & Row, 1973) is an easier book on man and plants.

Vision cycle

R. L. Gregory's *Eye and Brain* (N.Y.: McGraw Hill Book Co., 1968) provides the best introduction to this cycle. For a fascinating glimpse into another reality read Edwin A. Abbott's *Flatland* (N.Y.: Dover). The book is an imaginative journey into a place where the inhibitants lack the third dimension. The last books we will mention on vision are all the books about don Juan by Castaneda.

note for educators

The experiences provided by the sessions in *Earth Festivals* come under two new categories of education: *transpersonal* education and *ecological* education, in its largest sense.

Transpersonal education

Current teaching emphasizes acquiring information through such skills as reading, mathematics and other cognitive methods. These methods all deal with only the left hemisphere of the brain. In disucssing the two sides of the brain, Thomas B. Roberts states: "While the left half is verbal, analytic, calculating, reasoning, active, and linear, the right hemisphere is pic-

	arts and crafts	dance and movement	sense of smell	meditation	music	ritual	chant and sounds	talks	teaching stories	games
balancing self and nature	I-3*, II-1, I-7, II-8, III-2, III-3, III-4, III-5, III-8, III-7, III-8, IV-1, IV-4, IV-5, IV-6, IV-4, V-5, V-7	I-3, II-1, I-4, II-7, II-8, III-2, III-8, IV-1, V-1, V-2	I-2, III-7, V-6	I-3, II-1, III-5, IV-4, V-5, V-6	III-3, III-4, III-4, II-8	I-3, II-1, III-7, III-8	III-3, III-4, III-5, III-8, IV-1, IV-2, IV-6, IV-7, V-6	I-3, II-2, I-4, II-7, III-1, III-2, III-3, III-4, III-5, III-7, III-8, IV-1, IV-6, IV-8, V-3, V-4, V-8	I-8, III-8	II-4, II-6
body/ mind balance	I-7, II-8, II-9, III-2, III-8, IV-1, IV-4, IV-5, IV-6, V-3	II-7, II-8, III-2, III-8, IV-1, V-1, V-2, V-6	III-2, V-6,	II-3, II-7, III-5, IV-4, V-5, V-6	III-3, III-4, III-7, III-8		II-5, III-5, III-6, III-8, IV-1, IV-7	I-3, II-9, III-1, III-4, V-1	II-1, II-9, III-3, III-5, III-8	
ecology	I-3, II-1, I-7, II-9, III-2, III-4, III-5, III-6, III-7, III-8, IV-1, IV-4, IV-5, IV-8, V-3, V-7	I-3, II-1, II-2, II-7, III-8, III-2, III-8, IV-1, V-6	I-3, II-1, II-2, II-4, III-2, III-7	I-3, II-1, III-5, IV-4, V-5, V-6	I-3, II-4, III-7, III-8	I-3, III-7, III-8	I-3, III-5, III-6, IV-1, IV-2, IV-6, V-6	I-3, II-2, II-4, II-5, I-7, II-9, III-1, III-2, III-4, III-6, III-7, III-8, IV-1, IV-4, IV-5, V-8, V-4, V-6	III-8	II-4, II-5,
medicine wheel	I-1, I-3, II-1, I-7, II-8, III-8, IV-4, IV-5, V-6, IV-8, V-3	I-3, I-4, II-7, II-8, III-8, V-2, V-3			I-3	I-3, III-8	I-2, III-5, IV-7	I-1, II-4, I-7, III-1, III-3, III-5, III-8, IV-1, V-2, V-3, V-4	II-8, III-8	III-8
other states of con- scious- ness	I-7, II-8, III-6, IV-8, V-7	II-7, III-8, V-6		II-3, III-5, IV-4, IV-5, V-6	III-7	III-7	III-6, IV-1	III-3, V-3		II-5
right/ left brain	I-2, II-7, II-8, II-9, III-2, III-6, III-7, III-8, V-7	II-7, II-8, III-8, V-1, V-2, V-6	II-2, III-2	I-3, III-5, IV-4, V-6	III-7, III-8	III-8	III-6, III-8	I-2, II-9, III-2, III-8, IV-4, IV-8, V-1, V-3	III-8	
seeing from differ- ent view- points	I-1, II-8, III-3, III-4, III-6, III-7, III-8, IV-1, IV-4, IV-5, IV-6, IV-8, V-3, V-7	I-1, I-3, II-7, II-8, III-8, IV-1, V-2, V-3, V-6	III-7, V-6	I-7, III-5, IV-4, IV-5, V-6	II-4, III-7	I-3	I-2, III-3, III-5, III-6, IV-1, IV-7, V-6	I-1, II-4, III-3, III-4, III-7, III-8, IV-1, V-1, V-8, V-3, V-4, V-5, V-6	I-8, III-8, III-1, III-8, V-4	II-4, II-6, V-5
self- worth	I-1, II-7, I-8, III-5, III-7, III-8, IV-1, IV-4, IV-5, IV-6, V-7	II-7, II-8, III-8, V-6		III-5, IV-4, V-6		II-4	IV-7	I-1, II-4, I-5, II-8, III-3, III-7, III-8, IV-6, V-4	II-8, III-5	III-8
"the Powers"	I-3, II-1, I-3, III-6, III-8, IV-1, IV-4, V-7	II-1, III-8, V-6		III-5, V-6	III-8	III-8, IV-7	III-6, III-8, IV-1	I-3, II-8, I-9, III-5, III-6, III-8, V-2, V-4	II-1, III-8,	II-6

*Roman numerals refer to the cycles and the arabic numerals refer to the sessions in *Earth Festivals*. See Table of Contents.

torial, synthetic, intuitive, receptive, and holistic. We concentrate our teaching on the left brain functions, in effect neglecting the right half."[48] The left hemisphere of the brain splits the world apart to analyze bits of it; the right hemisphere sees things as interconnected, as whole. One-sided development of the brain which occurs with our emphasis on congnitive skills stifles creativity, not only in the artistic field but in science as well. The key concepts in many major scientific discoveries were made through use of the right side of the brain. Whole learning occurs through use of both sides of the brain. *Transpersonal* is the term used for the more complete learning.

The aim of transpersonal education is not just to add another type of education onto the existing forms but, according to Frances Vaughan Clark, "to expand our existing forms to include the development of those functions which have been neglected in order to bring about a balance between intellectual and intuitive, conscious and unconscious, verbal and spatial, physical, emotional, and spiritual processes."[49]

The use of the word, *spiritual,* does not mean that transpersonal education teaches any particular doctrine or belief but that it presents ways of transcending the individual self and grasping the larger whole. The preoccupation with left brain functions in our culture has created an almost pathological condition of separateness and aloneness. Transpersonal education helps the individual to find a "way to move from dependence through independence to interdependence."[50] In presenting this idea of interdependence *Earth Festivals* uses terms referring to the American Indian. This does not mean to imply that the Indian culture is the only source of these interdependent values. The values in question are common to many so-called primitive cultures, to many of the great Asiatic religions and are being rediscovered by modern science through such studies as particle physics. We refer to the Indian most often because children readily identify with Indians whereas they have no every-day contact with Eastern religions.

Education from the ecological point of view

Humanity plays a much larger role in changing the earth than was previously realized. The ecological point of view studies this interrelationship of man and the earth. Pointing out the importance of ecology, Thomas R. Blackburn, writing in *Science,* states that, "for at least the next decade, the most important, active, and heavily funded field of science will be ecology — in its broadest sense. Unless we reach a full and effective understanding of human society and its place in the biosphere, there will be no science worth speaking of in the twenty-first century."[51]

Because it is an innovative concept to combine these two fields of education, we have appended a table listing the specific learnings in transpersonal and ecological education which each session of *Earth Festivals* provides.

supplies

Someone has to get the supplies together if you are going to have a celebration or ritual. This problem of logistics stops some people from attempting celebrations because they, somehow, feel the whole thing should just happen without any preparation for it to be valid; however, in unified, whole cultures such as the Hopi, the preparation IS the first part of the ritual.

To ease the task of getting the supplies together we have compiled all the lists of materials needed at the end of each session into one carefully organized list.

• There are three types of materials.
   1. materials to be purchased. These are further subdivided and listed under the type of store where they may be secured.
   2. materials to be borrowed or acquired free.
   3. materials from nature. Because the impact of human population in and near cities is destroying our relatives, the living beings of the earth, it is no longer valid to use the natural things of the environment for every art activity. A great number of the activities in these sessions call for man made materials, often recycled. In the few instances where natural materials are called for in special ceremonies be sure that you secure the necessary quantity from a variety of plants. Never take all of any one species of plant from any one area.

• In order that you do not have to buy or arrange for everything at once we have broken each section of the list into two categories according to the way *Earth Festivals* is arranged:

FIRST HALF. This contains materials needed for the sessions in the first half of the book, from the Autumn Equinox cycle through the Relationship cycle (Winter Solstice).

SECOND HALF. This contains all the materials needed for the sessions in the second half of the book, from the Energy cycle through the Vision cycle (Spring Equinox and Summer Solstice).

• Some of the items listed below are to be used by the group as a whole. (ex. one can of white spray paint) The amounts listed are sufficient for groups of about 20 to 25.

Materials to be purchased

Art store or school supply store

FIRST HALF

- 1 piece (12 x 14 in.) railroad board for each person — Autumn Equinox 2.
- 2 pieces (22 x 22 in.) railroad board for each person — Autumn Equinox 3.
- 1 compass for each person. These may be ordered by mail from Edmund Scientific Co. See address below. — Autumn Equinox 3.
- gold, white and yellow tempera paint.
- several brushes for tempera paint.
- several sets of crayons.

SECOND HALF

- 1 scissors for each person. These are first used in Energy 4 but are used again later.
- several Craypas sets — Vegetation 3.
- several sets of Milton Bradley water colors — Vegetation 6.
- several fine brushes for above.
- 1 green crayon for each person — Vision 3.

Discount store or office supply store

These items are for general use throughout the sessions. Many of them should be kept on hand for each session.

First half

- 1 can of white spray paint.
- 1 roll of masking tape.
- 1 package gold Christmas tree icicles — Relationship 9.
- several soft pencils.
- one pencil for each person.
- several sets of watercolor felt pens.
- colored pencils.

Second half

- 1 package of round brass paper fasteners (brads).
- 2 medium sized packages of rubber bands — Energy 4.
- several ink pads — Energy 6.
- 1 small roll Scotch magic transparent tape — Vegetation 7.
- Rit dye for fabrics — See Energy 4 for more information.
- crepe paper: 1 small package each of black, green, yellow and white paper — Energy 8.
- 1 roll masking tape.

Fabric store

First half

- white yarn — Relationship 2.

Second half

- stitch-witchery bonding material — Energy 1.
- Each person needs three 6 in. squares of pellon fabric. The first one is used in Energy 2 and the others are used in later sessions.
- felt scraps. These may also be acquired at Goodwill. — Energy 6.
- 2 strands of yarn for each person of the following colors: red, blue, black, yellow and green.
- short felt strips in the following colors: black, white, yellow and green. — Vision 5.

Films to rent

Ordering information will be found under the materials needed at the end of each session requiring films.

First half

- *Requiem for Tibet* — Relationship 7.

Second half

- *American Time Capsule* — Vision 3.

Grocery store

First half

- Crystal brand liquid soap, 1 bottle — Relationship 10.
- 1 bottle Vano liquid starch — Relationship 10.
- 1 package containing 3 or 4 colors of vegetable dye.
- 1 bottle Sweetheart Lime dishwashing liquid — Relationship 2.

Second half

- 1 zip locking baggie for each person. This is a brand name for a special type of plastic bag — Vegetation 4 and following sessions.
- bones from the butcher. These should be free — Vision 1.

Hardware store

First half

- 1 large ball of heavy string.
- contact glue.

Second half

- Elmer's glue.
- colored twine — Vision 1.

Health food store

First half

- Sunflower seeds — hulled but unroasted — Autumn Equinox 1.

Second half

- miso, a Japanese soybean product. You can get instant miso soup from Japanese groceries or order instant miso from Finn Hill Arts. See below for address — Energy 4.

Paint store

First half

- bright yellow latex paint — Relationship 9.

Second half

- latex paint: red, black, yellow and green — Vegetation 2.

Paper

In general, much of the paper can be acquired free or at reduced cost. Sometimes you can get left-over or very cheap paper from printing shops, silk screen shops and offices. The list below gives the type of paper needed. In most cases it can vary considerably from the type listed. In only one listing, *the hard surface, white drawing paper,* there can be no substitute. No other paper will work for this use.

First half

- 1 piece for each person of stiff paper such as biology bond or architecture bond. Buy at college book stores.
- 1 piece of newsprint for each person.

- 2 pieces of drawing paper (18 in. square) for each person.
- 1 piece of black 8 x 10 in. construction paper for each person.

Second half
- 1 piece of drawing paper for each person.
- 4 pieces of 8 x 8 in. white hard surface good quality drawing paper for each person. Do not substitute for this — Vegetation 4.
- 2 white pieces of cardboard for each person. File cards are suitable — Vision 3.
- 1 piece of stiff white paper such as biology bond or architecture bond.

Sporting goods store
- 2 feet of fishline for each person. 1 foot is used in Relationship 9; the shorter pieces are needed for Relationship 3 and Energy 7.

Thrift store

First half
- bits of old jewelry — Vegetation 2.
- bits of old felt of various sizes and colors — Energy 6.

Special Items

Precision items may be ordered from:

Edmund Scientific Co., Edscorp Bldg., Barrington, N.J. 08007. Send for their free catalog.

First half
- compasses for each person if you cannot find good cheap ones locally — Relationship 7 and many other sessions thereafter.
- 1 magnifying glass for every two persons — Relationship 7.

Books, records and other media-type materials may be ordered from:

Finn Hill Arts, P.O. Box 542, Silverton, Colo. 81433. Books, records and particular items available nowhere else may be ordered from this company. Write for price list.

Books needed for the actual sessions

First half
- *Seven Arrows* by Hyemeyohsts Storm.
- optional: If you like the demons drawings in Relationship 7 send for the coloring book they came from, *Demons, a psychological coloring book* by Randy LaChapelle.

Second half
- *Windigo and other tales of the Ojibways* illustrated by Norval Morrisseau and told to Herbert T. Schwarz
- Supplementary books — These books are needed for reference for sessions and art activities. They may be borrowed from a library or substitutes may be used. Any of these books which you can afford may be ordered from *Finn Hill Arts*.

First half
- *Pueblo Designs* by H. P. Mera — Autumn Equinox 3 and other sessions later.
- *Your Symbol Book* by F. Wallace and E. Kirby — Autumn Equinox 3 and later sessions.

- *Indian Art of the Americas* by Le Roy H. Appleton — Autumn Equinox 3 and later sessions.
- an atlas of the world showing the various altitudes of mountains in different colors — Relationship 7.

Second half
- Borrow books from the library showing spiral designs used by Indians on art objects — Energy 7.
- the design book listed for the first half — Vegetation 2.
- *Mandala* by José and Mariam Argüelles — Vegetation 4.

Records

First half
- *American Indian Dances* — Folkways.
- *Spellbinder* by Gabor Szabo.

Second half
- *The Music of Tibet.*
- *Sidewinder* by Morton Subotnick.
- *American Indian Dances.*
- *Sonic Seasonings* (optional) — Vegetation 4.

Posters and other media

First half
- space slides showing spiral storms and the earth — Relationship 2.
- sun poster — Autumn Equinox cycle and often throughout the year.

Supplies for making ceremonial clothing and accessories may be ordered from:

Grey Owl's Catalog of Indian Craft Supplies 150-02 Beaver Road, Jamaica, N.Y. 11433. Send 35¢ for their catalog.

First half
- 1 small piece of leather thong for each person — Relationship 5.
- 1 mirror for each person, 2 in. in diameter — Relationship 9.

Second half
- ⅔ yard of 36 in. wide Buckskin Finish cloth for each person — Energy 1.
- several sets of Coloring Dye Pens — Energy 1.
- 8 in. circle of suede leather for each person — Vision 4.
- 12 in. long piece of leather thong for each person — Vision 4.

Optional photographs may be ordered from:

Hale Observatory

Second half
- spiral galaxy photos. See Energy 7 for further details because this is an optional item.

Borrowed or free materials

These items are usually in the home or may be borrowed to use for a specific session. These items are listed by sessions.

First half

Autumn Equinox 1
- gong or stainless steel mixing bowl.
- round bowl for sunflower seeds.

Autumn Equinox 3

- ingredients and utensils for Fried Indian Bread and natural tea.
- honey.
- margarine or butter.
- record player.
- paper punch.
- thread and needles.
- scissors.
- candle.

Relationship 1

- utensils for making and serving natural tea.
- honey.
- paper sack for each person — medium sized.
- pruning shears.

Relationship 2

- slide projector and screen.
- shallow flat bottom glass cake pan.
- milk.
- fork.
- knives and chopping board for chopping bark for dyes.
- hammer.
- stainless steel pots for boiling dyes.
- hot plate or stove.
- stirring sticks.
- plastic tarp or newspaper to protect floor.

Relationship 3

- leftover yarn: green, white, black and yellow. Short pieces are all right.

Relationship 4

- a green, growing plant.
- a vegetable such as lettuce or potato.
- record player.
- picture showing annual growth in the tree rings of trees.

Relationship 6

- a pillow.

Relationship 7

- movie projector and screen.
- flute or whistle.
- drum.

Relationship 8

- chisels and knives.

Relationship 9

- two plastic bread bags for each person.
- several needles and thread.
- one knife for each person. It must be sharp enough to peel branches.
- pictures of primitive drawings of the sun or Toltec designs of the sun or William Blake suns.
- latex paint. Leftover paint can be used as only a small bit is needed. Colors needed are bright green, white, yellow, blue and red.
- several paint brushes.
- newspaper.
- clean up water and towels.
- several egg cartons.

Relationship 10

- soap, water and rags for washing the floor.

- record player.
- pans for boiling water.
- stove or hot plate.
- tortilla ingredients.
- utensils for making tea.
- cups.
- honey.
- butter.
- cornmeal.

Second half

Energy 1

- leather punch.

Energy 3

- flashlight.
- small mirrors — as many as you can find.
- record player.

Energy 4

- gong or stainless steel mixing bowl.
- bowl which holds about a cup of water.
- 1 hot plate and 1 cooking pan for each group of 8 people. The pans should not be teflon.
- 1 pair of rubber gloves.
- label maker for putting names on the T-shirts.
- vinegar.
- 1 very long handled spoon or stick about 2 feet long.
- 1 plastic squirt bottle for every 4 people.
- 1 bucket or dish pan for every 4 people.
- 1 large plastic garbage bag for each person to protect clothing.
- plenty of newspapers.
- 1 plastic bag for each person to carry wet T-shirts.
- bleach for cleanup.
- paper towels for cleanup.

Energy 5

- candle in a holder.

Energy 6

- stereo record player.
- ball point pens.

Energy 7

- shallow flat glass bottom cake pan.
- milk.
- fork.
- any size screw for demonstration.
- projector and screen for slides.
- various kinds of paper: different colors and textures.

Energy 8

- record player and records. See session for kinds of records to borrow.

Vegetation 1

- small plastic bags to collect pollen — 1 for each person.
- large paper sacks to collect plant material — 1 for each person.
- 1 piece of twine or rope to use as a hanger for wall hanging — 1 per person.

Vegetation 2

- latex paint in black, yellow, green and red colors.
- pruning shears.

Vegetation 3

- vases or jars.

- wooden platter.
- sweet smelling plants: sage, aromatic leaves, thyme etc.
- dried eucalyptus, sage or pine needles.
- matches.
- record player.
- large brown grocery bag for each person.
- newspapers.
- at least 4 irons and extension cords if needed.

Vegetation 5
- scraps of cloth to use as blindfolds — 1 for each 2 people.
- record player. This is optional. If you decide to use the record which is listed, you will need a record player for the next 2 sessions also.

Vegetation 8
- yarn — a different color for each person.
- old rope, any kind of fibers, yarn, string, cord etc.
- pieces of 1 x 2 wood to make a rough frame.
- hammer, nails and other tools necessary to make the frame.

Vision 1
- paper towels.
- colored twine or yarn.

Vision 3
- projector and screen for film.

Vision 4
- leather punch.

Vision 5
- picture of Stonehenge or Chaco Canyon, New Mexico.

Vision 6
- small plastic bags for each person.
- scraps of cloth to wrap soil.

Materials from nature

First half

Autumn equinox 1
- 31 small stones.
- sage, fresh or dried.
- skull.
- natural herb tea or buy from health food store.

Autumn equinox 3
- corn husks or dried leaves.
- rough textured squash and an apple.

Relationship 2
- natural materials for dyes.

Relationship 3
- small sticks about 12 inches long or less and about one forth inch thick. Each person needs 2. You can buy wooden chopsticks or wooden dowels.

Relationship 4
- piece of tree wood.
- wood shavings.

Relationship 5
- 4 small bones, small enough to be hidden in a closed fist: chicken or turkey bones.

Relationship 9
- 1 small tree branch — 12 inches long by ¾ to 1 inch thick for each person.
- 1 forked branch to make slingshot.
- 4 white feathers for each person.

Relationship 10
- 1 large forked branch or small tree — five to six feet long.
- cedar branches or dogwood bark or other material which has a strong fragrance when boiled.

Second half

Energy 1
- small bones or get lamb bones from a butcher.
- natural objects for decorating ceremonial vests.

Energy 2
- 1 forked branch.

Energy 8
- 31 small stones.

Vegetation 1
- 1 branch or dowel 18 to 24 inches long.
- material for wall hanging.

Vegetation 2
- 1 flower
- 4 cattails or hollow reeds for each person.
- moss.

Vegetation 3
- wild food.

Vegation 4
- 1 flower for each person. It should have a deep cup like a tulip.

Vision 1
- 1 stick for each person about 12 inches long.

sources

Adler, G., M. Fordham, H. Read, and W. McGuire, editors, trans. by R. F. C. Hull, THE COLLECTED WORKS OF C. G. JUNG, Bollingen Series XX, vol. 9, *The Archetypes and the Collective Unconscious*, Princeton: Princeton Univ. Press, 1959 and 1969.

———, vol. 11, *Psychology and Religion: West and East*, 1958.

Alexander, Hartley Burr, *The World's Rim, Great Mysteries of the North American Indians*, Lincoln: University of Nebraska Press, 1967.

Ames, Adelbert, Jr., *The Morning Notes of Adelbert Ames Jr.*, New Brunswick: Rutgers Univ. Press, 1960.

Argüelles, José and Miriam, *Mandala*, Berkeley: Shambhala, 1972.

August Sky, Gino, "Searching for the Miracle," *Clear Creek*, 14, June 1972.

Basso, Keith H. and Ned Anderson, "A Western Apache Writing System: The Symbols of Silas John," *Science*, June 8, 1973.

Bateson, Gregory, "Alfred Korzybski Memorial Lecture 1970, Form, Substance and Difference," *General Semantics Bulletin*, vol. 37 (1970), pp. 5-13.

——, "Bali: The Value System of a Steady State," in Meyer Fortes, ed., *Social Structures: Studies Presented to A. R. Radcliffe-Brown*, N.Y.: Russell & Russell, Inc., 1963.

——, "The Cybernetics of 'Self': A Theory of Alcoholism," *Psychiatry*, vol. 34, no. 1, 1971.

——, "Pathologies of Epistemology," *Second Conference on Mental Health in Asia and the Pacific, 1969*, Hawaii: East-West Center Press, 1972.

Berry, Wendell, "A Composting Privy," *Organic Gardening*, December 1973.

Blackburn, Thomas R., "Sensuous-Intellectual Complementarity in Science," *Science*, 172, June 11, 1971.

Blofield, John, *The Tantric Mysticism of Tibet*, N.Y.: E. P. Dutton and Co., 1970.

Boas, Franz, "Ethnology of the Kwakiutl," *35th Annual Report of the Bureau of American Ethnology, 1913-1914*.

Brave Buffalo, quoted in Francis Densmore, *Bulletin of the Bureau of American Ethnology*, no. 61, 1918.

Brown, Joseph Epes, ed. *The Sacred Pipe: Black Elk's Account of the Seven Rites of the Oglala Sioux*, Norman: Univ. of Oklahoma Press, 1953.

Carroll, J. G., ed., *Language, Thought and Reality: Selected Writings of Benjamin Lee Whorf*, Cambridge: The M.I.T. Press, 1951.

Castaneda, Carlos, *Journey to Ixtlan*, N.Y.: Simon and Schuster, 1972.

——, *A Separate Reality*, N.Y.: Simon and Schuster, 1971.

——, *Tales of Power*, N.Y.: Simon and Schuster, 1974.

——, *The Teachings of Don Juan*, N.Y.: Simon and Schuster, 1968.

Clark, Frances Vaughan, "Rediscovering Transpersonal Education," *Journal of Transpersonal Psychology*, no. 1, 1974.

Cox, Harvey, *Feast of Fools*, Cambridge: Harvard Univ. Press, 1969.

de Angulo, Jaime, *Indian Tales*, N.Y.: Hill and Wang, 1953.

Deikman, Arthur E., "Bimodal Consciousness," *Archives of General Psychiatry*, December 1971.

Deloria, Vine Jr., *God Is Red*, N.Y.: Grosset and Dunlap, 1973.

Densmore, Frances, *Bulletin 61 of the Bureau of American Ethnology*, Smithsonian Institute, 1918.

Dillard, Annie, *Pilgrim at Tinker Creek*, N.Y.: Harper Mag. Pr., 1974.

Drake, Samuel G., *Biography and History of the Indians of North America*.

Dubos, René, "A Theology of the Earth," *Audubon*, July 1972.

Erdoes, Richard, *The Sun Dance People*, N.Y.: Alfred A. Knopf, 1972.

Fagan, Michael, "The Search for Authenticity," in Samuel Bercholz and M. Fagan, eds., *Maitreya I*, Berkeley: Shambhala, 1970.

Fagen, Joen and Irma Lee Shepard, eds., *Gestalt Therapy Now*, N.Y.: Harper and Row, 1971.

Fletcher, Alice C., "The Hako: A Pawnee Ceremony," *Bureau of American Ethnology Twenty-second Annual Report*, Part 2, 1904.

Gaskin, Stephen, *Monday Night Class*, Santa Rosa: Book Farm, 1970.

Gauquelin, M., *The Cosmic Clocks*, Chicago: Henry Regnery Co., 1967.

Gibbons, Euell, *Stalking the Healthful Herbs*, N.Y.: David McKay Co., 1966.

Giddings, Ruth Warner, *Yaqui Myths and Legends*, Tucson: Univ. of Arizona Press, 1959.

Govinda, Lama A., *Foundations of Tibetan Mysticism*, London: Rider and Co.

——, "Meditation and Art," in Samuel Bercholz and M. Fagan, eds., *Maitreya, I*, Berkeley: Shambhala, 1970.

Gregory, R. L., *Eye and Brain*, N.Y.: McGraw Hill Book Co., 1968.

Grossinger, Richard, *Solar Journal*, Los Angeles: Sparrow Press, 1970.

Hardin, Garrett, *Exploring New Ethics for Survival, the Voyage of the Spaceship Beagle*, N.Y.: The Viking Press, 1972.

Heisenberg, Werner, *Physics and Philosophy*, N.Y.: Harper and Row, 1958.

High Pine, Gayle, "The Non-Progressive Great Spirit," *Akwesasne Notes*, early winter, 1973.

Holder, Constance, "Altered States of Consciousness Conference," *Science*, vol. 179, no. 4077, March 9, 1973.

Howard, Helen Addison, *War Chief Joseph*, Caldwell: The Caxton Printers, 1941.

Huang, Al Chung-liang, *Embrace Tiger, Return to the Mountain*, Moab: Real People Press, 1973.

Huang, Wen-Shan, *Fundamentals of Tai Chi Ch'uan*, First Edition, Hong Kong: South Sky Book Co., 1973.

Humphrey, Clifford C., *Ecology Action Educational Institute*, Box 3895, Modesto, California 95352.

Hyland, Kathy, "Energy: Transactions in Time," *The Markets of Change Series*, Oakland: Kaiser News, 1970.

Jacobs, Paul and Saul Landau, *To Serve the Devil*, vol. 1, "Natives and Slaves," N.Y.: Vintage Books, 1971.

Jett, Stephen C., *Navajo Wildlands*, "as long as the rivers shall run," N.Y.: Sierra/Ballantine Books, 1969.

Johansen, Bruce, " 'America' was a continent away," *The Seattle Times*, May 10, 1976.

Jones, Richard, *An Application of Psychoanalysis to Education*, Springfield: 1960.

——, *Fantasy and Feeling in Education*, N.Y.: New York University Press, 1968.

Jung, C. G., "The Commentary" in Richard Wilhelm, tr. Cary F. Baynes, *The Secret of the Golden Flower*, N.Y.: Harcourt Jovanovich, Inc., 1970.

——, *Man and His Symbols*, London: Aldus Books, published in the U.S. by Doubleday and Co., Inc. 1964.

——, *Memories, Dreams, Reflections*, N.Y.: Pantheon Books, 1963. Page numbers in *Notes* from paper edition, Vintage, 1963.

——, "On Psychic Energy," in *On the Nature of the Psyche*, Princeton: Princeton Univ. Press, 1969.

Kapp, Ronald O., *How to Know Pollen and Spores*, Dubuque: Wm. C. Brown Co., 1969.

Kathleen, "Letter to An Indian Friend," *Challenge for Change*, Montreal, Quebec, Canada: National Film Board of Canada, Summer, 1973.

Keen, Sam, "Sorcerer's Apprentice, a Conversation with Carlos Castaneda," *Psychology Today*, December 1972.

——, *To a Dancing God*, N.Y.: Harper and Row, 1970.

——, "We have no desire to strengthen the ego or make it happy, a conversation about ego destruction with Oscar Ichazo," *Psychology Today*, July 1973.

Kopp, Sheldon, *The Hanged Man, Psychotherapy and the Forces of Darkness*, Palo Alto: Science and Behavior Books, 1974.

Kramer, Joel, unpublished source. Kramer's lectures have since been published: *Passionate Mind*, Celestial Arts, 231 Adrian Rd., Millbrae, Ca. 94030.

Kreig, Margaret B., *Green Medicine*, N.Y.: Rand McNally and Co., 1964.

LaChapelle, Randy, *Demons, A Psychological Coloring Book*, Olympia: Pure Diamond, distributed by Finn Hill Arts, 1975.

Lame Deer, John and Richard Erdoes, *Lame Deer Seeker of Visions*, N.Y.: Simon and Schuster, 1972.

Langer, Susanne, *Philosophy in a New Key*, Cambridge: Harvard Univ. Press, 1942.

Lawrence, D. H., *The Plumed Serpent*, N.Y.: Alfred A. Knopf Inc., 1926, 1951.

Lee, Dorothy, *Freedom and Culture*, Englewood Cliffs: Prentice-Hall, 1959.

Leonard, George B., *The Transformation*, N.Y.: Delacorte Press, 1972.

Leopold, Aldo, *A Sand County Almanac with other essays on conservation from Round River*, N.Y.: Oxford Univ. Press, 1966.

Le Shan, Lawrence, *The Medium, the Mystic and the Physicist*, N.Y.: The Viking Press, 1974.

Leveson, David, *A Sense of the Earth*, N.Y.: Natural History Press, 1972.

Lieff, Jonathan, "Music as Healer," *East West Journal*, vol. IV, no. 4, May 1974.

Luce, Gay Gaer, *Body Time: Physiological Rhythms and Social Stress*, N.Y.: Pantheon Books, 1971.

Maslow, A. H., *The Farther Reaches of Human Nature*, N.Y.: The Viking Press, 1971.

Matthews, Washington, *Navajo Legends*, 1897.

McHarg, Ian, *Design with Nature*, N.Y.: Natural History Press, 1971.

Metzner, Ralph and Timothy Leary, "On Programming Psychedelic Experiences," *Psychedelic Review*, no. 9, 1967.

Moon, Sheila, *A Magic Dwells*, Middletown: Wesleyan Univ. Press, 1970.

Nasr, Seyyed Hossein, *The Encounter of Man and Nature*, London: George Allen and Unwin Ltd., 1968.

Neihardt, John G., *Black Elk Speaks*, Lincoln: Univ. of Nebraska Press, 1961.

Oppenheimer, J. Robert, "Physics in the Contemporary World," in M. Gardner, ed., *Great Essays in Science*, N.Y.: Washington Square Press, 1961.

Ornstein, Robert E., ed., *The Nature of Consciousness*, San Francisco: W. H. Freeman and Co., 1973.

——, *The Psychology of Consciousness*, San Francisco: W. H. Freeman and Co., 1972.

——, "Right and Left Thinking," *Psychology Today*, vol. 6, no. 12, May 1973.

Oster, Gerald, "Moire Patterns and Hallucination," *Psychedelic Review*, no. 7, 1966.

Payne, Buryl, *Getting There Without Drugs*, N.Y.: The Viking Press, 1973.

Pearce, Joseph Chilton, *The Crack in the Cosmic Egg*, N.Y.: The Julian Press, 1971.

Pelletier, Wilfred and Ted Poole, *No Foreign Land*, N.Y.: Pantheon Books, 1973.

Petersen, James, "Lessons from the Indian Soul, a Conversation with Frank Waters," *Psychology Today*, vol. 6, no. 12, May 1973.

Pieper, Josef, *In Tune with the World*, N.Y.: Harcourt Brace and Jovanovich, 1965.

Powell, Peter J., *Sweet Medicine*, Norman, Univ. of Oklahoma Press, 1969.

Prabhavananda, Swami and Frederick Manchester, tr. *The Upanishads*, N.Y.: New American Library, 1948.

Reeves, P. R., "A Topological Approach to Parapsychology," *Journal of the American Society for Psychical Research*, 38, 1944.

Roberts, Thomas B., "Transpersonal: The New Educational Psychology," *Phi Delta Kappan*, November 1974.

Rothenberg, Jerome, ed., *Shaking the Pumpkin*, N.Y.: Doubleday & Co., 1972.

Schilpp, P. A., *Albert Einstein: Philosopher-Scientist*, N.Y.: Harper & Row, 1959.

Schwenk, Theodor, *Sensitive Chaos*, London: Rudolf Steiner Press, 1965.

Seton, Ernest Thompson, *The Gospel of the Redman*, Seton Village, New Mexico, 1966.

Shah, Idries, "The Teaching Story: Observations on the Folklore of our 'Modern' Thought," *Point*, no. 4, winter 1968-69.

Shearer, Tony, *Lord of the Dawn*, Healdsburg: Naturegraph Publishers, 1971.

Singer, June, *Boundaries of the Soul, The Practice of Jung's Psychology*, Garden City: Doubleday & Co., 1972.

Skinner, A., "The Mascoutens or Prairie Potawatomi Indians," *Bulletin of the Public Museum of the City of Milwaukee*, vol. VI, no. 1, 1924.

Snyder, Gary, *Earth Household*, N.Y.: New Directions, 1969.

——, *Regarding Wave*, N.Y.: New Directions Publishing Co., 1970.

Stanistreet, Edgar, "The Amazing Mister Stanistreet," *East West Journal*, September 1973.

Stilley, Brenn, in Samuel Bercholz and M. Fagan, eds., *Maitreya I*, Berkeley: Shambhala, 1970.

Storm, Hyemeyohsts, *Seven Arrows*, N.Y.: Harper & Row, 1972.

Taimni, I. K., *The Science of Yoga*, Wheaton: The Theosophical Publishing House, 1967.

Tomkins, Peter and Christopher Byrd, *The Secret Life of Plants*, N.Y.: Harper & Row, 1973.

Toynbee, Arnold, "The Challenge of Tomorrow," *Japan Times*, October 6, 1972.

Villaseñor, David, *Tapestries in Sand*, Healdsburg: Naturegraph Publishers, 1966.

Waters, Frank, *The Book of the Hopi*, N.Y.: Viking Press, 1963. Notes pages are from the paper edition, Ballantine, 1971.

——, *The Man Who Killed the Deer*, Chicago: The Swallow Press, 1970.

Watts, Alan, *Does It Matter?*, N.Y.: Pantheon Books, 1971.

Willoya, William and Vinson Brown, *Warriors of the Rainbow*, Healdsburg: Naturegraph Publishers.

Weill, Andrew, "Light on the Dark Side of the Brain," *Psychology Today*, vol. 7, no. 1, June 1973.

——, *The Natural Mind*, Boston: Houghton Mifflin Co., 1972.

Wood, Nancy, *Hollering Sun*, N.Y.: Simon and Schuster Inc., 1972.

Zimmer, Heinrich, *The King and the Corpse*, Princeton: Princeton Univ. Press, 1956.

notes

Because *Earth Festivals* involves both the adult and the child we have used a different system for providing the bibliographical information for each quotation used in the text. The author's name only is used on the quotations for the adults; the quotations in the material which is used when children are present are footnoted in the usual manner. In the *notes* all quotations for any given page in *Earth Festivals* are listed by that page number in the order they appear on the page. In addition, those quotations which were footnoted in the text have the number of the footnote before the bibliographical information.

Title page   "Grandmother Earth, hear me!": Joseph Epes Brown, editor, *The Sacred Pipe: Black Elk's Account of the Seven Rites of the Oglala Sioux*, p. 105.

ABOUT THE BOOK

page

6 "The organism which destroys its environment": Gregory Bateson, "Pathologies of Epistemology," *Second Conference on Mental Health in Asia and the Pacific*, 1969.

6 "Continue to contaminate": Bruce Johansen " America' was a continent away," *The Seattle Times*, May 10, 1976.

6 "To live out, for some special occasion": Josef Pieper, *In Tune with the World*, p. 23.

7 "That the stubborn land": Wilfred Pelletier and Ted Poole, *No Foreign Land*, p. 55.

7 "We became more involved": Tony Shearer, *Lord of the Dawn*, p. 170.

8 "Symbols that tell what to say": Keith H. Basso and Ned Anderson, "A Western Apache Writing System: The Symbols of Silas John," *Science*, June 8, 1973.

9 "I've run dozens of Western songs through": "Baba Ram Dass: I Hear You," *East West Journal*, December, 1973.

AUTUMN EQUINOX CYCLE

11 Frank Waters in James Petersen, "Lessons from the Indian Soul," *Psychology Today*, May 1973.

12 Sam Keen, "Sorcerer's Apprentice, a Conversation with Carlos Castaneda," *Psychology Today*, December, 1972.

12 C. G. Jung, *Memories, Dreams, Reflections*, p. 209.

13 C. G. Jung, *The Secret of the Golden Flower*, p. 113.

14 John G. Neihardt, *Black Elk Speaks*, p. 198-199.

15 C. G. Jung, *Man and His Symbols*, p. 102.

15 Andrew Weil, "Light on the Dark Side of the Brain," *Psychology Today*, June 1973.

16 Susanne Langer, *Philosophy in a New Key*.

16 Richard M. Jones, *Fantasy and Feeling in Education*, pp. 70 and 72-73.

17 C. G. Jung, *The Secret of the Golden Flower*, pp. 104 and 107.

18 G. Adler et al., editors, *The Collected Works of C. G. Jung, vol. 9, The Archetypes and the Collective Unconscious*, p. 388. Paperback, *Mandala Symbolism*, p. 4-5.

19 Josef Pieper, *In Tune with the World*, pp. 29-30.

20 Jaime de Angulo, *Indian Tales*, p. 242.

21 [1.] Tony Shearer, *Lord of the Dawn*, p. 4.

22 Joseph Epes Brown, editor, *The Sacred Pipe: Black Elk's Account of the Seven Rites of the Oglala Sioux*, pp. 37 and 115.

24 Peter J. Powell, *Sweet Medicine*, p. xxi.

page

RELATIONSHIP CYCLE

25 Seyyed Hossein Nasr, *The Encounter of Man and Nature*, p. 98.

25 Stephen Gaskin, *Monday Night Class*, p. 131.

25 [2.] John G. Neihardt, *Black Elk Speaks*, p. 21.

26 Ernest Thompson Seton, *The Gospel of the Redman*, p. 18.

28 Carlos Castaneda, *Journey to Ixtlan*, p. 43.

29 David Leveson, *A Sense of the Earth*, p. 26.

29 René Dubos, "A Theology of the Earth," *Audubon*, July 1972.

30 Seyyed Hossein Nasr, *The Encounter of Man and Nature*, p. 135.

30 [3.] Franz Boas, "Ethnology of the Kwakiutl," *35th Annual Report of the Bureau of American Ethnology, 1913-1914*.

30 [4.] Helen Addison Howard, *War Chief Joseph*, p. 84.

30 Richard Grossinger, *Solar Journal*, prefix.

31 [5.] Samuel G. Drake, *Biography and History of the Indians of North America*.

31 [6.] Joseph Epes Brown, editor, *The Sacred Pipe: Black Elk's Account of the Seven Rites of the Oglala Sioux*, p. 105.

31 Vine Deloria Jr., *God Is Red*, pp. 87, 294, 296 and 300.

32 Dorothy Lee, *Freedom and Culture*, p. 164.

33 Arnold Toynbee, "The Challenge of Tomorrow," *Japan Times*, Oct. 6, 1972.

33 A. H. Maslow, *The Farther Reaches of Human Nature*, p. 231.

35 George B. Leonard, *The Transformation*, p. 235.

36 Joel Kramer at a yoga workshop held in Vancouver, Canada in June, 1971.

37 Alan Watts, *Does It Matter?* p. 25.

38 Andrew Weil, *The Natural Mind*, pp. 131-132.

38 Oscar Ichazo in Sam Keen, "We have no desire to strengthen the ego or make it happy, a conversation about ego destruction with Oscar Ichazo," *Psychology Today*, July 1973.

39 [7.] Gary Snyder, *Regarding Wave*, p. 17.

39 Garrett Hardin, *Exploring New Ethics for Survival*, p. 62.

40 [8.] Hyemeyohsts Storm, *Seven Arrows*, pp. 5 and 120.

41 Richard M. Jones, *An Application of Psychoanalysis to Education*, p. 15.

41 [9.] Hyemeyohsts Storm, *Seven Arrows*, p. 221.

42 Marie-Louise von Franz in C. G. Jung, *Man and His Symbols*, pp. 212-213.

43 Gregory Bateson, "Bali: The Value System of a Steady State," in Meyer Fortes, editor, *Social Structures: Studies Presented to A. R. Radcliffe-Brown*, pp. 47 and 51.

45 John Blofield, *The Tantric Mysticism of Tibet*, pp. 37-38.

46 Carlos Castaneda, *A Separate Reality*, p. 187.

46 José and Miriam Argüelles, *Mandala*, p. 47.

47 C. G. Jung, *The Secret of the Golden Flower*, p. 106.

48 José and Miriam Argüelles, *Mandala*, p. 92.

49 [10.] The *Dance of the Four Directions* combines ideas from the following sources: various Tibetan chants, H. Storm's medicine wheel terminology, Argüelles' *Mandala* and Randy LaChapelle's, *Demons, A Psychological Coloring Book*.

50 C. G. Jung, *Man and His Symbols*, p. 82.

50 C. G. Jung, *The Secret of the Golden Flower*, p. 120.

51 Ibid., pp. 99 and 107.

51 [11.] Gerald Oster, "Moire Patterns and Hallucination," *Psychedelic Review* No. 7, 1966.

51 12. Ralph Metzner and Timothy Leary, "On Programming Psychedelic Experiences,"·Psychedelic Review No. 9, 1967.

51 13. Ibid.

52 G. Adler et al., editors, The Collected Works of C. G. Jung, vol. 9, The Archetypes and the Collective Unconscious, p. 357. Paperback, Mandala Symbolism, p. 73.

53 John Freeman in C. G. Jung, Man and His Symbols, p. 13.

54 Marie-Louise von Franz in C. G. Jung, Man and His Symbols, p. 187.

54 14. H. Storm, Seven Arrows, p. 16.

54 15. Ibid., p. 20.

55 Andrew Weil, The Natural Mind, p. 152.

55 16. H. Storm, Seven Arrows, p. 16.

55 C. G. Jung, Memories, Dreams, Reflections, p. 209.

57 Heinrich Zimmer, The King and the Corpse, pp. 34-35.

57 17. H. Storm, Seven Arrows, p. 125.

58 C. G. Jung, Man and His Symbols, p. 52.

58 18. H. Storm, Seven Arrows, pp. 126-127.

58 A. H. Maslow, The Farther Reaches of Human Nature, pp. 100-101.

59 Frank Waters in James Petersen, "Lessons from the Indian Soul, A Conversation with Frank Waters," Psychology Today, May 1973.

61 Lawrence Kubie in Richard M. Jones, An Application of Psychoanalysis to Education, p. viii.

62 Robert E. Ornstein, "Right and Left Thinking," Psychology Today, May 1973.

63 Harvey Cox, Feast of Fools, pp. 10 and 14.

64 Richard Grossinger, Solar Journal, pp. 65 and 67.

64 19. Ibid., p. 24.

66 John Lame Deer and Richard Erdoes, Lame Deer, Seeker of Visions, pp. 243, 244.

67 20. Joseph Epes Brown, editor, The Sacred Pipe, p. 105.

ENERGY CYCLE

69 Brenn Stilley, Maitreya I.

69 C. G. Jung, Memories, Dreams, Reflections, p. 338.

73 Wen-Shan Huang, Fundamentals of Tai Chi Ch'uan, pp. 419 and 421.

74 Arthur E. Deikman, "Bimodal Consciousness," Archives of General Psychiatry, December 1971.

74 Gay Gaer Luce, Body Time, pp. 263, 264, and 268.

75 Constance Holder, "Altered States of Consciousness Conference," Science, March 9, 1973.

76 Al Chung-Liang Huang, Embrace Tiger, Return to the Mountain, p. 12.

76 21. Euell Gibbons, Stalking the Healthful Herbs, p. xiv.

77 Joseph Chilton Pearce, The Crack in the Cosmic Egg, pp. 3 and 5.

78 Padma Sambhava, quoted in P. R. Reeves, "A Topological Approach to Parapsychology," Journal of the American Society for Psychical Research 38 (1944).

78 22. H. Storm, Seven Arrows, p. 214.

81 Edgar Stanistreet, "The Amazing Mister Stanistreet," East West Journal, September 1973.

82 Albert Einstein quoted in Henry Margenau, "Einstein's Conception of Reality," in P. A. Schilpp, Albert Einstein: Philosopher-Scientist, p. 246.

82 Lawrence Le Shan, The Medium, the Mystic and the Physicist, p. 77.

83 Stephen Gaskin, Monday Night Class, pp. 17, 28 and 91.

84 C. G. Jung, "On Psychic Energy," in On the Nature of the Psyche, p. 64.

85 Alan Watts, Does It Matter? p. 85.

85 Buryl Payne, Getting There Without Drugs, p. 83.

87 Annie Dillard, Pilgrim at Tinker Creek.

87 Buryl Payne, Getting There Without Drugs, pp. x and xi.

88 Joseph Chilton Pearce, The Crack in the Cosmic Egg, p. 176.

88 Al Chung-liang Huang, Embrace Tiger, Return to the Mountain, p. 6.

89 Lama A. Govinda, Foundations of Tibetan Mysticism, p. 46.

90 Kathy Hyland, editor, "Energy: Transactions in Time," The Markets of Change series, No. 3.

91 George Leonard, The Transformation, pp. 10-11.

91 Lama A. Govinda, Foundations of Tibetan Mysticism, pp. 25 and 47.

92 Benjamin Lee Whorf in J. B. Carroll, editor, Language, Thought and Reality: Selected Writings of Benjamin Lee Whorf.

93 Joseph Chilton Pearce, The Crack in the Cosmic Egg, pp. 113 and 162.

94 Robert E. Ornstein, The Psychology of Consciousness, p. 144.

94 Joseph Chilton Pearce, The Crack in the Cosmic Egg, pp. 112-113.

95 Lama A. Govinda, Foundations of Tibetan Mysticism, p. 47.

95 I. K. Taimni, The Science of Yoga, p. 69.

96 Lama A. Govinda, Foundations of Tibetan Mysticism, p. 61.

97 Michael Fagan, "The Search for Authenticity," Maitreya I.

98 Vine Deloria Jr., God Is Red, pp. 106-107.

100 Stephen Gaskin, Monday Night Class, p. 91.

103 Gayle High Pine, "The Non-Progressive Great Spirit," Akwesasne Notes, early winter, 1973.

104 23. H. Storm, Seven Arrows, p. 214.

105 Joseph Epes Brown, editor, The Sacred Pipe, p. 96.

107 Lama A. Govinda, Foundations of Tibetan Mysticism, p. 131.

108 Ibid., pp. 187 and 208.

VEGETATION CYCLE

109 Sitting Bull quoted in Paul Jacobs and Saul Landau, To Serve the Devil, p. 3.

110 Gayle High Pine, "The Non-Progressive Great Spirit," Akwesasne Notes, early winter, 1973.

110 Frank Waters, The Man Who Killed the Deer, p. 218.

112 Ian McHarg, Design with Nature, p. 68.

113 Stephen C. Jett, Navajo Wildlands "as long as the rivers shall run," p. 119.

114 Ronald O. Kapp, How to Know Pollen and Spores, p. 6.

114 Peter Tomkins and Christopher Byrd, The Secret Life of Plants.

115 Gay Gaer Luce, Body Time, pp. 290-291.

117 Margaret B. Kreig, Green Medicine, p. 9.

117 24. Washington Matthews, Navajo Legends, p. 109.

117 Jonathan Lieff, "Music as Healer," East West Journal, May 1974.

118 David Spangler, Attunement, pp. 8, 9 and 12.

119 José and Miriam Argüelles, *Mandala*, p. 83.

119 Gregory Bateson, "Alfred Korzybski Memorial Lecture 1970, Form, Substance and Difference," *General Semantics Bulletin*, Vol. 37 (1970).

121 25. Frank Waters, *Book of the Hopi*, p. 279.

123 Lama A. Govinda, "Meditation and Art," *Maitreya I*, pp. 9 and 10.

124 26. Angel Maria Garibay K., "A Song of Chalco," in Jerome Rothenberg, editor, *Shaking the Pumpkin*, p. 368.

125 Lama A. Govinda, *Foundations of Tibetan Mysticism*.

125 Sam Keen, *To A Dancing God*, pp. 59-60.

126 J. Robert Oppenheimer, "Physics in the Contemporary World," in M. Gardner, editor, *Great Essays in Science*, p. 189.

126 June Singer, *Boundaries of the Soul*, pp. 11 and 240.

127 27. José and Miriam Argüelles, *Mandala*, p. 63.

130 Hartley Burr Alexander, *The World's Rim*, pp. 164-165.

131 G. Adler et al., editors, *The Collected Works of C. G. Jung, vol. 9, The Archetypes and the Collective Unconscious*, p. 363. Paperback, *Mandala Symbolism*, p. 79.

132 28. Nancy Wood, *Hollering Sun*, unpaged.

133 29. José and Miriam Argüelles, *Mandala*, p. 77.

134 30. John G. Neihardt, *Black Elk Speaks*, p. 212.

135 Theodor Schwenk, *Sensitive Chaos*, p. 112.

135 31. H. L. Penman, "The Water Cycle," *Scientific American*, September 1970.

136 Michael Gauquelin, *The Cosmic Clocks*, p. 221.

137 32. Tony Shearer, *Lord of the Dawn*, pp. 39-44.

139 John (Fire) Lame Deer and Richard Erdoes, *Lame Deer Seeker of Visions*, p. 123.

140 Brave Buffalo, quoted in Francis Densmore, *Bulletin of the Bureau of American Ethnology*, No. 61, 1918.

140 Kathleen, "Letter to An Indian Friend," *Challenge for Change*, Summer, 1973.

141 Gayle High Pine in a letter to *Akwesasne Notes*, early winter, 1973.

141 33. Ruth Warner Giddings, *Yaqui Myths and Legends*, pp. 62-64.

141 Idries Shah, "The Teaching Story: Observations on the Folklore of our 'Modern' Thought," *Point*, No. 4 (Winter 1968-69).

142 David Leveson, *A Sense of the Earth*, p. 18.

142 I. K. Taimni, *The Science of Yoga*, pp. 65-66.

143 Arnold Toynbee, "The Challenge of Tomorrow," *Japan Times*, Oct. 6, 1972.

144 Lama A. Govinda, *Foundations of Tibetan Mysticism*, p. 228.

145 Buryl Payne, *Getting There Without Drugs*.

146 Nancy Wood, *Hollering Sun*, unpaged.

146 Frank Waters, *The Man Who Killed the Deer*, p. 27.

147 34. Aldo Leopold, "Odyssey," in *A Sand County Almanac with other essays on conservation from Round River*, pp. 104-106.

147 Werner Heisenberg, *Physics and Philosophy*, p. 107.

148 Gregory Bateson, "The Cybernetics of 'Self': A Theory of Alcoholism," *Psychiatry*, vol. 34, no. 1, 1971.

149 José and Miriam Argüelles, *Mandala*, p. 99.

149 35. John G. Neihardt, *Black Elk Speaks*, p. 43.

149 Swami Prabhavananda and Frederick Manchester, *The Upanishads*.

150 Alan Watts, *Does It Matter?*, p. xiv.

VISION CYCLE

151 Gayle High Pine, "The Non-Progressive Great Spirit," *Akwesasne Notes*, early winter, 1973.

153 Wendell Berry, "A Composting Privy," *Organic Gardening*, December 1973.

154 36. Nancy Wood, *Hollering Sun*, unpaged.

155 R. L. Gregory, *Eye and Brain*, pp. 104, 106, 108 and 109.

156 Gregory Bateson, "Pathologies of Epistemology," *Second Conference on Mental Health in Asia and the Pacific, 1969*.

157 Robert E. Ornstein, editor, *The Nature of Human Consciousness*, pp. 313-314.

158 R. L. Gregory, *Eye and Brain*, pp. 73-74.

159 Adelbert Ames Jr., *The Morning Notes of Adelbert Ames Jr.*, p. 162.

160 Annie Dillard, *Pilgrim at Tinker Creek*.

161 Richard Erdoes, *The Sun Dance People*, p. 21.

163 Gay Gaer Luce, *Body Time*, p. 264.

164 37. William Willoya and Vinson Brown, *Warriors of the Rainbow*, pp. 19-20.

165 Sheldon Kopp, *The Hanged Man*, p. 17.

165 38. John G. Neihardt, *Black Elk Speaks*, pp. 44-45.

165 39. Ibid., p. 280.

165 June Singer, *Boundaries of the Soul*, p. 141.

166 Sheila Moon, *A Magic Dwells*, p. 89.

166 40. Tahirassawichi, quoted in Alice C. Fletcher, "The Hako A Pawnee Ceremony," *Bureau of American Ethnology, Twenty-second Annual Report, Part 2*.

167 Gino August Sky, "Searching for the Miracle," *Clear Creek*, June 1972.

168 Carlos Castaneda, *A Separate Reality*, p. 39.

169 John (Fire) Lame Deer and Richard Erdoes, *Lame Deer, Seeker of Visions*, p. 46.

169 41. H. Storm, *Seven Arrows*, p. 119.

169 Carlos Castaneda, *Tales of Power*, p. 284.

170 Carlos Castaneda, *The Teachings of Don Juan*, p. 194-195.

171 Gay Gaer Luce, *Body Time*, p. 254.

172 Fritz Perls quoted in Joen Fagen and Irma Lee Shepard, editors, *Gestalt Therapy Now*, p. 38.

172 42. John G. Neihardt, *Black Elk Speaks*, p. 180.

172 C. G. Jung, *Psychology and Religion: West and East*, pp. 533 and 535.

173 David Villaseñor, *Tapestries in Sand*, p. 94.

175 43. A. Skinner, "The Mascoutens or Prairie Potawatomi Indians," *Bulletin of the Public Museum of the City of Milwaukee*, vol. VI, no. 1, 1924.

176 44. Clifford C. Humphrey, Director, Ecology Action Education Institute.

177 45. Gary Snyder, *Earth Household*, p. 128.

177 46. Gary Snyder at the Theodore Roethke Memorial Poetry Reading in Seattle, Washington, May 27, 1976, unpublished.

179 47. D. H. Lawrence, *The Plumed Serpent*, p. 178.

187 48. Thomas B. Roberts, "Transpersonal: The New Educational Psychology," *Phi Delta Kappan*, November, 1974.

187 49. Frances Vaughan Clark, "Rediscovering Transpersonal Education," *Journal of Transpersonal Psychology*, No. 1, 1974, p. 6.

187 49. Ibid., p. 5.

187 51. Thomas R. Blackburn, "Sensuous-Intellectual Complementarity in Science," *Science*, June 4, 1971.